CASSANDRA

at his finest and funniest

Preface by Hugh Cudlipp
Annotated by Paul Boyle

First published by Paul Hamlyn, 1967
Published 2008 By Revel Barker Publishing

This special edition of CASSANDRA AT HIS FINEST AND FUNNIEST is published with kind permission of the Editor of the *Daily Mirror* who has agreed that royalties should be donated to the Journalists' Charity (formerly the Newspaper Press Fund).

The Journalists' Charity is the leading charity for all journalists in need; it is there to assist them, their partners and dependants with grants and other forms of financial assistance where possible. Apart from allocating £300,000 plus to the needy every year, it runs a care home in Dorking and a sheltered housing complex nearby.

The new care home, built to the highest standards of the day, cost £4million and the charity is campaigning to raise the cash. For more information, see the website: *www.journalistscharity.org.uk*

ISBN: 0-978-9558238-2-4

Revel Barker Publishing
66 Florence Road, Brighton BN1 6DJ

Contents

About Cassandra
by Hugh Cudlipp

The man who should be writing the preface to this book by Cassandra is William Neil Connor. He knew his faults, and scarcely suspected his virtues. But they died at the same moment in the same bed at Bart's Hospital, London, earlier this year, and we'll have to make do without him. A pity.

For the past two or three years the medicos had re-arranged the internal plumbing and checked the haemorrhages as best they could, but we all knew (except Old Incorruptible himself) that in the early hours of some sad morning, surgery, drugs and the patient's formidable courage would have to give up the ghost.

The nursing sister in his room at High Wycombe Memorial Hospital, where he started the marathon series of operations and treatments, told me ruefully that she called him 'Sweet William'. Liberace, for one, would not endorse that tender tribute; arsenic yes, but not old lace.

Cassandra had a predilection for writing in the Last Words about the famous and the infamous. He had a morbid acquaintance with the chap who brings the obituaries up to date at *The Times,* or so he told me.

Connor phoned me the day before the funeral for Winston Churchill.

'I have my ticket for St Paul's. I have hired my morning suit from Moss Bros. I would like to add my two cents' worth to the Niagara of eulogy. Churchill once called me malevolent, but there is another side to my nature. He said hard things of me, but I am forgiving.'

'George Bernard Shaw is dead,' he wrote on an earlier occasion. 'The great dark gates of death that have been locked against him for so long swung open for a moment at dawn yesterday and the lean, derisive sage looked over his shoulder for a final twinkling trice and was gone.'

His farewell to Joseph Stalin was sombre.

> 'He died in his bed. That was the last triumphant, exultant trick of Josef Vissarionovich Djugashvili – otherwise Joseph Stalin, the most powerful man in the world…
>
> His seventy-three hideous years have been enough. In his time he did titanic things and the whole world was his chess board. No tyrant ever planned on such a scale, and continents rather than countries were his prey. Probably he was brave. Certainly he was shifty and cruel. His skill in power politics was unsurpassed.
>
> But his purpose was evil and his methods unspeakable. Few men by their death can have given such deep satisfaction to so many.'

For a writer who died at fifty-seven – he was three weeks from fifty-eight – Cassandra exuded a matchless zest for life. He held that no major event should occur in his absence, bereft of his comment in admonition or acclamation.

He was in orbit around the crust of the earth as a fine reporter long before Laika, the Russian dog, was projected into the stratosphere. He watched the Nazi jackboots clumping down the Unter Den Linden in Berlin in 1937, and peered over his spectacles with mounting misgiving at the Nuremberg rallies. He was on H.M.S. *Alert,* near Christmas Island, when the British tested their H-bomb and sent up that mushroom cloud above the Pacific Ocean – 'like an oil painting from hell.' He saw Eichmann in the glass dock at his trial in Israel. 'I will be in Washington,' he told me, 'for the Negro march on the White House.' He was in Dublin when Roger Casement's remains were returned to Eire ('the triumph from the felon's pit to the national shrine is complete'); and with Pope Paul VI in Nazareth in 1964 ('you can hear the beating heart of Christianity in this ancient town').

He'll be flaming angry now that he won't be able to write a column about Judgment Day.

Combat and satire were Connor's specialities. With due respect, the snarling kittens in the late-night TV programmes are still wet behind the ears in comparison, and most of them (certainly David Frost) would be big enough to admit it.

Outwardly he was stubborn, cantankerous, prickly. Except in the benign moments, which were not infrequent, conversation with him_was a boisterous affray; as a marathon reader of books and magazines, his mental ammo was abundant. But the explosive verbal combats ended as a rule with the twinkling eyes peering over the steamed-up spectacles.

Inwardly, he was a warm and friendly cove, always pressuring the firm and his friends to be generous to a pensioner or to a journalist who had fallen by the wayside. Hundreds of people up the creek turned to Bill for guidance, even on matrimonial crises. The people he dissected in his writings usually ended up on amicable terms. When the nails were withdrawn and the wounds had slowly healed the people he crucified were forgiving.

Cassandra joined the Services in 1942. He returned to his column on September 23, 1946, with the famous words: 'As I was saying when I was interrupted, it is a powerful hard thing to please all the people all the time.'

The Cassandra Column, non-stop for thirty years, apart from global hostilities, has now been interrupted again. So far as is known, it will not be resumed this time.

That is precisely why the millions of his followers throughout the English-speaking world will treasure this book of some of his finest and funniest writing.

I Remember, I Remember

Cass had a prodigious memory for the things of his youth. The toys, the games, the mighty cinema organs. The dashing Frazer-Nash with solid back axle that he owned – at speed it made a noise like tearing calico. The big brass telescope inherited from his father. And his one-time 'flat' in St Pancras which was always being phoned at 3a.m. in mistake for Camden Town Goods Station.

Conker time down south

September 21, 1948

I suppose I was mortally afraid of Mr Beulah for the best part of five years.

Dead scared.

And especially so at this, the third week in September, when the chestnuts hung heavily on the trees – when, in fact, it was conker time down in the south.

I have looked upon Mr Beulah's flat peaked cap from the upper branches of trees, and had the vertical wind up.

I have watched his great black spade beard from the long grass, and have been racked with anxiety.

I have noted his thick stick from behind the dahlias, and have felt weak at the knees.

Mr Beulah was the Head Park Keeper in Our Park – the symbol of Authority and the implacable enemy of every small boy between the ages of five and ten.

Yet I never saw him strike anybody. I never heard him raise his voice.

I never saw him chase anyone except at a slow and measured walking pace that didn't even jingle the little silver box that always hung on his watch-chain.

But his reputation struck almost permanent terror into several hundred young hearts. There were ghastly stories of the revenge he took on lads whom he was supposed to have caught lurking in the park at dusk, long after he had blown the whistle that preceded the ceremony of locking up the gates. Mr Beulah was credited with murder and mayhem after nightfall by scores of wide-eyed urchins when, in point of fact, he was placidly having a pint of mild ale at the local and gently complaining about his fallen arches.

But it was at conker time that his reputation for small-boy terrorism rose to its climax.

By hurling large sized sticks into horse chestnut trees, it was possible for us to bring down a substantial shower of the coveted conkers. A score of cunning by-laws displayed on the Park Notice Board rendered the conker collector liable to a series of ferocious penalties, in which the Sum of Five Pounds was mentioned in almost every other line. We wanted the best chestnuts. Mr Beulah's trees had them. Guerrilla warfare was ceaseless. Mr Beulah did sentry-go for hours on end. But young shavers with devilment in their hearts stalked him and created diversionary activities on the flower beds while the main parties went in on the conker raid.

We won.

Chestnuts were stuffed into pockets along with highly-prized bits of cork, old keys and lumps of toffee. Then they were taken home, put in boxes, matured and finally baked before being threaded on strings, for the great game of conkers in which the hardest nut wins.

Years afterwards I met Mr Beulah when he had retired.

He was sitting in his old park under the shade of a lilac tree. We got talking of times gone by – and the annual Wars of the Conkerers.

Mr Beulah took off his spectacles and wiped them.

'Funny you should talk about conkers,' he said. 'See this silver box?'

He opened the small trinket on his watch-chain. There was a tiny, black, gnarled object inside.

'Know what that is?' he said. 'It's a hundred-and-fifty-niner. This little conker's cracked a hundred and fifty-nine other chestnuts – had it since I was a nipper so high... hardest, toughest nut on earth.'

The toys of yesteryear

March 27. 1963

The other day an everloving – and maybe slightly overloving – father who had presented his young son with an expensive set of electric trains, was astonished to find the lad playing happily with a battered old clockwork engine that he had scrounged from somewhere. He ignored the elaborate electric trains and was delighted to lark about with something he could wind up. Dad was reported to be puzzled and slightly hurt.

There were no toy electric trains in my youth and anything that cost more than five bob was for millionaires' sons only.

But the toys of yesteryear were none the worse for that.

Oddly enough we were far more explosive than the lads of this nuclear age. I was surrounded by enormous bangs that were not confined to the open season of Guy Fawkes, but crashed and thundered the year round.

There was the Sulphur-Potassium-and-Flat-Stone Explosion. The pale yellow powder was placed under the stone and the sole of the boot brought sharply down in contact with the lot.

The noise was like a young air-raid and deeply satisfactory – except of course to the entire adult population within the earshot range of one mile.

There was the Key-Banger. Red powder scraped from match heads was plugged in the hole of the key with a nail as a detonator. The nail was tied to a piece of string which was knotted to the far end of the key in a sling.

Swing nail and key against a wall – and run for your life. There was the Wet-Carbide-in-a-Tin Eruption. The carbide was placed in the tin and the lid, with a tiny hole hi it, jammed on hard. Explosive gas resulted. A lighted match was then dropped through the hole and the ensuing crash convinced most householders that heavy quarry blasting was taking place in their front gardens.

There were Winter-Warmers crammed with brown paper soaked in saltpetre that got nearly red hot and there was the Steam Gun that took the roof off a greenhouse – especially when fired from inside.

There were Whip-Tops to be thrashed within an inch of their wooden lives; there were Humming-Tops that crooned and there were Peg-Tops that screamed when hurled to the ground.

There were great Iron Hoops propelled by metal hooks called 'skimmers' with which many urchins of five years old, shorter by far than the diameter of their hoops, could paralyse old ladies as the rascals belted and panted by.

There were the Heavy-Water-Bombs which were empty seven-pound paper bags which had contained corn, filled with tap juice and hurled from a high window at any living creature from cats to boys.

But not irascible fathers.

There was The-Deadly-Snake-of-the-Inner-Bicycle-Tube. It was in the nature of an elaborate booby trap.

What you did was this.

You invited a rival, or preferably a hated enemy, to hold the end of an inner bicycle tube that had been cut into one long open-ended rubber snake.

The bottom of the tube was tightly tied with string and the sucker-victim held it. From the top end, which you held from a higher plane, such as on the roof of a garden shed, you poured in water from a watering can.

As you continued, the lower end of the inner tube began to swell into the most enormous and bulbous rubber tumour filled with water that you have ever seen.

Gravity worked and the victim, still at the glistening receiving end, was entranced as the huge blister filled and swelled and filled again. Finally, to the immense joy of the youth on the roof, the whole thing burst with wet explosive force and the victim was half drowned in a drenching cascade of water.

Those were the days.

There were bows and arrows that would have scared King Harold.

There were cigarette cards and the marbles (called 'miggies' and 'alleys') and, of course, there was the great and traditional art of simply throwing stones.

The only rule about throwing stones was that they had to be hurled near windows and, preferably, in their direction.

Finally there was Toffee. Sticky Toffee.

Toffee that locked the jaws in a great gooey vice of delectable sweetness.

Toffee that lasted and lasted and lasted.

Toffee that could be chewed, stuck in the pocket, chewed, stuck in the pocket – and then chewed again.

Electric trains – my left potassium-sulphured foot!

A look at the Hook

June 23, 1954

Some people are forced to earn their living in boats, and for them I have nothing but deep sorrow. But it is the madness which seizes people and makes them go on launches, yachts, dinghies, skiffs, punts and canoes *for pleasure* that appals me most.

Nobody can be happy on these things. You have to work like a slave. You hit your head on the blasted roof – or whatever they call it – and it is impossible not to quarrel on a boat – many a romance has foundered for ever on 14ft of floating hell.

The cooking stove runs out of gas, oil, or whatever fuel you are supposed to put in it, and it always rains. The engine – if there is an engine – inevitably packs up. You can't sleep – the bed, berth or bunk is too small and too hard. You run aground. You can't wash. So wet, filthy, starved and sleepless you have to undergo the final mockery and torment of pretending it's great fun.

But I was lucky.

Supremely lucky. I got cured when I was young.

I got so cured that the only vessel that I will admit has the rudiments of comfort is the Queen Elizabeth – in dry dock.

Let me tell you about my lucky break.

When I was old enough not to know better a rich man invited me to go yachting with him for a long week-end. He said in that bluff salty manner that deceives nobody but the most land-locked fool:

'Nice freshening wind. We might pop over and have a look at the Hook.'

A look at the Hook! When you hear that remark abandon ship. Go over the side. Swim for home. It's easier.

The yacht was one of those very sharp lean things with an enormously high mast and was designed for racing on the sheltered waters of the Clyde. It was at Dover, and how it got there I'm darned if I know. There was a hired crew of three, locally recruited.

Once we got outside the harbour wall I felt seasick. I was seasick.

At once this accursed hooker put her nose down and tore into the sea. She heeled over. The owner, who knew about as much as I did about sailing, which was zero and then minus some, pretended that the alarming angle at which we were keeling over and the truly terrifying speed at which we were bucketing through the water was exactly what he had experienced in his long maritime career of half a dozen week-ends at sea.

The crew turned out to be longshoremen dressed up as sailors who had served their time at a whelk stall. They were as appalled as I was.

Within an hour the fresh breeze had become a fresh gale and it became sickeningly clear that the monstrous mainsail had to be lowered from the prodigious mast. Nobody knew which rope to pull.

The oldest fake in the hired crew advised that the only thing to do was to 'stand away from the shore.' All other craft had run for shelter. We got the mainsail down – with an axe. It roared down like the heaviest unsafety curtain in the world and half of it dragged in the water.

Then came The Conference. The furious and frightened owner summoned the whelk boys to the owner's cabin and bawled them out.

I was dying alongside on a bunk.

The charts were spread out on the table and examined upside down. Then somebody thought of the lights. We would be run down in the night.

They tried to fill 'em. The oil spilt all over the heaving chart table and the maddened owner mewed piteously with rage.

Water sploshed about and buffeted ominously against the bulkhead. Then one of the whelkers, in the spirit of finding a gas leak with a lighted match, opened the bulkhead door.

In it came – the most disgusting tide of seawater, oil, bilge and food. Delightful chickens from Fortnum and Mason's sailed legs upward across the floor. Veal and ham pies bobbed and jostled with broken bottles of mayonnaise. A crate of beer jauntily tumbled across the floor and a fresh salmon slopped its headless way towards the door.

Nobody was actually drowned and although we never saw the Hook the Royal National Life-Boat Institution was alerted on our soggy behalf.

Since then I have classed yachting with visiting the dentist, being sawn in half and going to prison for a prolonged stretch.

Camden Goods

September 24, 1956

Many years ago I had a Museum telephone number which ended with the number 56. The Camden Town Goods Station had a telephone number in those days which ended with the numerals 57.

The result was that I was continually rung up at all hours of the day and night – especially the night – and asked the most peculiar questions, such as what I proposed to do with forty-seven sheets of corrugated asbestos cement in Siding Seventeen.

At first I suffered the telephonic tortures of the damned, but after a while I used to lie awake longing to be rung up at three in the morning and be mistaken for Camden Goods.

A hoarse voice would get on and say – 'Arry?'

'Yus.'

'Twenty-seven rolls of netting wire. Sling 'em on Platform Three as usual?'

'Nooaw. Bung 'em out to Tufnell Park. Gunnight.'

I got to know and love these men.

We did enormous business together. In the wee small hours I shifted tons of stuff all over London. Especially I loved the crates full of pigeons.

The Voice would get on and shout: 'What abaht these bloomin' pigeons, 'Arry?'

'Ow many baskets?'

'Sevving.'

'Open five and let 'em fly 'ome. Sling the other two over to 'Arrods termorrer.'

'Oke.'

'Oke.'

I would deal in anything. Eggs. Plasterboard. Tiles. Dried milk. Gravel. Kettles. Cement. Pails. Tomato ketchup. Anything.

One memorable night The Voice and I did fine business with a crated pipe-organ.

'Thatchew, 'Arry?'

'Yus.'

'Gotter bloomin' organ 'ere. Wherejer wannit?'

'Old 'ard till I git the ledger. 'Ow many tons?'

'Levving!'

'Oke. Gottit. Write this dahn. 'Ackney Gasworks, 'Ackney.'

'Gripes! Wodder they want wiv a church organ?'

'Test the pipes wiv the gas, you big stoopid.'

'Oke.'
'Oke.'
Aaah, those Camden Town nights!

The surprise gag

April 24, 1958

Crooks are breaking their way back into our prisons. With magnificent cheek a gang of burglars broke into Walton Prison, Liverpool, and managed to burst open a safe.

They picked the wrong one, however, for it contained only a few documents while another safe containing £2,000 in prison wages escaped their audacious attention.

They then departed back to freedom over the high wall.

The break-in from freedom to confinement is a corking example of the surprise gag made famous in the United States by a fine, crazy chap I knew called Jim Moran.

Jim Moran, surveying the world in all its dull uniformity, decided to get to work among some of the more trite sayings that apparently had been annoying him for some time.

'Too many cooks spoil the broth,' was Jim's first target. He assembled a gathering of a dozen cooks and ordered them to make some soup.

It was magnificent.

From soup he turned to horses.

'Don't change horses in midstream,' said the adage.

Mr Moran hired two nags and drove them into the middle of a considerable river. He then leapt from one saddle to the other amid the cheers of the spectators.

Gathering speed he built a haystack, left a needle in it, and returned some days later to find it. Then, just to prove that nothing was impossible, he sold a refrigerator to an Eskimo.

When last heard of Jim was making tiny smoked glasses for pigeons.

To an innocent bystander, who mildly asked what was the point of it all, Professor Moran snarled :

'Be quiet, you ape. You are in the presence of The Unknown. I am the first man in the history of the Universe to have fitted smoked glasses to pigeons. Take your hat off.'

Bean and Bear-Cat

August 28, 1961

Yesterday and on Saturday large strips of Devonshire (formerly famous for rural delights such as clotted cream, cider – pronounced zider – and Uncle Tom Cobbleigh and all) were transformed into a vast noisome traffic jam.

The whole countryside is threatened with this great metal rash that breaks out every week-end.

The motor-car, once a means of seeing the trees and the grass and the hedgerows and the sky, has itself become a disfiguring blotch that cannot even fulfil its first function – which is to move.

The car factories are pouring out a great spreading tide of steel, aluminium, copper, wire, rubber and plastics that will put an end to the England as we knew it – the England of vales and hills and solitude.

The motor-car, in which you once went for a joyful ride, has become a machine to follow other machines with a good chance of your coming to an abrupt and nasty end.

Moreover, it is the standardized machine.

Today you have a choice of not much more than half a dozen factory groups from which to buy your car. Three of them, the British Motor Corporation, Fords, and Rootes, control about 80 per cent of the entire market. Standard and Vauxhall have another slice, and then you are limited to the Jaguar, Rover, Rolls class.

Henry Ford's old joke that you could have a Ford of any colour providing it was black, is becoming true of all makes of motor-cars. You can have anything you like – provided it is designed, made and sold by half a dozen immensely powerful arbiters of style, capacity, performance and price.

What a contrast with the old times!

Half a hundred and more makes fought for your patronage. Remember them?

The busy Clyno, the pernickety Calthorpe and the old Bean Fourteen, the great haughty Cubitt and the angular Moon. Their names often had an aristocratic ring about them: the Arrol-Johnston, the Siddeley-Deasey, the Belsize-Bradshaw and that old French swank-pot, the De Dion-Bouton.

When you went for a ride in a Waverley you were in a demure and pleasing little car. When you were in a Galloway the mood was solid and worthy. When you were at the wheel of an H.E. the tone was lofty and supercilious.

A Frazer Nash, with its solid back axle, its lift of chain, and its outside gear lever, was something to be reckoned with. The twin camshaft job did 44 m.p.h. in first and over 90 in top. It made a harsh churning noise on to which was superimposed the sound of tearing endless strips of calico.

The Autocar of those days described the Frazer Nash with a well-turned phrase of dignified restraint. 'It would indeed be difficult,' they said of this Fighting Temeraire of wheels, 'to find a faster point-to-point vehicle.'

Then there were the foreigners. What a bunch of mustachioed dandies they were!

The Metalurgique – with a sharp prow like a destroyer that could cut you in two. The Isotta-Fraschini with the smell of duels at dawn and reckless times on the tables of Monte Carlo about it. The Hispano Suiza with its curling contemptuous lip.

The Minerva that could look a Rolls straight in the eye. The Lorraine Dietrich that challenged all highsteppers.

And then the great Yankee cars strictly for cads: the Stutz Bear-Cat – nobody could be respectable in that. The Duesenburg, the Cord, the Auburn, and the tourer Maxwell, at one time a much favoured car with Chicago hoodlums.

Buzzing all round them with the hum of furious mosquitoes were the light cars.

The Salmson, the Amilcar, the G.N., the Mathis, the Carden, the Stoneleigh, the Rhode, the Gwynne, the Crouch, and the Tamplin.

A hornets' nest of buzz-boxes each with its own built-in legend.

They were made by hand. They brought trouble and joy to their owners and they were well loved. They, like the greater breeds of automobile, were also blessedly few on the roads and far between.

Give me the goggles and the leather coat any day.

August 31,1961

'Dear Cassandra,

'Never have you fitted me with such nostalgia! The Clyno, the Calthorpe, the Moon – the Galloway. When I was twelve you couldn't have driven a car near me which I wouldn't have recognized at fifty yards.

'Imagine someone else remembering the Mettalurgique! 'My favourite was the Stellite, later to become the Wolseley. My headmaster had one. None of us could drive, none of us knew how to start the thing, but when we were all supposed to be in bed we used to creep down to his garage and pretend to drive it.

'One night someone left the darn thing in gear. To start it, you had to crank it. Next day he broke his wrist. 'I wish you'd remembered the Stettite.

'Yours, L.H.*'*

But I did. It was a calm, confident motor with its oval name plaque looking you coolly in the eye.

And I remembered the Sheffield-Simplex, the Star, the Perry, and the Invicta, too.

And the old Vauxhall – not the glossy new jobs from Luton Town.

I mean the 'Thirty Ninety-eight' of course.

There was a motor.

You knew that underneath its bonnet an engine was alive. You were deeply aware of its presence; an iron lion lording it in a cave of power.

It was not tucked away in the boot or set squiffily sideways somewhere.

When the Vauxhall 30-98 started up, the long sloping wings gave a shiver of excitement at each revolution. Fast fun and furious fun was to come. The engine was not one of these compressed square packages of mechanical fussiness that you get today.

It had great long con-rods that rose majestically and sank again lolloping with easy leisure and dipping into the sump oil.

The old 'Thirty Ninety-eight', when you started her up, used to say 'Guddugety-Guddugety-Gonk, Guddugety-Guddugety-Gonk' and would speak to no other motor car – unless it was one of W. 0. Bentley's majestic green monsters who would civilly reply 'Berdoobely – Berdoobely – Bonk, Berdoobely – Berdoobely -Bonk.'

This classic Vauxhall looked like a sleek cruiser.

At slow speeds it loped along but when she saw the open road that old engine laughed in its metal guts and you were away leaving everything else far behind. The 'Thirty Ninety-eight' dreaded nought – unless maybe it was one of Monsieur Ettore Bugatti's wonderful cars from the factory – or I should say the engineering cathedral – at Molsheim.

There was a dashing Frenchman for you!

The triumphant red badge of speed on its beautifully machined elliptical brow; the precision-built massive wheels that looked as if they had come straight out of a gun-factory; the sporty sprung steel-and-wooden steering wheel; the dashboard instruments talking technicalities right back at you in French.

You simply had to wear a beret with a Bugatti and the girl beside you, if she had any sense, squealed 'Ooo-la-la!' as the supercharger on the 'blown 2-3' began to sing its fearsome song.

And I remember the Jowett and the Trojan, too. The gormless, faithful Jowett made by sturdy Yorkshiremen at Idle.

It ticked like a sewing machine. It looked gawky and foolish, but it took you there and it brought you back.

The Trojan also came from a similar school of hard-unrelenting designers, who yielded nothing to style and fashion.

It looked like a lumpy box, was driven by chains, had solid tyres and could never get rid of an albatross-of-a-joke hung round its neck that said that once you got in the tram-lines you stayed there until you reached the Depot.

Alas, they are gone and dear Delage and proud Peerless and their friends Hotchkiss, Napier, Bianchi, Horstmann, Darracq, Overland, Essex, Deemster, Itala and O.M. too.

'Up the Calley'

March 28, 1962

This day we mourn the passing of 'The Calley' – or rather the hallowed site where it used to be.

'The Calley' – as if you Cockneys didn't know – was that magnificent market in Islington, where all the world gathered to buy, to sell, to twist, and, quite often, to cop a rare good bargain.

The Corporation of the City of London has this week finally decided to release the twenty-nine acres where once some of the finest huckstering in the world took place.

Houses, a school and an open space will take the place of the old Caledonian Market.

What a place it was!

I knew it well. You could buy anything from codfish to daffodils, from paint to pianos, from netting to gramophones, from old bicycle tyres to willow pattern tea cups with anti-moustache ledges.

There was a tremendous one-man-slum of a chap who stood there for years in all weathers, presiding over a heap of dusty rubbish that apparently was entirely composed of dirt, paper and rags. When I first saw him, I wondered what he was doing and why, if he just wanted to stand in the rain, he didn't move to a tidier corner.

It took me some time to grasp that he was actually SELLING the stuff.

In this miniature slag heap there were things like rusty nails, ancient umbrella frames, bits of wire and old picture hooks. It was a help-yourself supermarket in reverse, with only the best rubbish available.

Two of my friends – both ex-actors on hard times – ran an antique stall in 'The Calley' – or rather 'Up The Calley,' as we used to say.

They were in the 'make-it-old-quick' business. Brand new chairs were aged overnight by the use of chemicals. Woodworm was applied at a rate that would have astonished the fastest woodworm.

Pewter fresh from a Birmingham factory was 'antiqued' into the Middle Ages in about the same it takes to sing *Love's Old Sweet Song.*

Eighteenth-century clocks had somehow skipped a couple of centuries. They were 200 years old ten days after they had been made.

Paper was transformed into parchment and many a happy American went back to the States with a rare old painting lithographed in thousands of copies, and a collection of old coins reaching back to the reign of Queen Anne that were hardly cold from some faker's secret mint.

'The Calley' had a pride of its own in that it could supply almost anything.

A lens from an astronomical telescope; piston rings for a two-stroke engine; brown paper dipped in salt-petre for winter warmers; china eggs for reluctant Buff Orpingtons; a copy of *Small Electric Motors,* published by Percival Marshall; a roll of the *Bustle of Spring* for a 1923 piano-player; a stone of beef dripping; eight copies of Ruff's *Guide* to *the Turf;* a bargain lot of empty creosote drums.

'The Calley,' the dear and now dead 'Calley,' could supply the lot with the impassive calm that comes from being in the business for a long, long time.

The empty chair

July 7, 1950

Cross the bridge at Henley and get over on to the Berkshire side.

Now walk downstream.

Past the enclosures with the Regatta tents.

Past the lovely girls thinking of photo-gravure pictures of themselves in the glossy magazines.

Past the old men with rowing caps looking like schoolboys with bald heads and beards, and past the strident-voiced young men with megaphones and bicycles and manners that are too confident to have much charm.

Now on to the towpath.

This is the English scene at its best. One of the loveliest stretches of fresh water in the world. Gaiety and serenity never walk better hand in hand than here along the side of the sweet Thames.

But come a little farther. See that empty chair there by the river's edge?

Nobody has taken much notice of it all day except perhaps a couple of spectators who may have idly wondered why it is there and who it is who has not turned up. Only one or two of us know.

Way back in the 'eighties a man came here on this very spot and saw his first Henley Regatta. He was a man who knew about the pleasures of mucking about in boats, who understood things about canoes and lock-gates and reeds and kingfishers and all the malty delights of riverside pubs. He was a man with a rather cold blue eye and more conviction about most things than is usually good for people, although he had the grace which is beyond price to admit (sometimes rather angrily) that he might be wrong.

This first Regatta evidently pleased him although he was pleasantly rude about the rowing with the fierceness of someone born with an oar in his hand.

He decided to come again – to let another year slip by and return to see whether the watermen of England had more muscle, endurance and skill than they had a twelvemonth before.

The gas-lit 'nineties with the chink of gold sovereigns, the gleam of top hats and all the tight-lipped confidence of the little old Royal lady in Buckingham Palace were born. There was the smell of distant war in the air – of proud Colonial war and fierce anger against someone called Smuts.

But the man who liked mucking about in boats still went to Henley every year; still took his chair to the same place and still raised a critical cheer as the flashing, dipping oars went by.

The century turned and the stink and rattle of the horseless carriage was the new music of having fun. The unsinkable Titanic went down. And a vain man with a withered arm at Potsdam postured as the Lord and Master of War. But the man who loved the wind in the willows still went to Henley.

Ten, twenty, thirty, forty years on, he was still seated at the river's brim in the early days of each July.

William Bliss, in his eighty-fifth year, saw his last Regatta in 1949.

It was his sixty-fourth.

Some of us mourn that empty chair.

Surf on the shore

January 30, 1964

What happens to old water-wheels, used acetylene lamps, elderly elephants, surplus steam locomotives, unwanted magic lanterns and superannuated cinema organs when they are no longer required?

Where is the secret burial ground?

To what unknown resting place do they creep away to die in dignity and solitude?

For the most part I cannot tell you.

But I can tell you about a mighty cinema organ, whose bones had been cast all over London, that has been resurrected, reassembled, restored, redeemed and forgiven and is now triumphantly trumpeting again.

Like Walter Mitty and Billy Liar, I have always nursed a secret dream to play one of the gorgeous brutes and when I hear that a mighty Wurlitzer that was defeated and dispersed has been victoriously reassembled, then I too make a joyful noise.

What happened was that from the bones of the Wurlitzer that used to peal forth from the Metropole Cinema, Victoria, and a lovely great sonorous brute that used to sound forth at the Troxy, Stepney, a new and composite mellifluous monster has been assembled in the Town Hall at Buckingham – of all places.

From The Picture House in Maida Vale, from The Rink at Sydenham, from the twin Gaumonts at Finsbury Park and Luton, and other musical centres hardly distinguishable from Salzburg and Malvern, the old bones were collected and the new flesh grew again. A band of gay enthusiasts under the musical command of Ralph Manchester and Ralph Bartlett rebuilt the old chap and monthly concerts now burst from its retuned and reconstructed heart.

It's got the lot. A three manual ten ranker – excuse these lovely terms. The blower weighs 7½ cwt. and the whole accompanying chorus of equipment is pure delight.

There is the Chrysoglott (build me a better word if you can); the Tubular Bells; the Tuned Sleigh Bells – as opposed, of course, to the Untuned Sleigh Bells; the Cathedral Chimes; the Castanets; the Horses Hooves (no information supplied about instrument for extracting stones therefrom); the Bird Whistle; the Fire Bells; the Cymbal Crash; the Snare-Drum; the Chinese Block; the Tom Tom; the Solo-to-Great; the Great-Unison-Off; the Steam Boat Hooter and the Krumet T F – God bless her whoever and wherever she is – and my old and dear friend from the Plaza, The Surf on the Shore.

Boy am I on my way to Buckingham and are those old monks in the Monastery Garden and the spivs in the Persian Market going to have a whale of a time!

The clock at St Pancras

September 14, 1966

Being fought, with that quiet bitterness and elegant ferocity that we have come to admire in the columns of *The Times,* is a hand-to-hand engagement with no quarter asked or given. It concerns the architectural merits of St Pancras Station.

Roughly speaking – and rough speaking is the order of the day – there are two views.

One: That the station named after the boy saint, who was martyred in Rome at the age of fourteen, is one of the greatest abominations ever wrought by the hand of misguided man.

Two: That the station is unique and 'possessed of visual richness and excitement' that would challenge St Peter's if only they had five platforms and a ticket office in the nave.

Those who wish to raze St Pancras to the ground are led by Sir Edward Playfair, who positively loathes the building, and the preservationists are strongly rallying to the staunch flag of Mr John Betjeman, who would, if he had the chance, grill his opponents to an agonized frazzle on some low quality ironwork discarded from the Coal Exchange.

Even the original builders have joined in and have rhapsodised about their honourable craft of brickwork involving such delectably named items as 'king closers, queen closers, rubbers, squints and noggins.'

I am solidly for keeping St Pancras from the destructionists and their unspeakable accomplices the developers, but for reasons that I do not think will be duplicated.

Nearly forty years ago I lived in what I rather grandly called a flat in Herbrand Street which was really more of a dusty attic than anything. It was on the top floor and overlooked the roofs of St Pancras. Sir Giles Scott's famous red brick clock tower, which dominates St Pancras, was about half a mile distant.

In those days jobs were very hard indeed to get and I lived as riotous a life as I could on about forty bob a week in a world of gas-rings, kippers, home-washed socks, tin-openers, lamentably restricted quantities of mild beer at threepence a pint and ferocious shopping expeditions to the

Caledonian Market with bitterly contested arguments about the price of a haddock.

I had a spare room with no furniture and not even a yard of worn lino with which to conceal the hard lines of life, where I permitted several disreputable unemployed friends to doss down provided they did the washing up and swept up the place – including their girl friends.

There were no pictures, some Penguins – the books not the birds – a disgruntled radio set, a huge Soyer soup tureen that I swore had seen service in the Crimea, and no clock. Not even a watch or a long-distance egg-timer.

But there was a telescope.

A beauty left to me by my father, who apart from painting water-colours, being permanently at war with an allotment, singing in Westminster Abbey choir and inventing a revolting stew called 'Steuchie', evidently mistrusted the stars in their courses. He kept a sharp eye on them on clear nights when for some obscure reason he concentrated on The Pleiades, who may in the past have given him cause for celestial umbrage. This excellent instrument – it was at least seven feet long and mounted on a tripod – he left to me.

Not being able to afford a clock I observed that the L.M.S. (or was it the Midland Railway then?) could afford a giant clock and had it mounted at the top of the tower of St Pancras for all to see. What could be more sensible than to have my well-loved telescope permanently trained on it from my private observatory or doss house in Herbrand Street.

The magnification was enormous and in reply to a request 'Wosser time Bill?' I was able, after careful scrutiny across the roofs of St Pancras, to say, 'It is seven and a quarter minutes past eight including the blue-bottle on the hour hand, and the young lady we saw undressing last night has drawn the blinds, you filthy beast.'

As you know, the great clock of St Pancras is illuminated at night; a soft amber colour made positively radiant when once a year we cleaned the windows. Do away with St Pancras?

Grind to rubble those king closers, queen closers, rubbers, squints and noggins?

Not if I and the ragged cohorts and timeservers and timeseekers of yesteryear can help it.

I was recounting these times recently with a friend of mine who remarked that he too had lived in a small block of flats and had no clock.

'But I had a bugle,' he said, 'which I also inherited from my father. It was most useful for telling the time – especially at night.'

'Pray how do you tell the time with a bugle at night?'

'It is quite simple. You open the window and blow a tremendous blast. The neighbours leap from their beds and bawl right back at you: "What the Lenny Bruce do you mean by blowing your blasted trumpet at 2.43 in the morning?" '

When Box meets Cox

September 17, 1966

I was clearing out my desk yesterday and came across some rather odd things which reminded me of the time long long ago when I shared a desk, a huge roll-top affair, with a man who worked at night and whom I never saw.

We lived a Box and Cox existence and I once wrote a description of my unseen nocturnal desk-fellow which I built up from his possessions.

There were lottery tickets, pocket puzzles, photographs of Derby winners, a lavish catalogue of champagnes, an unused portion of a first class railway ticket to Ascot, a small spirit level, a quantity of copper wire (22 S.W.G.): and a copy of Whymper's *Scrambles Among the Alps.*

Fitting this jigsaw together I formed a composite picture of a florid sporting thirsty gent (not a gentleman) who was thinking of going to Switzerland. The spirit level and the copper wire didn't fit very well in the pattern but I defiantly reassured myself that there was no reason whatsoever why florid sportsmen should not go up the Jungfrau all wired up to test levels.

When at last I did meet Cox – or was it Box? – he was plainly annoyed with my deductions which I had published. He was short, rather harsh-voiced, very efficient, despised the racing fraternity, disliked champagne and had no intention of going to the Alps either on the level or all wired up.

What I exhumed yesterday from my desk made me realize how vulnerable I was to any amateur Sherlock Holmes who might try to reconstruct me from my possessions alone.

There was a blow-lamp; an empty wooden seed box; a great brass letter B four inches by three; a chain for an eyeglass holder in a box labelled 'Spec-Band', and a huge photograph of a printed announcement that said that Marcus Aurelius the Roman Emperor, David Hume the historian, Daniel Defoe the writer, Emma Lady Hamilton mistress of Lord Nelson, Artemus Ward the humorist, Sir Alliot Verdon-Boe the aviation pioneer and John James Audubon the ornithologist were all born on April 26.

It added, somewhat mysteriously, that King George the Sixth and Queen Elizabeth were also married on April 26, 1923, and that in 1521 the Diet of Worms ended.

There was also a naval rating's hat; a map of the Western Isles printed in Venice by one Antonio Zatta in 1779; a bottle of marking ink and a thousand words on how to cook an egg ('Boiling eggs isn't all that elementary' is the ominous opening sentence) followed by instructions as to how to coddle, poach and scramble eggs.

There was a great brass paper clip measuring seven inches by two inches and a menacing looking little phial which read: '300 mg. Ferrous Gluconate B.P. 30 m.g. Ascorbic Acid B.P.' Now rebuild me from that lot.

I'm just an ordinary chap who suffers from elephantiasis of the paper clip, has a phobia about the letter B, sends birthday greetings to the ghosts of Emma Hamilton and Marcus Aurelius, celebrates the Diet of Worms, wears naval hats in secret, tortures his secretary with a blow-lamp and coddles eggs which he eats out of a seed box.

One Man's Wars

Cassandra was a wager of wars, great and small, public and private. His most notable campaigns included skirmishes with senders of Christmas Cards, wearers of Beards (who were threatened with instant imprisonment under his Hirsute Practices Act), British Railways, the Football Pools, Estate Agents, the Public Hangman, GPO Telephones, Electricity (or, as he called it, The Letrit) and a monstrous hot-water system that became known as The Thing In The Hall.

The Christmas card artillery

December 21, 1953

During the next three days about 350,000,000 Christmas cards will be fired in the British Isles.

Most of them are aimed at targets at home, for the long-ranged salvoes for overseas have been loosed off and are nearing their point of impact.

Now I am an old gunner in the Christmas Card Artillery, and it seems to me that more should be known of the military postal science of causing Yuletide mortification, annoyance, irritation, inconvenience, vexation, offence, resentment and deep anger.

The whole practice is such a thundering nuisance that it is high time that some practical advantage such as causing unhappiness was extracted out of the wretched business. I think I can point the way.

The first – and one of the most essential things to decide – is when to shoot. Timing is of critical importance. A premature Christmas card is not only ineffective but can be downright humiliating to the sender. It reveals one's position, discloses the size and weight of the ammunition and often provokes a devastating counter-attack.

On the other hand a late Christmas card (we gunners call them hang-fires) is liable to explode harmlessly, for the enemy has been given time to take cover. It is better to be on the early rather than late side, for the get-in-quick Christmas card sets the pace and compels the opposition to reply.

The next thing to understand is the value of size in Christmas cards.

Important people – and people who think they are important – send big and important-looking Christmas cards. This makes the recipient feel small – which is precisely what was intended. Expensive Christmas cards can be deadly, too, for they are usually fired by expensive people to make their victims feel cheap.

This is often quite costly but well worth it.

The really big Christmas card can be immensely infuriating. It barges its way into your house, glows with the swank and pride of its sender, crowds everything off the mantelpiece and makes strangers cry 'Ooooh' as they pick it up to see who is so rich, so powerful and so magnificent, as to be able to afford it.

The very small Christmas card can be pretty insulting, too. Don't underestimate its destructive value.

It shows what you think of the addressee – practically nothing. It is a mistake to make them too small as they then become rather cute and are liable to give pleasure. Avoid this dangerous mistake.

A really contemptuous size is about three and a half inches by two and a half inches. They are a bit difficult to obtain in the shops just now but are well worth the suffering they cause.

An old gunner's trick can be used very effectively, if, when you've sent a really whopping great card, you get an even bigger one in return.

You fire a second round.

You wait till after Christmas and then you send off the most squalid printed missile you can find. Address it incorrectly – but not so inaccurately as to confuse the postman – and then carefully spell the target's name wrong.

By these crafty means you create an unbearable impression that the first card was all a mistake and that the grubby follow-up is the true appraisal of your contemptuous feelings. Much misery and deep and very valuable loathing can be created by this well-proven and disgusting practice.

Now from size and cost to content.

With a little thought, the malevolent Christmas-carder can gain the upper hand of whole nations at a time.

Do you know any of those characters who live in Scotland? Then no doubt you burn to have your revenge.

It is quite easy.

Buy a Christmas card with a Scotsman on the front of it. Automatically he will be red-nosed (whusky), horns-woggled and be-sticked (Harry Lauder) and kilted (fra the Hie'lan's). The red nose will offend, the stick will be criticised for its music-hall background and, as for the tartan, nothing can stop its being 100 per cent wrong. Nobody, least of all designers and printers, gets the patterns right.

But these are minor (although valuable) irritations. The real razor slash is in the inscription. Now the way to tear Scotland apart and wrap it up in a torn Christmas card, is to smash into the Rabbie Burns business. What goes under the doddering alcoholic crackpot from Auchtermuchtie, runs something like this:

Ah the whaupit, burnin' dochter
Frae the brawlie speering dichter
Sonsy goes the loupin' beastie
Whaur's the crowlin' ferlie cochter.

Now that's pretty good Burns. The real Midlothian buttermilk touch. The Scots-wha-hae-wi'-Wallace-bled mob see this patriatic stuff and immediately start arguing as to whether the poem came from *Man Was Made to Mourn* or *The Lass of Blallochmyle* by the immortal R.B.

They quarrel. They fight. They fall out. 'It wasn't frae *The Lass of Ballochmyle,* nor from *The Kirk of Lamington.'* In their Hie'lan' disagreements they even hit each other. This is deeply gratifying south of the Border, because anybody can write Burns. I can write Burns. And that delectable sonnet on the card is my particular piece of Burns.

Another intensely valuable and hurtful approach is The-Out-of-Season-Touch. This studiously and carefully avoids robins, holly, snow, log-fires and wassail.

People stuffed with Christmas pudding, South African Port and crystallised ginger can be turned dizzy, green and reeling with the vertigos by one glimpse of the front of a Christmas card of the Cutty Sark in full sail.

This number, which even hi mid-summer is enough to give you the dry heaves, is available almost everywhere at a reasonable price.

Strongly recommended and of great emetic value.

Anti-dog lovers (Britain, contrary to popular conception, is laden down to the gunn'els with 'em) can be estranged for evermore with Christmas cards of lop-eared spaniels and unbearable Pekes with hideous insulting tails like furry aspidistras. Likewise, anti-catmen and anti-catgirls can be sent howling and spitting over the tiles by presenting them with carefully selected pictures of Tiddles, Cuddles and Snookey – the yelling sharp-clawed, slit-eyed limbs of Satan.

December 21, 1955

This year I have relied on the Mass Saturation Attack. I have fired more missiles than ever before. Nobody is safe. Men who have never heard of me and are happy in that state have suddenly been hit by printed matter of incomparable hypocrisy. I have taken care to spell their names wrongly and I have reminded them of the wonderful Spam and Constituted Egg Lunch Reunion that we all had in the Refreshment Bar at Peterboro' North in 1942. To people who ask only that I shall be imprisoned for life, I have sent unbearably hearty good wishes thanking them for their loyal support over the past nineteen years.

To neat, taut women whose moment of truth is a pale, sour sherry in the lounge (O Lovely Word!) of their suburban, chintzy superiors, I have sent gruff, belching cards of thirsty oafs knocking it back in Blackpool.

Even that pestilential Partridge in a Pear Tree has been dislodged from his throaty perch. The prize-winning Cadet from the Battle School managed to depict him on a shameful piece of soggy cardboard as a dishevelled parrot squawking filthy words in a pub in Peckham.

The Hirsute Practices Act

February 5, 1957

I'm getting a bit tired of the Duke of Edinburgh's beard.

I've had enough of these Royal whiskers and more than enough of the various imitative young gentlemen accompanying him who, with hairy flattery, have also grown these disguises. The Britannia must be a very hirsute place with all this face-fur about.

I am agin all this stubbly camouflage and I think there ought to be A Law. And that Law, which I have drafted myself, shall be known as the HIRSUTE PRACTICES ACT.

'WHEREAS the Lords Spiritual and Temporal and Commons assembled at Westminster freely representing all the Peoples of this Realm shall under the Provisions of the HIRSUTE PRACTICES ACT deem it unlawful for all male persons above the age of twenty-one to grow hair upon their upper lips, their chins and their chops for the purpose of disguising themselves as being more bountifully blessed with Virility and Masculinity than with which they have naturally been endowed. SUCH CITIZENS contravening the HIRSUTE PRACTICES ACT with growths intended to impress young female persons shall be accounted guilty of impersonation and be subject to a PUBLICK SHAVING with cold water and blunt blades. SUCH CITIZENS contravening the HIRSUTE PRACTICES ACT with growths intended to impress frequenters of ale houses with uncommon powers of suction shall be expelled from all licensed premises and consigned to forced labour in the PUBLICK WATERWORKS.

SUCH CITIZENS contravening the HIRSUTE PRACTICES ACT with growths and immoderate reminiscences of improbable feats of Valour in Her Majesty's Royal Air Force shall be forcibly ejected and required to GO FLY A KITE ELSEWHERE.

That will do for the moment, but further Sections are being drafted that will make it exceedingly perilous for certain young men to face the world as if peering through a furze bush darkly.

February 7, 1957

I note with grave satisfaction that immediately after the publication of my Hirsute Practices Act, the Duke of Edinburgh and Lieutenant-Commander Michael Parker have become clean shaven.

It is untrue that I have been offered a seat on the board of the Gillette Razor Blade Company.

April 11, 1957

I recently outlined proposals for my new Hirsute Practices Act under which it will be an offence for any person to disguise himself by wearing facial undergrowth – or rather overgrowth. This progressive measure is of course based on Section 28 of the Larceny Act of 1916 which provides that persons found on enclosed premises with blackened faces between the hours of dusk and daylight with intent to commit a felony are up to no good.

My own view is that all whiskered people, ranging from bearers of the thin vicious hairline moustache to the face hidden in deep and impenetrable fur are highly suspect. Rightly doubting of then[1] own virtue they pretend to be entirely different parties in order to conceal their own defects.

I once knew a most deplorable man – he was one of my closest friends – who wore a beard. It was golden and terrible and at my urgent request he shaved it off. Then was revealed a hairless physiognomy of such depravity that I pleaded with him to grow the beard again. This, with a characteristic rapacity, he refused to do until I gave him a rental of five bob a week 'for the facial shooting rights' as he expressed it, to keep the beastly thing on.

I paid up.

The Six-Five Special

February 21, 1958

What's the good of having a column that you've plied for twenty years, man and boy, if you can't use it for a private beef?[*]

Here comes the beef and slice it as thin as you may, it's still not boloney.

The papers are now adorned with a series of large-scale advertisements describing the virtues of British Railways. These lavish exhortations describe how trains are not a 'harassing scramble'; how 'going by train is not only quicker, it's so much more comfortable'; how you can 'stretch your legs'; how you can 'eat a meal or a snack at your ease'; how you arrive 'fresh as a daisy'; and how you can at certain times save 'four shillings in every pound'.

This rosy dream is paid for by you and me.

Every word of it. Every silly untrue blandishment.

Now I, together with countless other people, use this shabby transport.

---

[*] Beef: Vivid American slang for grudge, complaint or sense of injustice.

Together with millions of other people I hold a season ticket and ply to and from London Town five times a week.

I pay over fifty pounds a twelve-month for this dirty ordeal. I travel from High Wycombe to Marylebone year in and year out and I want to say that it is an abysmal experience. Thousands of other people do likewise and are charged through the nose for this degrading journey. I have done it for over a quarter of a century and I have paid the railways the best part of a thousand pounds to pursue this squalid, slimy trail.

The distance is less than thirty miles. The average time taken to accomplish it at scheduled speeds is just under an hour and the occasions that it takes over an hour are legion.

High Wycombe is a prosperous town of over 42,000 inhabitants, yet it has only three non-stop trains all of which are hours away from the rush times. The rolling stock is filthy and to wear a light suit is to risk rising from a seat smothered in grime.

For twenty years the inhabitants of this unfortunate town (of whom I am one of the more patient) have been attempting to get the 6.18 pm from Marylebone to Sheffield to stop at High Wycombe. Our M.P.s have tried. Our mayors have tried. Our councillors have tried.

The season ticket holders, who are far more important financially than the occasional long-distance traveller who rides in comparative comfort and cleanliness, have tried.

We've all failed.

This busted down, wheezy, sooty, slow alleyway into London continues its slothful, unsanitary way at speeds which are slower than those achieved twenty-five years ago.

These ludicrous advertisements paid for by the taxpayers to paper over the cracks of suburban travel say that the process is not a 'harassing scramble'.

Absolutely untrue.

I've had people standing on my feet and I've stood on other people's feet since the early thirties.

They say that going by train is quicker.

Absolutely untrue. The wretched Wycombe line is slower than it was before the war and twice as costly.

They say that you can arrive as fresh as a daisy.

Some daisy.

In all this sooty scene the only shaft of sunlight is the courtesy of the staff at Wycombe and Marylebone, who presumably sympathise with us on our protracted pilgrimage of polluted pain.

For ten years, war raged between Cass and the Railways. Then, suddenly, in 1963, peace came as the result of an improved service between his house and London.

Huddle-dee-dee Huddle-dee-dah

May 17, 1963

Things have changed and where all the blame in the world would not have been enough for this dreadful iron road of squalid misery and delay, this Golgotha of transport to the West, I pour out my praise for the great and welcome change that has overtaken us this last year.

I will now describe what happens on the new flyers from Paddington to Wycombe.

At the head of the long-distance train is a gigantic diesel locomotive that wears no smile on its formidable face. It has the same expression as an eighty-ton fighting-tank – only more so.

It looks as if it feeds on ingots and drinks molten metal, and its mighty tribe of fellow locomotives bear challenging names like *Western Courier, Western Explorer* or *Western Thunderer*.

We move off at a low hum and slip through Royal Oak station easily enough, and past a grey panorama of gas-holders, radio factories, dry cleaning establishments, and brave white and pink laundry flaunting from the backs of terraced houses that were old when Gladstone was reforming the world.

We move through grey brick-walled canyons where once there were iron enamel advertisements that said without comment SKETCHLEY DRY CLEANING or, more laconically, PETER'S OIL ENGINES.

Other printed notice boards in the splendid days of the once-wonderful Great Western Railway used to say to the footplate men SHUNT or, more mysteriously to the laymen, ENGINES MUST CONDENSE. Now a low moaning begins beneath the carriage wheels and the steel dinosaur ahead of us, with the greyhound legs, takes charge. The acceleration sooms and the scent of the hare of Old Oak Common, three miles ahead, gets into the nostrils of the speeding brute.

Over many years on the Great Western I have noticed that when locomotives smell Old Oak Common, they are really off. Our wheels start the famous chant that Reginald Gardiner made famous years ago in his gramophone record about trains. They say 'Huddle-de-dee, Huddle-de-dah. Huddle-dee-dee, Huddle-dee-dah' ever faster and ever faster.

We are away to the West. The telegraph wires start their swaying up-

and-down dance. The switch points and the crossing chant with syncopated glee: 'Honkely Donk, Honkely Donk, Honkely, Honkely, Honkely, Honkely Donk-de Donk-de. Huddle-dee-dee, de Huddle-dee-dah…'

We roar up to that strange station called Denham Golf where for twenty years I have stopped, often near midnight, to allow the non-existent golfers to play golf and where it is reputed that many years ago a director of the Great Western Railway lived and ordered all trains to stop for his own convenience.

This station, as with Seer Green Halt, a few miles ahead which also caters for a golf club, is not even a blur outside the window now. Not even a smudge or a smear.

Gerrards Cross and Beaconsfield, the Shangri-las of the stockbrokers, are fuzzy backward disappearing streaks. Then on to the tunnel (O blessed tunnel) that lies two miles east of Wycombe. I have for decades used it as a waker-up. In the old day the sound of it as we drifted lazily in said 'Whaaa… Whaaa… Whaaa... Whaaa… Whaaa… Whaaa...' and so on.

Now, as we rocket through it at eighty miles an hour, it simply says 'WHOP!'

And that's it. Twenty-eight miles sometimes accomplished in twenty-six minutes. Thank you, B.R.

No X.43196 replies

October 27, 1955

I have to report that Mr Cecil Moores, the millionaire chairman of Littlewoods Pools, has given up the struggle to win thin tanners from out of my ragged pockets.

The great typhoon of idiot circulars and printed drivel has apparently blown itself out.

Somehow Mr Cecil – if I may be so familiar – has managed to get his lurching, swaying business under control, and I have been left in peace for several weeks.

I am much obliged.

But what has happened now?

A brilliant flanking attack has been launched which has crashed into my defences. Brother Cecil Moores having failed to add me to his millions of pools suckers has retired, but Brother John Moores, with a great sweeping arc of violent hostility has opened fire on me from a totally unexpected direction. He seems a determined man and has decided that where Cecil, the Pools King, was unsuccessful in making me into a luckless gambler, he, John, the King of Littlewoods Mail Order Stores, will triumph in making me a salesman for his business.

The first salvo of literature was terrific – and dead on target. It consisted of a 300-page Mail Order Catalogue weighing 2 lb. 2 oz. that cost one shilling and threepence to send to me through the mail.

With it was a personal letter from John Moores (of this more later); a Mail Order Book with Order Forms; a Collecting Record; eighteen Club Subscription Cards; A Payment Card circular promising me two pairs of nylons *(all right Moores, I'll get you yet);* a Free Voucher; an Invitation to join a Home Shopping Club; two Addressed Envelopes; an Offer for Free Introduction Cards; a Reminder to include full payment with orders; a Request to make a correction on page 98 to the effect that a rug is 'Wine with Grey Motif, not as illustrated'; a paste-over Amendment Slip about Black Velveteen Mules *(you can say that again, Brother John)* and three severe little items about sheets, dresses and 'a charming occasional table'.

Quite a start for a beginner.

All I want now is a free motor-car in which to call upon my clients, a crate of light ale to bolster me up, and a fund of filthy stories for the long, dark winter evenings in travellers' hotels.

Mr John Moores, my new Managing Director, is pretty sure he has got me for keeps, for already I have a stencilled plate somewhere up in Liverpool that addresses me as 'Mr Cassandra.' I must be pretty securely pinned down in my new job for I have also got a number – X.43196 – just like any gaolbird being mugged by the police.

Managing Director Moores has his human moments, however, for he addresses me as *'Dear Organiser'*, and although he continues his letter with a direct lie – *'This is the catalogue you asked for'* – that *'Organiser'* touch has just the right hint of flattery I rather fall for.

Although how the heck I'm going to organise myself out of this job, I haven't figured out yet.

In the meantime, according to Brother John, I'm at your service. You want a low-priced Axminster of utterly appalling design? I have one right here, lady – seventy bob.

You want some crockery to chuck at the old man? What about the *Crinoline Lady* 21-piece set for fifty shillings? It has just the correct old-fashioned note for the missus who feels a bit old-fashioned.

Or a bird-cage that is described as *'Comfy'*? What you are suffering from, madam, is an attack of uncomfy bird-cages about the house.

Or maybe a quietly menacing bedroom suite that will disturb your peace of mind for all time; a three section frying pan; a blackboard and easel; a

Graceful Galleon Coal Vase (ugh!); a pair of long-legged, warm-plated underpants just suitable for Spitsbergen – or a storm lantern, maybe?

Lady, I got 'em all.

And it looks as if I'll be stuck with the lot.

That is unless my new Managing Director abides by his promise in the final paragraph of his letter:

'*If there is any way I can help you,*' he writes, *'drop me a line... I shall be delighted to hear from you.*'

You will, buddy? You will?

Well take your great postal caravanserai of pots and pans and brushes and umbrellas and twisted-oak candlesticks. Desist, sir! I say DESIST!

Adjoining Green Belt

January 31, 1966

Now that the Government is going to pass a law making accurate trade descriptions of goods for sale in shops compulsory, I hope its legislation will extend to houses.

Estate agents who are in the home-sweet-home business have evolved a language of their own to describe properties. They have distorted words and completely twisted them out of their original meaning, so that the luckless prospective buyer cannot believe that the house he is looking at is the same one that has been advertised.

You need a glossary to understand the lingo.

'Easily maintained' means it badly needs propping up.

'Superbly restored with no expense spared' means that the price is so outrageously high that even the vendors dare not mention it.

'Miniature' means no room to swing a cat.

'Within thirty-five minutes of Waterloo' means eighty miles to the south-west of London flying by specially chartered helicopter.

'Charming' means revolting.

'Picturesque' means the same as charming – only held together with poison ivy.

'Delightful' means disgusting.

'Compact' means suitable for dwarfs.

'Home of the future' means unsold in the present and likely to remain so.

'Adjoining green belt' means Slough.

'Immaculate' means badly needs a lick of paint.

'Antique oak-beamed' means new black-painted pine.

'Manageable Garden' means gnarled nasturtiums with room to swing a dead rat on a short string.

'Important' means pretentious.

'Imposing' means menacing.

'Secluded' means set in swamp in the middle of a forest.

'Spacious' means anything from ten to twenty damp bedrooms with a coal-fired boiler that was originally designed by Brunel for his monstrous ship the *Great Eastern.*

And 'enchanting surroundings with modem conveniences' means there's a pylon at the bottom of the garden.

Euston station

July 20, 1951

I remember when I was very young that I thought of Euston Station as being the Temple of the London and North-Western Railway, the gateway to Fleetwood and Belfast and a place that was as romantic as Treasure Island and as dirty as the chimney of hell.

I remember when I was young, but not so very young, that I thought of Euston Station as being the Temple of the London and Scottish Railway, the shrine of Sir Josiah Stamp, and a place that was not so romantic as Treasure Island and as dirty as the chimney of hell.

Now that I am no longer young and I try to forget Euston Station, which is the Temple of the British Railways Executive and a place that is an insult to mention in the same breath as Treasure Island, I only observe that the scene changeth not and it still remains as dirty as the chimney of hell.

Late last night (that is late by English standards, although it was not yet midnight) I was back again in this smutty maw that leads to the North.

Once through the Euston mausoleum arch, with its hint of a journey from which there may be no return, I found the same studied care to repel the traveller that existed thirty years ago.

The smell of sulphur and bananas that I remember from the days when Dempsey knocked out Carpentier.

No bookstalls open.

What! want to *read* at this ungodly hour?

Tired old ladies sitting wearily on porters' trolleys.

What! want to *sit* at this ungodly hour?

Not a bar open.

What! want to *drink* at this ungodly hour? Orange peel and paper and litter and filth all around.

What! want the place *clean* at this ungodly hour? The inquiry counter, barred and grilled with only an empty teacup standing on squalid sentry-go, defies all comers and silently hints that this is no time to ask foolish questions.

What! Want to *know* anything at this ungodly hour? All around the Festival signs proclaim with pathetic joy the happiness that may be found across the Euston-road.

Bales of netting wire, baskets of blackcurrants, crates of machinery, motor-cycles, mail bags, trunks, suitcases and sacks and all the tired cargoes that move in and out of this mournful place lie hopeessly around.

On the far platform drunks are squabbling.

Someone is trying to climb through a carriage window and a raucous Glasgow voice is yelling its wearisome obscenities. Tipsy soldiers and patient policemen are scuffling and arguing the dreary toss.

The new £20,000 Train Arrival Indicator tells a stunned and defeated public with bright and clinical efficiency how much later their friends will be.

Lights are switched out. Porters yawn and ticket collectors stare at travellers as if they are evil-doers who should have long been home abed.

Maybe it was better in the twenties.

The smell of sulphur and bananas seemed more exciting then and at least you *could* get the bananas.

Ruth Ellis was convicted of shooting her lover in a blaze of vengeance. Cass pleaded for the law to show her mercy; in vain. She was hanged.

The woman who hangs today

July 13, 1955

It's a fine day for haymaking. A fine day for fishing. A fine day for lolling in the sunshine. And if you feel that way – and I mourn to say that millions of you do – it's a fine day for a hanging.

IF YOU READ THIS BEFORE NINE O'CLOCK THIS MORNING, the last dreadful and obscene preparations for hanging Ruth Ellis will be moving up to their fierce and sickening climax. The public hangman and his assistant will have been slipped into the prison at about four o'clock yesterday afternoon.

There, from what is grotesquely called 'some vantage point' and unobserved by Ruth Ellis, they will have spied upon her when she was at exercise 'to form an impression of the physique of the prisoner'.

A bag of sand will have been filled to the same weight as the condemned woman and it will have been left hanging overnight to stretch the rope.

IF YOU READ THIS AT NINE O'CLOCK, then – short of a miracle – you and I and every man and woman in the land with head to think and heart to feel will, in full responsibility, blot this woman out.

The hands that place the white hood over her head will not be our hands. But the guilt – and guilt there is in all this abominable business – will belong to us as much as to the wretched executioner paid and trained to do the job in accordance with the savage public will.

IF YOU READ THIS AFTER NINE O'CLOCK, the murderess, Ruth Ellis, will have gone.

The one thing that brings stature and dignity to mankind and raises us above the beasts of the field will have been denied her – pity and the hope of ultimate redemption.

The medical officer will go to the pit under the trap door to see that life is extinct. Then in the barbarous wickedness of this ceremony, rejected by nearly all civilised peoples, the body will be left to hang for one hour.

IF YOU READ THESE WORDS OF MINE AT MID-DAY the grave will have been dug while there are no prisoners around and the Chaplain will have read the burial service after he and all of us have come so freshly from disobeying the Sixth Commandment which says 'Thou shalt not kill.'

The secrecy of it all shows that if compassion is not in us, then at least we still retain the dregs of shame. The medieval notice of execution will have been posted on the prison gates and the usual squalid handful of louts and rubbernecks who attend these legalised killings will have had their own private obscene delights.

Two Royal Commissions have protested against these horrible events. Every Home Secretary in recent years has testified to the agonies of his task, and the revulsion he has felt towards his duty. None has ever claimed that executions prevent murder.

Yet they go on and still Parliament has neither the resolve nor the conviction, nor the wit, nor the decency to put an end to these atrocious affairs.

When I write about capital punishment, as I have often done, I get some praise and usually more abuse. In this case I have been reviled as being 'a sucker for a pretty face'.

Well, I am a sucker for a pretty face. And I am a sucker for all human faces because I hope I am a sucker for all humanity, good or bad.

But I prefer the face not to be lolling because of a judicially broken neck.

Yes, it is a fine day.

Oscar Wilde, when he was in Reading Gaol, spoke with melancholy of 'that little tent of blue which prisoners call the sky'.
The tent of blue should be dark and sad at the thing we have done this day.

The small red room

February 13, 1962

An extraordinarily large part of my life is spent holding a black plastic object that stretches from my mouth to my ear.
I talk, shout and whisper down it for hundreds of hours a year.
Much of the time when I do this I am in a small red room that is usually filthy, always uncomfortable and frequently ill-lit.
This constricted house of pain is called a telephone kiosk.
I pay money for doing this. And so do my employers. Between us we lay out hundreds of pounds a year for the minus quantity of fun I have in the small red room.
There are 74,000 public call boxes in Great Britain and although I have not been in every one of them, I feel as if I have. I am completely familiar with these rectilinear hells.
And yet there are not enough of them. I know. I have waited outside watching the expressions of the customers using them. If it is a man, you will usually see the dark shadow of pain cross his face as he endures having to use the monstrosity that Edison began.
If it is a woman, you will all too often discern the light of endless garrulity in her face. You can observe her slanderous pleasure as her female telephonic accomplice hurls back a piece of malicious gossip to be gnawed over later in leisurely reflection.
When finally you DO get admission to this vermilion, vertical coffin, as often as not the door won't close properly, there is cigarette ash in the return-money pocket and the place smells of dead goats on a hot afternoon in Kabul.
At times the slot where you try to thrust your money is blocked with cardboard, paper or chewing gum (which is not the fault of the GPO) and the release aperture which attempts to give you your money back may also be clogged.
If you carry a hairpin about (and what well-trained business executive does not?) thrust the point upwards and you may win a jack-pot of pennies which have been denied exit because of a plug of chewed bread, that the get-rich-quick boys have been using.

The other day in this column I said some harsh things about the GPO Telephone Service, the main point of which was that a go-slow could be borne with equanimity by the public because they were hardened by what they got for their money.

Not unexpectedly, I was sharply rebuked and challenged to visit a typical telephone exchange. I went yesterday to the Museum Exchange.

I was received with courtesy that at times was in danger of ripening into cordiality by no less than six officials ranging from a union representative to talented technical men. I felt like an important condemned prisoner who was going to be treated with the utmost civility on a specially laid red carpet right up to the trap door.

They proved, which I never queried, that the GPO Engineers are getting a raw deal. They claimed, which I never doubted, that the service is being eroded for lack of funds.

And they insisted, which is undeniable, that it was the Post Office Engineers, and I quote them, 'who first led the field in opposing the dishonourable and arbitrary action of the Government by staging the biggest demonstration march seen in London since the General Strike of 1926'.

Now the work-to-rule which results in the go-slow is gathering speed – and I offer you that paradox with great pleasure. I was shown one of the thirty or forty tomes that tell unionists how to give bad value for money and not to infringe the rules.

There are two views about this doleful practice.

One: It is the only way the GPO Engineers can legitimately and effectively make their grievance felt.

Two: They are short-changing their employers, the public (and maybe ultimately their own reputation), by giving bad value for money.

You can take your choice – but I warn you you will get no reduction on your phone bills for being at the slow-receiving end of this dispute.

In the meantime, it's back to the small red room for me.

December 15, 1964

Hullo there! Hullo there! You can't hear me? I'm not surprised. I'm telephoning you from my subterranean hideout. I've gone to ground.

But let's go back to the beginning. On December 3, 4, 7 and 9, I published in this column criticisms of the GPO telephone system describing it, among other things, as 'costly', 'incompetent' and 'all too frequently manned by indifferent staff'.

Very well. Now let's see what happened. On Monday, December 7, I began to receive telephone calls at my home address. The name

'Cassandra' is not in the Directory. The bell rang and I, or a member of my family, lifted the receiver.

There was no answer.

These persecution calls continued at the rate of about one every two hours, the earliest being at one minute past five in the morning and the latest at seven minutes to midnight. I do not like being woken at five a.m.

Where these cowardly anonymous calls came from is anybody's guess.

But, judging by my mail, the switchboard operators are not pleased with what I have to say, although I have the names and addresses of some who agree with me. The general public, who are subscribers, are largely delighted at my criticisms.

After the third day of being pestered. I wrote to the Superintendent of the Reading Exchange asking him to try to stop the calls.

He received my letter on Thursday, and with commendable speed asked whether he could come and see me that night. As it was around 9pm I said that ten o'clock the next morning would do perfectly well. He turned up on the dot. Let me say here that if all GPO employees were as prompt and efficient and courteous as Mr D R E Wilcox, our GPO telecommunications would not be in the tattered disrepute they are.

He suggested that I should go to ground, that my old number should be disconnected and a new number known only to me and selected telephone operators should be substituted. I at once agreed.

The persecuting calls ceased and I was safe in my aural bunker. True, outside friends, unless they had been warned by me, were cut off, but the bells that rang in the deep of the night and wan hours of the early morning had been silenced.

This malevolent use of the phone is, of course, fairly commonplace, and to people who live alone it can be terrifying. Big Ear is always listening. You are being watched. There is someone there. You can always take the receiver off the hook, of course, but to rent the telephone equipment and be unable to use it is not what I call a satisfactory business deal.

I was able to avoid using this troublesome machine until Sunday, when I was compelled to get in touch with my office.

Little did I know.

At 2.31pm, carefully noting the time I dialled my exchange, asked for a transfer-charge call to FLEet Street 0246 and gave my local new under-cover number and my name. The operator then asked if I had said that 'Bradfield' was my exchange which, not in any syllable sounds remotely like my local switchboard. I repeated the correct name and number once more, clearly and slowly, with not a trace of sorrow or anger that have long been drained out of me in this melancholy business.

After a pause she said: 'Are you quite sure you have given me the right number?'

I said I had. She said that the number was unobtainable. I said it wasn't.

She said: 'It's a ceased line.' I said it wasn't.

After a pause she said: 'There's so much to remember and I'm not used to this Sunday afternoon work.'

My heart bled a little.

She put me through to FAULTS, and in just under six minutes I was all the way through to London Town, a remote city at least forty miles away.

It may be worth recalling that Mr T A O'Brien, who is the PRO of the GPO, wrote to my Editor saying that 'Operators write down numbers as they are given and there is rarely need for them to ask for a number to be repeated.'

Well, you can repeat that again Mr O'Brien.

But on with my winged tale...

At 6.39 on the same evening I again tried to get in touch with my office, I dialled the exchange, and the ringing tone commenced.

For exactly eleven minutes I hung on with nothing happening to see what was the endurance record for the course. Then at 6.50 I fell off through sheer exhaustion. Next, I dialled the number for FAULTS and got through to the *Mirror* at 6.52. At 6.57 I was cut off in mid-flight, but managed to get back to London two minutes later.

Now I don't think this is good enough. I am one of the nine million subscribers to the GPO telephone system and over the last few years I have paid hundreds of pounds in telephone bills.

My employers, the *Daily Mirror,* are also customers. The amount paid by the *Daily* and *Sunday Mirror* last year to the GPO for telephone services is in the neighbourhood of £135,000.

The profit on GPO telecommunications last year was £38,583,846.

I think the public deserves a better deal and I don't propose to be silenced by anonymous bunglers at the top of the GPO.

It's the Letrit!

March 7, 1958

I oppose electricity. Whether the stuff will continue to exist after my condemnation is problematical.

I learned to loathe electricity many, many years ago. An old car I once owned broke down and had to be towed into a garage.

The mechanic was an ancient chap who was probably brought up on steam cars and attributed all the troubles of the motoring world to electricity.

He was probably right.

He took one look at my paralysed four-wheeled hulk and said with scorn and dislike: 'Betcha it's the letrit!'

Try pronouncing the word 'electric' as 'letrit'! It is very satisfying.

It gets the real note of contempt that all true electricity leathers feel about the stuff.

He opened the bonnet, pointed to the petrol pump and spat out the word 'Letrit!'

He jabbed an accusing finger at the distributor and snarled: 'Letrit!'

He looked at the fuse-box and found it guilty with one word: 'Letrit!'

He glared at the starter motor and said: 'Letrit!'

He sneered at the headlights and jeered: 'Letrit!'

Then he gave his all-embracing verdict: 'Letrit! Letrit! Letrit! Nothing but this pesky Letrit! No good will come of it, mark my words.'

And no good has come of it.

'Letrit' has not helped this world.

Without 'Letrit!' we could be free from television. Without 'Letrit!' we could be emancipated from the telephone. Without 'Letrit!' we could escape radio, aeroplanes, high-voltage guitars, hairdryers, buzzing razors, neon signs, guided missiles and simply enormous shocks that amateurs like myself receive when we try to put a new plug on the vacuum cleaner.

We could also have fewer newspapers because with the 'Letrit!' one printing machine alone can belt out 60,000 copies an hour.

When I start my own newspaper it will be powered by a water wheel with the splashing of the stream drowning the noise of the horses clip-clopping up to take away the first edition.

When we on the Water-Wheel Press wish to communicate with anyone we will have no telephone so we will put our hat and our coat on and we will summon the four-in-hand to take us to our informants.

Megaphones and ear trumpets will be available for those who just wish to gather the news by sitting and shouting at the passers-by from open windows.

Down with 'letrit!'

The Thing in the Hall

October 13, 1960

In the hall there is The Thing.

My hall.

The Thing is in the same line of business as Dr Jekyll and Mr Hyde, the Abominable Snowman and what they are doing at Cape Canaveral.

It is about three and a half feet high, two feet wide, nearly a yard deep, gleaming white and looks more like a refrigerator than a boiler – which it is.

The Thing has been the greatest spreader of alarm and despondency I have ever bought, with the possible exception of a certain television set which reported great TV occasions, like the Coronation, with nothing more than a thin, bitter, horizontal line across its sneering face.

This particular Telly (which even its despairing manufacturers called 'a rogue-elephant set') had nothing on The Thing.

The Thing makes hot water and is stuffed with British Thermal Units, electric eyes, thermostats, switches, and feeds on what smells like low-grade sump oil mixed with ground-up pterodactyls.

It sits there silent and aseptic like one of those operating theatre cabinets full of long knives and oval trays for swabs they mean to leave inside you.

Then, without warning, The Thing erupts.

There is the sudden Kerrrrrrr-UMP! of a two-thousand-pound bomb going off in the middle-distance followed by a deep, guttural roar.

If you have the radio set switched on it twitches and if you have the Telly on, the blood runs from its electronic face.

Milk turns sour and even strong, tyrannical men within earshot who have won prizes in weight-lifting contests lock up their daughters.

If you listen carefully I swear you will hear a faint, menacing metallic voice doing the Cape Canaveral count down…

'Seven... Six... Five… Four… Three… Two… One… FIRE!'

The house trembles and you expect to see The Thing rise slowly from its launching pad and then, as the blast-off reaches its mighty crescendo, roar off into the night via the first and second floors and the tiled roof.

The cat, normally a confident, insolent animal by the name of Bulgy, happened to be passing when The Thing first exploded into action.

So did Bulgy with a vertical take-off from Runway Four. He is now a trembling psychiatric case who fears to pass The Thing by day or night.

The sound it makes is a deep, catastrophic rumble of impending doom.

You get it in the boiler-rooms of sinking battleships with men dying of scalding steam.

You get it in organ lofts behind the thirty-two foot diapason pipe which is pumping out poison gas.

You get it when you are entombed after an earthquake and the local gas main bursts into flame.

Windowpanes splinter and old walls crack, and spiders with deep, bass voices emerge. Then, as suddenly as it began, The Thing stops.

The silence is an explosion in reverse, and even more unbearable than the hideous grumble of intolerable profundity.

You long to hear something.

A baby screaming with terror.

A tocsin. A shrieking owl.

A prayer for the dead.

The slam of a dungeon door.

The sigh of doomed men.

But The Thing says nowt.

It crouches there in the hall with its thunderous tongue torn out.

Waiting . . . waiting . . . waiting.

What can I do with The Thing?

There is only one recourse.

I will entomb The Thing.

I will have the hall exorcised.

And then, and only then, will Bulgy and I get a decent night's rest.

December 18, 1960

In response to overwhelming public demand for morbid details of the final interment of The Thing in the Hall, I have decided to succumb to my worst instincts and release details of the last sombre and affecting scenes.

Mourners and revellers alike who have been following the story of my fight against an electrically-operated, oil-burning hot-water boiler will recall when I first installed it in the hall this box of thermal pain regularly exploded with a KERRRRRRUMP! that shook the plaster off the ceiling.

This was followed by the diapason roar of a distant avalanche abruptly cut off when a million tons of snow were roaring down the side of Mont Blanc. The worst part was wondering in the deathly hush that followed at three in the morning, how the snow stopped and whether it rolled back upwards on to the summit again. The secret decision to bury The Thing alive in a tomb of brick, acoustic tiles and walls of fibre glass was taken in Highgate Cemetery in the rain just behind Karl Marx's grave. Dark glasses were obligatory, the muttered password was 'Jingle Bells' and sodden plimsolls were worn.

When at last we had the brute cornered, grunting, spitting and slavering like a trussed wild boar, and the last stones were being cemented in, a scholarly mourner with a sense of history remarked: 'Not since Tutankhamen was entombed in his golden coffin in Egypt near the last resting place of Rameses VI has there been an event of comparable significance. Surely it would be fitting that alongside The Thing we placed certain symbolic articles of the year 1960 that would add a topical note to man's triumphant contempt for the machine and a memorial to the heroic spirit of The Owner who, with courage and splendid vision, finally managed to put a sock in it.'

I was compelled to agree.

Through the last aperture and down into the hole were lowered the unsurrendered portion of a day return ticket from King's Cross to Finsbury Park via the Copenhagen and Gasworks Tunnels – the squalid and pathetic symbol in the sixties of man's suffering on the Golgotha of British Railways.

The Thing evidently spotted this grimy passport to travelling pain and strained at its bolts and spewed up like Moby Dick. 'Thar she blows!' remarked one nautically-minded pall-bearer.

My cats who had had the daylights scared out of them when The Thing was at large and first terrorized the whole house with its hideous rumblings and its favourite party imitation of Vesuvius blowing its top, arched their backs and screamed.

The wind sighed and the rain beat down upon the windows. A pair of filthy mud-enslimed Wellingtons were stuffed into the steaming catafalque, and a deaf mute from the Exeter region of Devonshire coughed hoarsely and sneezed.

From the heated sepulchre came a snuffling and a snoring, but it was muffled, distant stuff like a mild influenza case in a coal mine heard from pit-head level.

Someone keened and blubbered:

'Strew on your roses, roses
And never a spray of yew.

In quiet it reposes,
Ah would that I did, too!'

The Thing lay still.

The head mourner tested the casing with a stethoscope. There were no heart-beats. Respiration had ceased. But it still lived with its tongue torn out and its eardrums pierced.

The soft sweet silence tip-toed down upon us with engulfing, swaddling calm.

The clocks nervously hammered away with their thunderous ticking. A tap dripped and sploshed with noisy, liquid joy.

The cats clumped and stamped across the carpet like the Guards at foot-drill on the square at the Depot at Caterham.

A fly roared up on to the picture rail noisier than a Boeing 707 jet, and a stray, tipsy coroner, who had just stumbled in, prayed earnestly for silence – on the grounds that he could not hear the sound of his toe-nails growing.

The Thing was in.

The Thing was down.

The Thing was out.

Professor Brown-fingers

So many things went wrong in Cassandra's garden that Philip Zee, the cartoonist, christened him Professor Brown-fingers. Then one year he grew a giant sunflower over ten feet tall. Readers had to endure a day-by-day account of the brute's progress. But first, the epic of the Army Boots he bought to work in…

Boots-boots-boots

May 21, 1962

I hate digging. I can endure mowing, a bit of hedge-clipping, a modicum of planting and a short spell of weeding. I am at my best in a greenhouse – hidden from the outside world by the foliage of tomatoes and drinking a bottle of beer while reclining in a deck chair.

But I hate digging.

Last week I set out to do some digging. I put it off time and time again.

I kidded myself that it was going to rain.

I looked at the fork and tried to persuade myself that the tines were too short.

Things became desperate so I laid a trap for myself. It's rather like playing single-handed draughts against yourself. I went and bought a pair of gigantic studded and steel-tipped boots that made ex-Army clod-hoppers look like ballet shoes. They were obviously built for stamping things to death – like full-sized crocodiles. They would have made a dinosaur look clumsy in them. I unloaded these gigantic crushers into the shed and waited. The self-goading plot ripened. I could not get those boots off my mind. There they stood gaping, gawking and yawning at me. You couldn't avoid seeing them even when you averted your eyes. There they were – thirty-nine shillings and sixpence worth of accusation.

Something extremely nasty in the tool shed. Two enormous rebukes in steel-encrusted leather. Twin boats of pedestrian derision. I heard Kipling chanting his 'Boots-boots-boots-boots – movin' up an' down again', except that these boots stood stock still staring at me.

Ultimately I broke down and put my foot gingerly into one like a bather, testing the water with his toe.

I tried to walk but I felt as if I were in the stocks. Maybe the boots were nailed to the ground. Perhaps the steel studs were attracted by some enormously powerful underground magnet. But somehow we got moving and a small patch of ground has been slightly scratched on the surface with deep imprints where the boots-boots-boots-boots have sunk deep into the cringing soil.

April 4, 1963

Yesterday I heard the rustle of spring.

The grass was muttering. The crocuses crooned sweet and low. The buds stirred and the blackbirds shouted aloud with joy.

But from the garden-shed came a rumble of thunder and The Boots bellowed: 'Come into the garden, Bill, we are here in the shed alone.' So I obeyed the order.

But could I get into the great pedestrian containers? Not a chance.

They were as rigid as iron. I could just stand on tip-toe on the heel part. The remorseless beetle-crushers were as inflexible as steel ingots. Compared with them The Iron Boot of Grotingen was a ballerina's silken slipper lightly dipped in champagne.

So once again we don't plough the land and we don't scatter the good seed on the ground.

Yippee!

Happing it up

December 3, 1962

I have been designing, planning, constructing and maintaining a bonfire.

It has now been burning for eight days and has been pronounced by an eminent bonologist as 'truly one of the finest specimens seen in the Home Counties since they made a bonfire in South London in 1936 that included, among its ingredients, the Crystal Palace.'

I inherited my talent – some would say genius – for bonfires from my father, who said that life without a bonfire wasn't really living at all.

He would get up in the night to attend an important bonfire. In his own words he 'happed it up' and that meant applying more weedy clods to the great steaming mound with a heart of three or four hundredweight of red-hot ashes.

When the bonfire was properly established, which was usually within about forty-eight hours, he loved it to rain, remarking: 'That bonfire is laughing at the rain. Doubt whether any fire brigade could put it out.'

His final seal of approval of his own handiwork was to observe with a mysterious smile: 'Maybe I'll bake some hedgehogs in it. Do 'em in clay y'know. Finest dish you ever set your teeth into. Never missed it when I was younger.'

There are no hedgehogs in my bonfire.

But there are – or rather there were – about half a ton of rotten apple tree; enough hedge-clippings to obscure the forest of Dunsinane; more leaves than the Babes in the Wood ever saw; a mound of those horrible cardboard cases that nobody can ever get rid of; a cartload of weeds unfit for compost; four rows of frost-bitten chicory; a quantity of straw, string, old magazines; two pairs of soleless shoes; a broken picture frame and a nice trimming of the dead stalks and leaves of a failed runner-bean crop.

Its plume of smoke and steam, strongly reminiscent of the wisp of smoke and steam that garlanded Vesuvius after the great eruption of 1944, rises vertically into the cold winter air. The Red Indians in the Chiltern Hills are said to be reading smoke-signal messages from it.

I shall probably throw my bonfire open to the public with a small admission fee to go to charity.

It has been a rewarding week.

A ray of sunshine

May 14, 1962

It always surprises me how much enjoyment people can get out of other people's mishaps.

I have just given immense pleasure to many of my friends. I have brightened their lives. I have let sunshine into dark places. I was in the tap room of a pub noted for the fierce conversations that go on about gardening, and an acquaintance of mine, with whom I have horticultural rivalry, said:

'Growing sweet peas again this year?'

'Yes, I am – I mean, yes, I was.'

'Come again?'

'My sweet peas are strictly in the past tense.'

'Frost?'

'No, they are in the greenhouse. Or rather they were in the greenhouse.'

'What happened?'

'I watered them with liquid weed-killer.'

'Pray say that again.'

'I watered them with a can that had contained weed-killer.'

A roar of pure delight shook the pub.

'Intentionally?'

'No, you great dolt.'

'The tomato plants... I trust they are well?'

'They are dead. Burned to a frazzle. Withered. Finished.'

Thunderous laughter. Men with dirty great pints in their hands are choking with glee.

'May I inquire into your zinnias?'

'They look as if they have been nursed by a blow lamp.'

'And how are your dwarf dahlias?'

'Wiped out.'

People are crying with laughter. They are sobbing with glee.

'Your asters? Your sun flowers? Your marrows? Your cinerarias?'
'Scorched, Doomed. Had it.'
Complete strangers come up to me and shake me by the hand saving:
'Funniest thing I've ever heard of. You've really made my day. Thanks awfully old man. You've properly bucked me up.'

March 3, 1964

About a year ago when the rustle of spring was so deafening that you had to shout to make yourself heard above the clamour of the daffodils, the thunder of the onrushing tulips and the uproar of the advancing wallflowers, I apparently gave great and abiding pleasure to my readers by describing how I committed horticide.
You readers apparently loved all this. You fell off your bar stools, your beds, or your bare boards in prison cells – or wherever it is you read the *Daily Mirror*. My misfortune was your pleasure. My disaster was your ribald paradise.
So, as Operation Greenhouse seems so popular, I shall tell you about how I moved my greenhouse.
Until recently my greenhouse was one of those metal jobs in which the glass reaches right down to the ground – which is a mistake. The glass should only come to about three feet from the ground and be placed preferably on a brick base.
So I gave myself the job of shifting the brute. Now the normal sensible way is to dismantle the thing, take the putty and the glass out and start from scratch again. Not with this particular boyo. Oh no.
I decided to take the broad view. To hacksaw the framework roughly in half and then convey the top section and dump it on the brickwork. I worked it out that since we didn't need the bottom panes of glass we could take what the insurance world call 'a high rate of breakage'. We could smash up to eighteen panes of glass without batting an eyelid.
What we had to do was to saw the glazed skirts off the greenhouse, use the spirit of Drake, never look back and charge with the Light Brigade.
We did.
I got two blokes to help me. I explained to them that although they had read about men going into orbit, this was a far greater bolder sweep of the new horizon of limitless adventure.
This was the soaring courage of eagles; the way through hardship to the stars and, if they heard the smashing of glass, they should press on.
I equipped my two storm-troopers with brooms. The idea was that when we had got the ship off the sandbank they should then, like expert salvage men, carry the great glass ark to the near-by brick base.

There was a 10-knot gale blowing when we took off. My miniature Crystal Palace became airborne all too easily under the brooms.

Then the cross wind caught us.

Ever held the top part of a greenhouse over your head with a broom?

Ever heard the avalanche of exploding glass?

Ever heard the language of men who have sailed before the mast in greenhouses and don't need to throw stones?

Never have I heard such abuse in my profane life.

'To the right! – you spray of bloodstained lilac!'

'Hold it, diseased lout of my dreams.'

'May Allah curse you and destroy you you painted poisoned spray of deadly nightshade from the remoter parts of sulphurous hell.'

We lurched.

We staggered.

We stumbled.

Shattered glass burst into shards and splinters all around.

The great swaying transparent caravanserai finally ended up on its brick base looking like a bent steel skeleton surrounding rectangular places where glass once used to be.

Some of us do it the hard way.

Diary of a sunflower grower

August 9, 1965

In my passport I am prosaically described as a journalist. I am thinking of changing this and substituting 'sunflower grower'. Stand by for a little boasting.

In a small stone courtyard in my garden, I have two sunflowers which I grew from seeds. They emerge from two small earth patches that are little more than crevices, for they measure only three inches by five. The larger of the sunflowers is 8ft 6in high. The stem (or should I say the bole?) is 2½ in. in diameter.

These giants are reaching for the sky and are growing at the rate of three inches a day. The flowers are forming and, in the few hours of sunshine we have recently had, they have learned to turn their noble heads to follow the arc of the sun.

To me these sunflowers are the greatest, the most, the tallest and the handsomest ever grown by man.

I now await an avalanche of letters about sunflowers that are 21ft tall and grow at the rate of six inches a day.

August 11, 1965

When I climbed the step ladder yesterday my sunflower was 9ft 2 in tall – a gain of eight inches in three days.

Pressure suits are being prepared for further height and altitude calculations.

August 16, 1965

The control centre that has now taken charge of my mighty sunflower has reported that all systems grow and the count-up indicates a height of 10ft 1in with the plant exactly on vertical course. Some anxiety was caused during the weekend by a strong south-easterly wind and guy lines had to be attached.

At the moment, these are made of high tensile hemp, but steel hawsers are being considered.

The warhead (or main sunflower in the nose) is not yet fully extended but is expected to be about the size of a searchlight. The maximum girth of the hole is 8¼ in.

The J Beanstalk Corporation have been appointed consulting engineers.

August 21,1965

My sunflower is now soaring up into the rain-sodden skies and is well over 10ft. high. The paving stones in the courtyard from which it is emerging look as if they may be dislodged by the terrific force of this vertical vegetable growth.

Quite near me and very visible from my room in the *Daily Mirror* building is the new Post Office Tower. This stunted construction is only about 600 feet high and on the top of it Sir Billy Butlin's son is engaged in organising a revolving restaurant.

I now warn Sir Billy that I am organising a revolving restaurant on the top of my ascending sunflower.

Excelsior!

Reporter at Large

Cassandra was more than a brilliant columnist: he was a born reporter of news and happenings. At regular intervals 'he took his column by the hand' (as he put it) and travelled the globe to record its foibles and follies. What follows is a tour out of time, a geographical ramble of jumbled date-lines in which he records his impressions of people and places, high dramas and low comedies.

This was Part One of a three-day investigation by Cassandra into drug-taking.

Part One: The case of the poisoned baby doll

June 14, 1966

People get nervous about walking under step-ladders. I get nervous about walking up or down steps. For instance you might fall, or trip up, but for me there's something faintly more ominous about it. You walk up steps to sing in a choir.

You walk up steps to receive a book and a handshake at the annual school prize-giving.

And you walk up steps to go to the scaffold.

You walk down steps to go to dungeons, to vaults and to catacombs.

So when I walked down a flight of steps the other day near Shepherd's Bush I got that old feeling again – that faint mood of ill-omen. This, in gentle words, was the home of a lady of easy virtue – or, in rougher terms, a whore's parlour. And the occasion was at once absurd and sombre, cheerful and tragic. It was to meet and talk to a young drug addict, to inquire into The Case of the Poisoned Baby Doll.

Eleven steps down, push the bell, open the door and into the basement flat.

The room had a well-lived-in look and the protector of the child who was only seventeen was a cheerful middle-aged tart who, like most of her profession (note how hostile society elegantly and scornfully uses the word 'profession' instead of 'trade') was kind and cheerful and flourished like the green bay tree.

The place was full of animals, or rather livestock, ranging from a goldfish and cats – that tense association – to dogs and a tortoise and an arbour of leathery-looking plants.

Ladies of leisure (again the stilted euphemism) are fond of living things around them, with the possible exception of men, and always seem to be in the midst of barking and mewing and the silent gulping of baffled goldfish.

Often there is a twittering of caged birds and I remember the words of a man who used to resort to this form of love-life with some regularity.

He said: 'I can stand the strangeness of waking up and not knowing where you are. I can stand the thick greasy locks on the pillow beside you. I can even stand the bright sunlight. But what I can't stick, at any price, is the twittering of the idiot canary or, worse still, a parrot insisting on being revealed on his perch beneath the green baize cloth.'

In the corner, seated in an armchair and dressed in jeans, sat Baby Doll.
She was, as I have said, only seventeen – not old enough to be a prefect at Roedean and some hopes at that. She left her home in Dorset a few months ago, had come to London and had not seen her parents since.
'Why haven't you seen them since? Had a row or something?'
'No, not that. No trouble at all. But you don't keep going back, do you?'
No, I suppose you don't. But what are mere kids doing in this sort of place? I left the question unasked.
The child had got a job at six pounds a week as an assistant-dresser in a West End theatre. She had, as the police say, no fixed abode, but slept here at the flat about three times a week and the rest of the time with friends or anywhere – or just with 'boys'.
She took 'pep' pills and had already had a handful although it was only midday.
She was on 'purple hearts' or 'bennies' or 'goof balls' or 'copilots', which are all stimulants based on the amphetamine group of drugs.
'When did you first start on purple hearts and how did you get them?'
'A woman gave me a boxful in a lavatory.'
'Why did she give them to you?'
'I don't know.'
'Did you know her?'
'Never seen her before or since.'
Baby Doll sat relaxed and apparently quite unconcerned with the rights and wrongs of drug-taking but just enjoyed it.
'What effect do these purple hearts have on you?'
'Oh wakens me up no end. I can dance all night.'
I thought *of My Fair Lady* and Julie Andrews and bloody Pygmalion and the theatrical days when they didn't need goof balls to do that.
'Do they give you a hangover?'
'Not really. I just get tired after them and sleep and sleep and sleep.'
'How many do you take a day?'
Baby Doll thought a bit and said that it was about 200 a week.
'As many as 30 a day?'
'Yes I suppose that's it – if it works out like that.'
'Where do you get them?'
'Oh, you can get them anywhere. No trouble at all. Pubs, cafes, coffee bars.'
'How much do you pay for them?'
'Oh, it varies. A bob. One and six. You know…'
She was vague about all this, but not about wanting to leave drugs alone.
'Don't you want to pack them up?'

'No. Why SHOULD I?'

At this point 'a boy friend', a tall anxious-looking chap who I felt might have been in love with this thin parcel of pathos, came into the room, and chimed in.

'You see, she doesn't WANT to. We try to stop her. But she doesn't seem to care. She'd find it hard to turn it in all right.'

I asked him if he took stimulant drugs. He replied: 'No, I keep clear of them. I like a drop of Scotch but not these things.'

Her protector said with her hoarse laugh and her tough smile: 'She just DOESN'T care.'

It was an odd set-up. The tart mothering her. The boy friend genuinely much concerned.

But like most people who live these rather desperate aimless lives, you felt that they felt – and certainly Baby Doll felt – that that was the way things are.

Fate had fixed it all up. So there was really NOTHING you could do about it. Was there? Life IS like that, isn't it? Isn't that the way the cookies crumble?

I felt appalled by the casualness of it all; the inevitability; the amoral negativeness of a seventeen-year-old kid caught in a net that she couldn't feel; the remorseless pattern of life that could not be altered even if you wanted to alter it; the one-way path with high unscalable walls that you had to walk whether you wanted to or not; the certainty of future unhappiness and the hopelessness of not being able or wanting to change the misery that lay in store. Tens of thousands of mostly young people take these amphetamine drugs in their different forms – which range from giving you a hefty kick to buck you up to a soothing mental caress to calm you down with a tranquillizing effect.

Athletes, actors, students and musicians use them and so do waifs and strays and misfits and aimless innocents like Baby Doll. Sometimes these drugs are prescribed by doctors, but much of the stuff is stolen from the manufacturers or the retailing chemists.

They are usually believed to be non-habit forming, but they are addictive in that their effect can only be sustained by increasing doses. The main menace does not lie in their use and effect. It lies more in the society that uses them.

The amphetamines, with all their fancy names, the 'Black Bombers', the 'French Blues', are obtained by theft and fraud and those who take them, whether they know it or not, are not far from the fringe of crime.

In 1959, 5,600,000 authorised medical prescriptions were for preparations of amphetamines or phenmetrazine. Since then the number has vastly increased and so have the robberies and thefts.

The current black market price for purple hearts is about £16 a thousand, so the vendor of them at 1s 6d each stands to make about £60 profit.

The police are immensely handicapped in their power of entry and search.

In Manchester, where there is legislation that gives the police far greater freedom than they enjoy in, say, London, the situation is under much better control, but Parliament has not yet woken up to the evil power and curse that these new drugs have on our society. The amphetamines belong to the comparatively harmless end of the spectrum of drugs wrongly taken.

The other colours are more sinister – marijuana or hashish or cannabis or bhang, is the beginning of far more potent drugs that lead to the appalling addiction of heroin and the new and unknown horrors of lysergic acid.

The little Baby Doll with the supreme futility of her aimless life is not yet hooked to the terrors that lead to madness, total character disintegration and often to death itself.

But the kind of people who swallow their purple hearts are the kind of people who can be led to fantasies and hallucinations that can change personality completely and introduce them to 'more devils than vast Hell can hold'.

For decades the British have congratulated themselves, and the Americans have explained their gigantic problem of narcotics by saying that in England, unlike the United States, we have a thoroughly integrated society with the family and the home as the basic unit and the stability that comes from having no great crime problem and no racial difficulties.

This comfortable doctrine may have been true once but it is infinitely dangerous balderdash now. The people of this country are in deep disarray.

Part two: The appalling paradise

June 15. 1966

The man who sits smiling and pleasantly articulate on the seat opposite me is twenty-nine, born on the fringe of Harlem, white, well above average intelligence, plays the trombone.

And has spent ten years in the appalling paradise of heroin addiction.

Jim (we'll leave the surname out of this) was, at the age of fourteen, playing on the streets of the slums of New York City, when out of kid's bravado he smoked his first marijuana cigarette.

It had no effect.

He pretended it did. He was trying to be 'one of the boys.' He should have felt 'high', 'up', or 'away'. He felt neither high nor low, up nor down, here nor away.

Only very slightly sick.

As he was not working and still intermittently at school, somebody suggested that he might earn himself a few honest bucks and avoid soul-destroying laziness by selling good dope. Dope was, at that time in New York, plentiful and easy.

The cops were comparatively lax, and before he was seventeen Jim was an accomplished peddler of heroin. A 'pusher' for the 'junkies'. In 1954 he took his first 'snort'.

Heroin is a white powder and he sniffed it up like snuff.

The scene of the first step towards one of the most terrible experiences that a human being can undergo was in a movie house. Instantly the smell and taste of the drug raced round the back of the nose, the throat and almost down into his lungs.

Jim was frightened.

The 'shot' was working.

Then the tight springs within him slackened, the cigarette that he was smoking seemed infinitely smooth and relaxing.

He felt serene yet powerful, detached yet wonderfully involved.

The hard lines of life were being rubbed out and something calm, contemplative and infinitely and sweetly aloof had taken its place.

Jim had got a job in a quintet playing the trombone and then a better position in a band, where the leader announced that he 'did not want no part of alcoholics or "junkies" and that if any of them were on the bottle or the needle, they had better get to hell out of it right now, and save a lot of trouble all round.'

Jim said nothing.

Since the first 'snort' in the cinema he had graduated to become a 'mainliner'. Somebody had said to him: 'Why waste all that good dope sniffing at it? Take it straight from "the works"?'

The 'works' consisted of an eye-dropper, a needle and an ordinary metal bottle top.

The heroin powder is dissolved in water, heated in the bottle top, and then injected through a puncture made by the needle, usually in the muscular part of the upper arm.

Jim told me: 'When I had my first fix, I thought I was going to die. I was afraid that this time I had done it, and that the answer coursing through my veins was Death.'

Apart from his nervousness and feelings of guilt, which were natural, there was good solid reason for anxiety.

Last year in New York over 300 heroin addicts died from an overdose. Jim was now securely 'hooked'.

The sentence of his fate had been passed and the statistical odds of Jim ever recovering completely at that time were about 100 to 1 against.

Of all the narcotics none is more fearful in its power to destroy human happiness and human dignity and to make a bearable pattern of life quite impossible than heroin.

Trying to give up heroin is known as taking 'cold turkey' and it is a nightmare process.

The consequences of the total removal of heroin from an addict are so terrible that the victims are frightened to face them.

There is cramp and vomiting, to such a degree that it may drown the patient, nasal discharge and diarrhoea, shivering and sweating, itching of the skin and muscular spasms all working under a dreadful pressure of melancholia and despair.

Jim, taking his secret with him, went on tour with the band.

They left New York and travelled south to Carolina where his supplies began to run low.

He rationed himself, but his system nagged for more.

His trombone playing rapidly fell off, his confidence disappeared and he began to be afraid.

Then he noticed that two of his companions were in similar straits. They, too, were 'junkies'.

'Had I known then what I know now,' said Jim, 'I could have got on to a codeine cough mixture which would have held me together.

'But by the time we reached New Orleans, I had broken apart.

'I couldn't blow a note and, as for the girl singer who was also a "mainliner", she was finished and sweating and shivering it out in bed.'

In New Orleans he got back on the 'shots', but was afraid of being cut off from his sources of supply.

He made for home in New York with all speed.

'I couldn't wait to get back,' said Jim.

'Once in the city I took a taxi to the nearest "pusher" I knew and settled back on in.'

He was unemployed, started peddling heroin and was swiftly in the hands of the police.

Heroin drives people to crime. They must have the stuff and it costs in the United States at least £20 a week for a comparatively mild case to keep going and avoid the almost unbearable strain of withdrawal from the drug.

The men are forced to steal. The women are driven to prostitution. His first sentence was thirty days.

By great good fortune, Jim began the methadone treatment under the care of Dr Marie Nyswander, of the Rockefeller Institute.

Methadone is a new addictive drug that takes the place of heroin and, according to Dr Nyswander, is as necessary to the heroin addict as insulin is to a diabetic, with no physical after-effects.

The results after three years' research, judging by Jim and other patients I saw under Dr Nyswander's care, are brilliantly hopeful.

But Jim's luck is exceptional, with the odds of being in his position rather like winning a football pool.

For every lucky Jim in the United States there are 10,000 unlucky Jims.

In 1964 the Federal Bureau of Narcotics announced that there were 55,899 addicts of all types of drugs in the country.

The figure is wildly conservative, and many authorities, including Dr Nyswander, believe that the real figure may be nearer 1,000,000.

In Britain the problem of heroin addiction is, by comparison with the United States, minute.

In 1964 the official figure was 342.

Last year the total number of addicts to all dangerous drugs had risen to 735.

The real figure may be much larger. The major source of supply has been the activity of a very few doctors, who have prescribed excessively for addicts.

In 1962 one doctor alone prescribed almost 600,000 tablets of heroin.

But such recklessness is quite the exception, and efforts to get heroin banned entirely have been, very properly in my opinion, strongly opposed by the profession.

Heroin is unrivalled in its capacity to counteract excruciating pain such as is often present in the last stages of cancer, and dying patients can leave this life in a haze of sweet euphoria.

The sinister thing about heroin is that, although it is at present isolated and still under control in Britain, it can swiftly become a central and hideous part of the spreading pattern of drugs.

What may begin as an apparently harmless adolescent thrill obtained from swallowing 'Purple Hearts', 'Red Devils', 'Blue Heavens', or 'Yellow Jackets', can extend through the secret social structure of addicts to the profound evil of heroin.

In the United States, the linked process is already firmly established. More and more heroin addicts also use barbiturates.

Over 50 per cent of all drug addicts are believed to use combinations of narcotics, which are more dangerous than heroin alone. In Britain, as in America, most drug addicts are young people. They are adolescents fighting authority.

In order to assert themselves they want to defy the established order, to shock their elders and to challenge the accepted standards.

Drugs, beginning with pills and then smoking marijuana, are the ideal new and exciting form of defiance.

There is a kind of inverted snob respectability about taking drugs, made more attractive by the fact that artists, writers and intellectuals indulge in them.

They should read their *Kubla Khan* written by Samuel Coleridge while in a magic trance of opiates:

That sunny dome! Those caves of ice!
And all who heard should see them there,
And all should cry 'Beware! Beware!'

Part three: The mushroom man cometh

June 16, 1966

On April 27, 1966, Roger Leonard Lewis was fined £25 for aiding and abetting the sale of a quantity of the hallucinatory drug known as L.S.D.

The case went largely unnoticed by the public – but not by the Narcotics' Branch of Scotland Yard, the Home Office and certain members of the medical profession.

The business of taking and selling drugs is, in nine cases out of ten, a squalid, dirty and often pathetic affair with humans being degenerated and doomed to a life of crime and despair. But the case of Roger Leonard Lewis is significant because it heralded the introduction and spread of a type of drug that has an intellectual and almost religious backing.

The full dress name of the drug is lysergic acid diethylamide tartrate, otherwise known as L.S.D., and it is a synthetic compound basically derived from a black fungus that grows on rye heads.

L.S.D. is not new and has been known to doctors and mental specialists for nearly thirty years. It was developed by Dr Albert Hoffman of the Swiss drug company Sandoz.

It belongs to the group of mind-expanding drugs called psychelics of which the ancient forerunner was the Mexican mushroom, eaten long before the time of the Aztecs and which was called 'Teonanacti' – or The Divine Mushroom.

The mushroom man was then a high priest and the religious ceremony of visions was known as 'eating God's flesh'.

This is the stuff of dreams such as only madmen know.

L.S.D. is a clear, tasteless, odourless liquid that is easy to make, cheap, and convenient to use.

By pouring a few drops on a lump of sugar you may take temporary leave of this world and all its conventional measurements and sensations and experience an unknown part of the mind that has never been fully explored before.

The results of taking L.S.D., as compared with the effects of barbiturates, tranquillizers, and marijuana, are as a fully symphony orchestra compared with a tin whistle; the roaring cataract foaming over the rocks compared with the dripping tap.

It is the prince of the chemistry of madness and hallucination. The addict speaks in ecstasy:

'I met God walking in a garden. His eyes burned like coals of fire. The petals of the flowers moved in a slow cascade towards me and they shone with a deep but sleepy brilliance such as I had never known before. The landscape danced with a slow rhythm and the peaks of the hills were jewel encrusted.

'I had long since died and God smiled upon me. Existence was holding its breath. The walls dissolved to the sweet chiming of dulcimers. I was suspended in mid-air. The dark sky sang and the stars were at their prayers.'

All lysergic acid visions are not as exalted as this one and often they are very similar in their beauty – and their horror – to the experiences that schizophrenics undergo.

Here is a description by a mental patient that Dr Sidney Cohen of the University of California records. The patient had taken no drug but the mental disturbance is strikingly similar:

> 'As to the visioned creations, these were of finer, thinner stuff than iridescent bubbles, in all the details of their forms more minute and miraculous than anything on earth.
>
> 'Indeed, they would have had little significance had they been such as could conceivably have been provided or invented from the experience of a human lifetime.
>
> 'There were small suns and strange twilight worlds of lakes and islands – not conceived of spinning balls, like our earth, but having definite yet changeable limits as drops of oil that float on water.

> 'Planets with their peculiar signs came near, the sun was broken and the face of the earth was changed, the landscape was never so enchanted.
>
> 'An ancient cave, passage or hollow ladder seemed to connect new earths; perhaps this was such as Jacob saw, for it was an image of remote antiquity.'

Now back from schizophrenia to the all-coloured, all-moving, all-tasting, all-touching delirium that comes from a lump of sugar soaked in the synthetic liquid that Dr Hoffman developed. This is a tape recording of a patient under the influence of L.S.D.:

> 'Now the movies are really starting. Some wonderful multicoloured geometric patterns; brilliant fireworks, too. And they are coming and changing a thousand times a second. They are all taking place twenty thousand leagues under the sea.
>
> 'There is something tremendously exhilarating about the underwater scenes – from pleasant to unpleasant, then pleasant again, then once more unpleasant, in rapid rotation... Some really beautifully illuminated fish, not like any real fish I ever saw before, but moving by the millions as if they were real illuminated fish.
>
> 'On the unpleasant side, when my beautiful fish flow away, there are some gigantic underwater spiders' webs composed of luminous threads, pretty to look at but threatening at the same time – as are the huge and delicately coloured sea anemones lurking near by. ...'

The L.S.D. addict will sit, lie or stand in a trance staring fixedly at any object – an electric light bulb, a bowl of fruit, a toy on the floor, a wallpaper design, a speck of dust, a single letter on a page of type.

The hallucination or 'trip', as it is called, may last as long as ten hours and the victims, or the disciples as they prefer to regard themselves, feel no marked after-effects and no hangover.

In the United States the high priest of all this chemical and visionary religion is a Doctor Timothy Leary, PhD, who is a saint to some and a menace to others – including his old university, Harvard. Also he is a problem to the police who have recently managed to get him sentenced to the excessively punitive and spectacular penalty of thirty years' imprisonment. But here is Dr Leary as he appears to one of his followers:

'He struck me immediately as a man who would never again be without disciples. Greying, appearing a little older than forty-two, he patiently tried to explain his aims.

'He looked at us out of bluish-grey, penetrating eyes that glittered at times when he concentrated on a question. Timothy Leary had that abstracted look of a person who can see with absolute clarity what no one else will believe is there.

'I noticed a beautiful young woman gazing at him and learned that she had come down from Boston. When the presentation was finished she slipped her arms through his and gazed up at him.'

The good doctor is not without his fans.

The enormous potency of this clear liquid is in keeping with the prodigious scale of its effects.

You could carry in one drum enough L.S.D. to hallucinate every man, woman and child in this country if you could distribute it through the water supply – a fact that has not escaped the military in their researches into chemical warfare.

It can induce feelings of omnipotence that have driven its victims to walking into moving vehicles believing that they are immune, and has also resulted in suicides by people who believed that they possessed the powers of immortality.

One of the strangest manifestations of this appalling substance is described by Dr Sidney Cohen in his book *Beyond The Within.*

'A strange malady of L.S.D. is an affliction not of the receiver but of the giver. This peculiar disorder might be called therapist breakdown.

'An unusual number of those dispensing these drugs have themselves come down with psychiatric disturbances.

'The manifestations are variable. After intensive though sometimes only after brief contact with the drugs a few have gone on to a psychotic breakdown or to megalomaniacal ideas of grandeur.'

It is said that people who have experienced the modern form of the sacred mushroom are never the same persons again. Like those who have electrical shock-treatment of pre-frontal lobotomy, they may change permanently.

Dr Leary says, not in defence of L.S.D. but in praise of it: 'It becomes necessary to go out of our minds in order to use our heads.'

And he goes on to laud those 'who have risked all social sanction to write about their new experiences. Some have lost their jobs, many have risked their reputations.

'Theirs has been the fun of the adventure, the excitement of the discovery, the fascination of the paradox.'

It is a strange form of fun not to be left to the new amateurs and addicts who have got hold of this substance and are now beginning to appear in our magistrates' courts with increasing frequency.

No one, least of all our young people poisoning themselves with their wretched Purple Hearts, Blue Heavens and marijuana, should graduate to the 'Remembrance fallen from Heaven and Madness risen from Hell.'

The moment of ecstasy vanishes in endless suffering and the slow, certain destruction of those who succumb to it.

Cassandra, the Dame and the Press Council

Sark, Channel Islands, September 14, 1954

Today I may be flogged from Newgate to Tyburn, clapped in the stocks, locked in the pillory or loaded up into the tumbril and carted off for summary professional execution.

I am charged by His Excellency the Lieutenant Governor of the Bailwick of Guernsey, and through him by the Dame of Sark, Mrs Sibyl Mary Hathaway, that, on the 17th day of August did I write an article the 'tone of which was objectionable'.

To consider this charge Colonel the Hon J J Astor, the Chairman of *The Times,* and twenty-four other newspaper executives, good men and true, who are the General Council of the Press, will assemble this day at Number 1, Bell Yard, Fleet-street, London.

Oyez! Oyez! Oyez! Loyal citizens! Assemble ye and hear this dread charge.

What have I done?

Written a foul libel?

Made a gross mis-statement of fact?

Used the thin dagger of innuendo? Not so.

I have, with my little pin – all unwittingly – punctured the balloon of pomposity and pierced the bladder of pride.

Before I fall squealing on the mercy of the Council, before I go a-grovelling to the Dame and a-touching of my forelock to His Excellency the Governor, I beg you to hear my tale. You have to speak like that these days or some buzzing Queen Bee will lay you by the heels for impertinence.

My story in these columns – you may even have read it – was the jaunty derisive tale of Alfred Baker, a cabby, who was charged with being tipsy on the island of Sark. Alfred was collecting Lord Oaksey from Mrs Hathaway's house – it is called La Seigneurie – and in the expressive phrase of the Dame who was seeing her guest off, was 'shaking about on his feet'. Later Baker was fined ten shillings at the Seneschale Court for being drunk and was banned from all the licensed hotels and inns on the island for six months.

I thought the whole affair was ridiculous – and delightful.

I went further. I ventured to hope that the distinguished visitor in the old cab drawn by the ancient mare Polly might not have taken it too seriously. I even suggested that Lord Oaksey, better known as Lord Justice Lawrence who heard the Nuremberg Trials, could take it in his stride and could perhaps smile at the case of the coachman who was 'shaking about on his feet'.

I congratulated 'the happy blessed isle where one coachman in charge of a fifteen-year-old nag can cause such heart-searching and concern' and which has so little else to worry about. But I was wrong!

When Lord Randolph Churchill realised that he was politically ruined he said mournfully about Sir William Goschen, who had helped to bring about his downfall: 'All great men make mistakes. Napoleon forgot Blucher, I forgot Goschen.'

Well, I forgot Dame Sybil Mary Hathaway of Sark.

I forgot that Dames (will the General Council of the Press allow me to call her an Old Dame? – for she is sixty-seven) are at their most formidable when Kismet places their dignity as hosts on a banana skin and then goes away quietly in a corner to watch the result and shake with silent laughter.

I forgot that feudal old ladies – she said on her departure to America, 'They are dying to hear about the last feudal State in the world' – do not take kindly to the smelling salts of outside opinion.

I forgot that elderly ladies who rule islands where religion, agriculture, fishing, land and transport are completely under their thumb, unless the Queen of England in Council intervenes, and where the Dame alone may keep a female dog (bitch to you) and where she alone can prohibit female pigeons (Coo!) may be inclined to export their ill-tempered and frivolous complaints to the mainland.

I forgot that criticism – even if it is confined to a wry smile about cabbies and judges and bottles – is like a rude word in the Visitors' Book to those whose opinion of themselves is rarely exposed to the asperities of a larger world than a thousand acres and five hundred people living in a toy kingdom.

I forgot that running to the bosses is as old as the hills and that the squawk of anger finds solace in the squeak of complaint. Well, I am here to try to repel the attack.

I am here – even if unsuccessfully – to say what I like within the laws of libel and the bounds of accuracy and fair comment. I am here to see that these rights, which are more important than the sex of pigeons, the conduct of horse-drawn vehicles and the number of female dogs, are not gnawed away by flustered old ladies put in a bad temper by the unsuccessful departure of important guests.

As for the General Council of the Press, across their aching backs there is laid the preposterous and staggering load of approving or disapproving hundreds of thousands of words sprayed out over millions of copies of newspapers every day.

It may be that their burden will not be made unduly heavier by the arrival of this petty, shrivelled peanut, shot from a vinegary peashooter from this tiny Channel isle.

Henrietta and the new mink coat

Paris, May 8, 1953

I am in Paris – and Henrietta is the talk of the town. In France, when the honour of a lady's name is involved and the tarnished road to divorce is concerned, there is a strict law which forbids more than the mention of anything other than Christian names.

Henrietta she was. Henrietta she is. And, by the blush of every guilty man's cheek, Henrietta she now remains.

Henrietta fell in love twice.

The first time was with a middle class tradesman from Aix-en-Provence. They married and they lived in moderate happiness.

Henrietta loved him. He loved Henrietta.

It was a dutiful, faithful love, and, as so often happens to dutiful, faithful lovers came the old, outrageous challenge of piratical, faithless love.

Henrietta fell. The Casanova was – and indeed he is – a rich leather manufacturer.

Henrietta, sweet and lovely and confronted with the most terrifying prospect of all to sweet and lovely women – the continuation of being sweet and lovely to an audience of one – fell for the Prince of Handbags… also suitcases, belts and leather jerkins.

She gave him all, and, as lovers do these days, he gave her fondness, passion, admiration, affection – and a hell of a fine mink coat.

It happened to be a long, slinky panther of a mink coat with a sign of ecstatic guilt in every hair.

And Henrietta – the sweet, neat and overflowing little parcel of love – was afraid to take it home.

Love, and especially French love, laughs at locksmiths. And Henrietta hit upon a tight, taut, vixenish little plan. She bought a cheap leathery suitcase.

She crammed the mink coat into it. Next she went to a railway station. Henrietta dumped the bag in the left luggage office and took the ticket home.

She rumpled it. She crumpled it. She stamped on it with her tiny high-heeled shoe. Then she rubbed it in the dust and with the serpent of the Garden of Eden grinning close beside her she showed it to her husband.

She told him she had found it in the street.

It was a cloakroom ticket. Why not claim it – for fun?

The Lord and Master of more households than he knew said 'Yes.'

He himself went to the station, handed over the ticket and collected the bag.

He took it home – unopened, he said – and Henrietta, coy, cute and unbearably anxious, watched him open it.

Out of it fell a pair of old pyjamas. And a shaving brush. And a pair of busted slippers.

Henrietta didn't know several things...

One – That all mistresses love mink coats.

Two – That husbands as well as wives can have lovers.

Three – That mink coats casually found in old suitcases can be diverted away from lawful unsuspecting spouses – diverted by husbands to their own mistresses.

Henrietta yelled blue murder. The action for divorce has begun.

And the ownership of the mink coat is high on the legal list of shattered love.

It is springtime in Paris. Intriguing, double crossing, conspiring springtime in Cupid's First City of Love.

Crash, bang, cackle, quack, moo!

Port de la Selva, Spain, September 21, 1957

When that accomplished and courageous American airman went up about nineteen miles in a balloon the other day he remarked on the absolute quiet of the stratosphere. The silence was complete and only the sound of his own breathing broke it.

This he contrasted with life on the surface of the earth where there is always some sort of aural disturbance.

I should like to confirm that.

I am staying in a little pub that is very clean, very cheap – and unquiet in a big way. In fact there is a Spanish Concerto going on here that must be something of a record.

I have been listing all the various sounds you can hear from my bedroom. Here is the record so far, but I am sure it is not complete and I will be able to add to it before I leave:

Donkeys braying. There are two of them within forty yards of my bedroom window and they have long and challenging hee-haw contests that start before dawn.

Cows mooing at a range of perhaps fifty yards – not more. Pigs grunting a cricket pitch away. Poultry crowing and clucking on the flat roof above me where they are permanently kept. This comes in, very loud and clear – reception perfect.

Ducks quacking outside the back door. Dogs barking from a range of ten to a hundred yards; the dog population of this place seems to be about one per square yard.

Babies crying very loudly in Spanish. There are seven of them in the hotel.

That ends the livestock side of this clamorous business. In addition we have church bells; the town siren (air raid type); thunderous dish-washing (all day); wood-sawing at nearby saw-mill; motor-scooters (Italian type, very penetrating); radio playing (non-stop tuned in on Barcelona); doors slamming and, as a permanent twenty-four hour background, the sound of the sea forty yards away and the whistle of the wind which sets up a mournful whooshing noise.

Not all these sounds occur together but sometimes three-quarters of them are in action at once. Sir Malcolm Sargent ought to come and conduct.

I had a rather alarming experience here that shows the virtues of silence and immobility.

I went to the local fish-market which is a building about the size of a church right by the harbour.

In the evening just before dusk some twenty or thirty small ships come in and unload astonishing cargoes of Mediterranean fish of lurid colours and designs; great velvety brown monsters with thick lips and glaring eyes; vermilion fish with blue spots; striped barrel-like customers with huge fins on top; prawns as big as forks; lobsters; crabs and fearsome rattling creatures with five legs and whip aerials.

All this maritime array is spread out on the floor of the fish-market and two auctioneers begin a dutch auction starting off with a deliberately high price and then come rattling down at enormous speed – 70 pesetas, 65 pesetas, 60 pesetas and so on – until a buyer shouts 'Me!' Or rather somebody just twitches and the auctioneers with lightning speed knock the stuff down.

It is very nerve-wearing and became more so when I had the audacity to cough.

At once the auctioneer wheeled on me and turned himself into an accusing question-mark.

I was terrified.

One more tremor out of me and I would have been the owner of several hundredweights of the most alarming fish you have ever seen.

The auctioneer glowered and then pointed to a large notice hanging on a board from the roof. It read: WE SUPPLICATE YOUR SILENCE.

I faded rapidly away.

Square-wheel English

March 21, 1958

I have been consulting an Anglo-Italian dictionary that was rushed out during the war to help improve the relations between our lusty soldiers and the apprehensive Italians.

It is a beautiful example of square-wheel English.

The emergency guide, produced in Naples, shows the speed and pace with which the Italian girls expected to be wooed.

Here is the script together with an exact transcription of what this beautifully abrupt little volume advises:

The girl is relaxing backwards. I now respectfully quote:

SCENE: FALLINGS WIT A PERSON.

'Good morning, madam.'

'How do you do?'

'How beautiful you are!' *(Quanto siete bella!)*

'Beautiful eyes have you!' *(Che begli occhi avete!)*

'Fascinating you are!'

'I love you. And you?'

'How old are you?' *(Quanti anni avete?)*

We will now have a pause in this breathless wooing. Lay the girl aside.

But not for long; the deadly dialogue clumps on:

'How bad are you?' *(Come, siete cattivo?)*

Oh, the darlin' wickedness of it all!

'How could you dare to tell me these words?' *(Come arditte dirmi queste parole?)*

Lady, we knew 'em all the time.

'How content I should be to marry you!' (Long brooding pause.)

'Can I see you? Here? When?' *(Possono vedervi? Quando? Dove?)*

The Lollo-Loren-Magnani tempo then speeds up with a shattering erotic tempo.

'Have you a bridegroom?' *(Siete fidanzata?)*

And if he is here, let's flush the rascal out from beneath the matrimonial couch. The pace quickens.

'My desire overloads!'

'Will you smoke?' *(Volete fumare?)*

'Are you cold?'

'Are you warm?' *(Aveti coldo?)*

The Snake of Suspicion arises again.

'What woman do you know?' *(Quale donna conoscete?)*

'Something has been told to me!' *(Qualche cisa mi estate detta.)*

'From whom have you had this present?' *(Dachi avete avulo questo regalo?)*

No reply.

'At whose house have you been?' *(Dachi siete stato?)*

At this point, our battered English friend has nothing other to say than to make the traditional remarks of our forefathers abroad. It worked in Edwardian tunes when the old rascals climbed out of the bagios of Vienna and didn't quite know where they were.

They wanted the advice of the *gendarmerie* so they said with slurred simplicity:

'Cabby! I greatly fear that my postillion has been struck by lightning. Kindly drive me to the police station!'

February 9, 1962

The square-wheel English that Italian hotels often use in their holiday brochures is so delightfully rocky that I think some literary genius, fully conversant with excellent English, must be making the stuff up.

Here is a description of an Adriatic resort which came addressed to me on the envelope as 'Dear Sir'.

'Cattolica, pretty and elegant town, offer you the delight living and the attractives of is naturals beauties.'

The geographical situation is: 'On sea. Enchanting and quite position modern and comfortable,' while the hotel is 'for everyone's pretension.' Then comes a flash of endearing candour: 'Eighty rooms with bad garden'.

The private beach is 'attainable in the bathing suit'.

With a filial flourish dealing with prices and pension rates there is a magnificent paragraph which reads: 'NOT INCLUDED: Nothing of nothing.'

I find the place irresistible. I think I shall go there and try the delight living in one of the eighty rooms with bad garden, contemplate the beach attainable in the bathing suit, all the time being reassured that not included in the bill will be nothing of nothing.

February 20, 1962

I must mention that my recent theory that foreign guide-book English is written by scholarly dons has been hotly challenged by Mr Paul Boyle.

These primitive writing forms, he maintains, are done by ill-paid clerks at a central *Oficina de Turismo* who know not more than a dozen words of English and sit there sweating away at dictionaries as they build their preposterous sentences far into the night for a few pesetas.

Boyle quoted his favourite work on the subject. It is a booklet published in Spain for English visitors. The title: *Up! To the Bullfight!*

In the interests of semi-intelligibility I have corrected the spelling.

Forward into the world of Toreadors, Matadors, Picadors and Banderilleros in the Plaza de Toros :

> Very interesting is hero the acting of the master bull fighter drawing the bull's attention upon himself. Here is the famous bullfighting brothers Carlos and Paco Corpas to ready set to the bull the harpoons in a giant bull-noon in the monumental ring in Barcelona City incomparable luck and of giant dangerous already that to provoke the animal body to body without deceit for to go out from the luck.

Are you with me? On with the fight:

> To pass by the chest the human box heart, than to offer to the bull for greater irony of the man dexterity of the beast. The bull is dominated, by the bullfighter; that in the dangerous position have been nearer of the sharp deadly bull horn, his triumph is to obtain and before of the final moment of the stab, to show himself erect and majestic or to caress to the tremendous animal that his power ferocity to remain convert in the nobleness most calm and pleasant.

July 25, 1956

I get a lot of publicity material sent to me most of which I am delighted to hurl away. But as a student of the English language – especially when it rides on the square wheels of foreign translation – I am very pleased indeed to give you, and to quote you, news about the Fair of Messina which is being held this year hi Sicily:

Cataclysms and sad events destroyed monuments of historical and remarkable character, but indomitable and tenacious work of this people, replied always with a strong promise and throb; rise again.

Many times buildings, churches and works are raised again, and Messina Fair, now large and magnificent international exhibition on the beautiful Straight of Messina amongst East and West traffics is turn again; this our famous for always times Fair is representative of our soul's people that every year passionately and interestingly follows this manifestation that is now justly 'international' market, either by merit its managers or by merit characteristical and economical function. For gracious publication. Thank you.

And thank you too, old Sicilian friend.

Nervy night in Nervi

Nervi, September 9, 1959

During the war, here in Italy, two place-names stuck in my mind. The first was Nervi.

The second was Angri.

I felt that Nervi and Angri between them just about summed up a quarrel which was at times distinctly nervy and angry.

Angri is a little impoverished place South of Naples not far from Vesuvius. The last time I saw it hi 1944 it was under about a foot of volcanic dust because Big Brother up the hill had just blown his top.

Nervi, which I visited much later in the war, is a seaside suburb of Genoa that has aspirations to be regarded as a Riviera resort. But it is stuffed too full of trams to succeed.

Last night I returned to Nervi. It was raining and getting dark. All the obvious hotels were booked to the eyebrows.

I am not over-fond of sleeping in a car, and when I saw one last remaining sign which said Hotel in forthright electric lights I drove straight in through a huge gate and found myself in a large garden. Standing way back from the road hi the shadows was a dim mansion.

There was no life to be seen except two clutches of chickens nesting in huge ornamental flower-holders on each side of the large flight of steps that led up to the main door.

As I approached the chickens stood up in the geraniums, yawned, and sat down again.

I felt that they were extending to me just that touch of respect that you can expect from a well-bred chicken.

I rang a bell which clanged massively far away inside the echoing house. No answer. The place had the mood of the Fall of the House of Usher. I walked in. Still no one about. A man with a beard suddenly peered round the door and was gone. I never saw him again.

Then far away came a woman's voice clacking and crying and soon after, shuffling down the stairs, came an amiable old duck fussing and making funereal welcoming noises.

Yes, she had plenty of rooms and the German gentleman ('English, you crone!') should have the best apartment in the whole house.

I dragged my way upstairs, arrived on a vast landing on the third floor and, through double doors, entered an enormous room. 'This,' she said, 'is the best bedroom and the German gentleman shall have it all to himself.'

She smiled the Smile of Golgotha and I thought of the Place of a Skull. And then she was gone. I was alone.

I think it was about the oddest room in which I have ever spent a night.

It had everything.

On each side of the bed there was a motto. Both were in English.

The first said: A FRIEND IN NEED is A FRIEND INDEED.

The second: WHERE THERE'S A WILL THERE'S A WAY.

They had a slightly sinister effect on me – just that menacing shade of meaning you might attach to them had you seen them in a condemned cell.

'Which friend?' 'What need?' 'What will?' 'What way?'

There was a locked door leading to the next chamber of horrors.

The keyhole had been carefully stuffed with paper.

Because I am the Mosquito's Delight I carry one of those small insecticide spray canisters. I gave the room a squirt or two. Within a minute a vast black cloud of tiny, dead flies floated down and covered everything – including the wash basin. To clean it out I turned both taps on. The bottom of the basin fell out and clattered on the floor in a drenching heap of broken china.

There was something odd about the electric light, too. When you switched it down, which is the normal on position, it went off. When you switched it off, it came on.

The doors opened outwards and the newspapers which lined the chest of drawers were in Greek. There was a cracked broken plate with a design of what looked like stuffed cormorants perched on the picture rail. A half-filled, dirty cup of coffee was under the bed. Kilroy had evidently been here.

Going to bed was faintly reminiscent of snuggling up in a grave.

All night long a thunderstorm rumbled and flashed and I swear a peacock screamed at dawn.

But I liked those old chickens in the geraniums. They stood stiffly to attention again when I left. They recognised bravery when they saw it. Not many people sleep in the House of Usher by choice.

The damp professor

Campo S. Salvatore, Venice, September 16, 1959

Thirteen years ago I used to live in Venice within a stone's throw, or rather a pail's throw, of the Campo S. Salvatore in this splendid town where the streets are paved with water.

I shared an apartment with a chap who got mixed up with me in The Case of the Damp Professor and, since I am right back on the spot again, I shall tell you the dripping tale of a rather odd encounter long ago.

In 1946 – as indeed in September 1959 – Venice was a town where you couldn't sleep, for although there are no motor cars in the alleyways that take the place of streets, the citizens, or some of them, jabber all night right outside your window.

Now this was all right with me, but I drew the line at hand-to-hand fighting after midnight. After several slight forays by gangs of pre-Teddy-boy hoodlums, Italiano-style, not much more than twenty feet below the end of my bed we decided on the old-fashioned reprisal of chucking a pail of water on the blighters.

The first night this worked well.

There was a yell of sodden rage and the enemy departed. The second night there was also a yell of sodden rage followed by a thunderous knock on the front door – by a great echoing hammering such as the secret police use when they come for a dawn arrest.

I went down the flight of stairs, opened the door, and there, to my astonishment, saw a small, neatly-dressed elderly man dripping from head to foot. Worse still, he was accompanied by a small neatly-dressed woman. Also dripping from head to foot.

He opened fire in perfect English:

'Are you the ineffable barbarian who occupies the first-floor flat of this place?'

For a flickering moment I was tempted to say I wasn't, and to reply: 'No. It's my brother Alf – and a bigger cough-drop you never saw in a day's march.'

But I thought the better of it, and merely said: 'Lo, it is I.'

He went on: 'My wife and I were having a quiet, final stroll and have been grossly assaulted by buckets of water indisputably thrown by you.'

He quivered with rage and his small neat wife reproachfully dripped to prove his point.

Now I ask you. What would YOU do?

What do YOU do with a damp professor very late at night in the Campo S. Salvatore in Venice? And his drenched missus?

I said, simply, 'Who are you?'

He replied with the faintest hint of aqueous pride: 'I am the Professor of Etruscan and Archaeology at Padua University.'

Pause.

'Won't you come in?'

It was the fatuous invitation, *par excellence,* made trebly worse by the fact that he and his watery spouse promptly walked in.

I introduced the water-logged pair to my room-mate who, catching up with the mood of hideous inconsequence, said politely: 'Will you have a dry sherry – and a dry towel?'

There was no stopping them from then on.

We mopped them both up and they mopped the sherry down.

They sat on our best chairs and left pools of tell-tale water. We heard about Padua University and the excavations near Vincenza as they dripped on the carpet.

The small, wet wife had a great, dry thirst.

The Prof – he was a kind of Italian equivalent of Churchill's great friend Professor Lindemann – had a prodigious command of fiery English and a considerable contempt for the Anglo-Saxon race.

Except for one man.

'And who might that be?' said I.

'Neville Chamberlain,' said he.

'And why might that be?' said I.

'Because he always carried an umbrella,' said he.

Good health, St Peter

The Bar, St Peter's, Rome, August 26, 1960

Kindly note the address. Few people will believe you when you tell them that there is a bar, deep in the heart of the holy, consecrated structure of St Peter's on the left bank of the Tiber.

Even fewer will believe you when you tell them that in the holy precincts this bar is open at 6.30am, is pretty wide awake in the morning, and continues its healing ministry long after noon.

In case you want to go there (which I hope you do), walk halfway up the nave, turn smartly to the left, and nip in next door to the Treasury.

All are welcome.

In command, Signora Peroffe. A charming mature lady who has been there for just over thirty years.

And the price is less than in most Roman bars.

Would you like a rum only a few yards from the most sacred part of the first basilica of the Roman Catholic world?

It's yours for the asking. It is called – perhaps a shade indelicately in these racial times – 'Nigger Rum', and, if you feel faint, the tot from the bot is available long before the Roman dew is off the grass.

This sweet little alcoholic chapel, where you can get thirty-nine different drinks ranging from Danish lager to the more potent brews of the Highlands, is a most practical refuelling station.

You can get huge buns, great slabs of milky chocolate, chips, coffee, Coca-Cola (ah! sweet face of America) peanuts, and fruit.

Sinners go there – I have paid my guilty respects – and priests go there. A nip of brandy at 8.30 in the morning is not an unforgivable sin in this most lovely and unrelenting town.

Pope John, the present incumbent of this greatest and most formidable parish in the world, has not yet been to the Bar of St Peter's.

But his predecessor, Pius XII, is said to have had a coffee with a strengthener in the ante-room next door.

His present Holiness, Pope J, with his simplicity, with his grace, with his abiding humility, may well be there one of these days quite early in the morning. Say about 9am, when today I was raising my glass to my own health, to St Peter, to forgiveness and to all who dwell in strange and saintly and unsaintly places far away.

The plough and the gun

Jerusalem, February 3, 1958

The name is Mordecai. The age is twenty-three. The occupation, farmer, and the appearance big, blond and handsome.

Two decades ago, had he lived hi Germany, those who specialise in racial idiocies might have been misled into calling him 'a typical Aryan type'.

Had they inquired a little further into his antecedents they would hastily have changed their ugly minds and marked him down as fodder for the Nazi gas chambers.

Mordecai is an Israeli born in Palestine, as Jewish as Joshua and Judas Maccabaeus – and like his famous forebears, he, too, is a fighting man.

I met him the other day where he farms 2,500 acres near Mefalsin, within a rifle shot of the Gaza Strip.

This very young man is the head of a community of a hundred people who grow wheat, potatoes, beet, vegetables, hay and apples and who run a herd of sixty cattle.

This is a strange farm.

It has silos and slit trenches; barns and an armoury; tractors and watch towers; a nursery and sub-machine guns; flood-lights, which burn all night, and flowers; a laundry and an air-raid shelter.

One hand holds the plough while the other grips the gun.

In the nursery the babies are playing or sleeping. In the air-raid shelter, thirty foot deep, built of massive concrete, wired for electricity and with ample supplies of food and water, there are cradles for the kids.

I asked Mordecai, who has only recently completed this underground fortress, whether he was expecting air raids.

He replied that you never could tell but in any case heavy artillery could be moved up into the Gaza Strip at any time and the Gaza Strip was just over the other side of that ridge. Every night there is guard duty for both sexes, for every woman strong enough to use a broom can use a gun.

How much is Mordecai paid for running this bristling company of men and women who are equally handy with a spade or a rifle?

The answer is nothing.

This is one of Israel's 'Kibbutzim' – the famous dedicated communities who pool their skill and their labour for the common good.

There is no such thing as wages and the money that is earned from selling produce is all ploughed back into a central fund for the improvement of the communal farm.

They live together, work together – and are prepared to die together. These are Israel's front-line pioneers, and they have seen the vision and the glory of a united Holy Land. It is a truly staggering conception.

Israel, a tiny lovely country almost cut in two in the middle where the waist is less than ten miles wide, is hemmed in by enemies on all sides. In the North by Lebanon, in the East by Syria and Jordan and in the West and South by Egypt. All are fanatically hostile and burning with Arab hatred.

Yet Israel prospers and is not afraid. Within ten prodigious years – a decade of compressed history – during which she has fought and won two major wars, the Jews have more than doubled their cultivated area and have more than trebled their irrigation.

Almost every crop ranging from citrus fruits, wheat, vegetables, potatoes, bananas and olives to grapes, tobacco, pulses and seeds has increased.

Eggs, milk and cattle have all become vastly more plentiful as have sugar beet and cotton.

Foreign trade has risen steeply, new roads have been built and public health has expanded beyond all recognition.

Outside Jerusalem there is rising one of the most splendid and beautiful universities in the world – a truly magnificent building set in a lovely surround that any nation would be proud of.

When I visited it I saw some of the Dead Sea Scrolls beautifully preserved in air-conditioned showcases. They were a triumphant reminder of the power of survival of this tenacious race.

There is more equality of sex in Israel than in any other land I know.

I flew up from the Red Sea port of Eilat which is Israel's new lung breathing against the Egyptian blockade. We were in a Douglas airliner and I was told that up front the pilot was a lady – one of two regularly operating on Israel's airlines.

I replied that I wished the best of luck to our 50 per cent of the national team – and especially to her passengers.

Water is the life-blood of Israel. Wherever you go you see pipe-lines being laid, pumping stations being erected.

Prom Lake Galilee the stream of life stretches her steel and concrete veins way down to the Negev in the South and into the edges of the desert.

Plans are afoot to extract fresh water from the sea – and arid tracts of what seem to be dead sands are transformed into fertile lands by scientific know-how, by courage, and by fierce, grinding toil.

Israel has a more than efficient Army – as the mountebank Nasser well knows. Its leaders are young men of the highest intellectual capability and are often scholars as well as soldiers.

But the Army serves a twofold purpose. There is conscription for both men and women – the boys serving two and a half years while the girls do two years.

Apart from the purely military side, however, the defence forces serve to fuse young people together who speak different languages and are used to different customs.

In the services they are all taught Hebrew and they are all indoctrinated with the famous – and terrible – story of Israel. These young people are firmly but sensibly disciplined and they emerge united, healthy and believing in their destiny.

Out of persecution, out of tragedy and out of the horrors of Hitlerism this great and historic return has been achieved.

I asked Ben-Gurion whether, against the long perspective of 3,000 years of Jewish history, it might not be permissible to take the view that the tragedies of Hitlerism and the unspeakable persecution might, after all, have been the only thing to have made the reunification of Israel possible.

The wise old man – he is seventy-three – looked at me with his wrinkled, deep-set eyes and said: 'How will I resurrect the six million Jews who died in the last war?'

The story of the new-born Israel is, I believe, the most massive achievement of the century. It is, however, by no means certain that it will succeed.

Israel is surrounded by implacable enemies and has her back to the sea.

Famine cannot conquer her. Disease will not now prevail.

She needs only one thing to preserve the shining story – PEACE. It is no coincidence that the word of greeting used on almost every occasion in Israel is 'Shalom'.

'Shalom' means peace.

There is a green hill

The Holy Land, February 5, 1968

Before I went to the Holy Land I had an exact mental picture of Jerusalem, of Nazareth, of Lake Galilee, of Calvary, of Bethelem, of the Mount of Olives, and a score of other places made sacred and immortal by the Bible.

It was so precise that I felt that I had been there before.

The real thing is different.

Take the Mount from which Jesus delivered the Sermon.

In my mind's eye it was a dark and terrible place: a sombre, stony-mountain with the peak lost in black clouds.

I was there last week.

It is little more than a hillock and is as fresh and green as a Yorkshire wold. The anemones show their crimson petals, the irises are out and the mimosa is shining in this fair and lovely scene. A verdant pulpit from which the most tremendous words ever uttered were given to mankind.

What of Nazareth?

I envisaged a tiny hamlet – a place of simplicity and charm. In point of fact Nazareth is a sizeable, dusty town crammed with Arabs to whom Christianity is anything from a feeble myth to an abomination. Coca-Cola signs proclaim the American faith in that odd beverage.

Swarms of guides abound and start reciting their automatic and almost meaningless descriptions, and sheets of corrugated iron cover the entrance to the place where Joseph the carpenter is said to have lived, I am sorry to trample on your dreams.

And the Sea of Galilee?

It is not unlike Ullswater – only more beautiful. The hibiscus was in bloom and the oleanders gave shade from the hot Mediterranean sun. I had a meal in the open and ate fish newly caught from the lake. It happened to be a Friday and I kept St Peter well in mind. I don't suppose the fish have changed much in the last 2,000 years. I regret to report to you that they were tasteless and coarse.

The near-by restaurant was in a whirl of cheerful activity being redecorated for the Tenth Anniversary of the founding of the State of Israel, which is being celebrated this year.

Somehow this vibrant country reminds me of the United States in its urgency – the main and slightly grotesque difference being that the Americans have grown up in a virgin land once populated by Red Indians, whereas the Jews are toiling in the very cradle of world history.

There is a green hill far away
Without a city wall.

So went the old hymn, referring to Calvary and Golgotha where they crucified the Lord.

You cannot see the green hill from Israel today and barbed wire entanglements and machine guns will stop you if you try to make the pilgrimage, for Golgotha is in Arab territory.

So is Bethlehem.

So is the old part of Jerusalem.

In fact, the main part of the sacred territory of Christianity is Out of Bounds. At Christmas time certain carefully vetted parties are allowed through the bristling frontiers that divide Jewish and Arab Jerusalem, and you may go to the places of the birth and death of our Lord only if you are visa-ed up to the eyebrows and apparently well disposed to the crackpot empire that Nasser is jerry-building in the Middle East.

More disillusion, I am afraid, for you.

I was shown the room where it's reputed The Last Supper was held. It is a rather shabby chamber (not that I was expecting highly polished premises), faintly reminiscent of a small annexe in the Alexandra Palace. You get a feeling that possibly some rich Mohammedan gentleman has a financial interest in the place but has not troubled to see that it is regularly dusted out.

Having been brought up in the Presbyterian Church of England, I was rather tickled to see St Andrew's Church of Scotland in Jerusalem.

It was as smart as a pin, as uncompromising in its architecture as anything that Aberdeen can show, and very much the 'Kirk awa frae hame'.

King David's tomb looked like something out of Drury Lane – the great stained glass let through shafts of ugly vegetable light – and Mount Zion was a good deal too small for my preconceived notions.

But Israel is endless in its fascinations. I had a glass of unassuming beer at a place called Ashkalon, and after a half-hearted game of table tennis with a companion I was suddenly told that I was standing more or less on the spot where Samson was born.

Later on, in an aeroplane flying down to the Red Sea, I was told to look out of the window.

Far below in the reddish brown desert were what appeared to be track marks and excavations.

'See those workings?' said my companion. 'King Solomon's Mines.'

Only Rider Haggard was missing.

Back home again after 3,500 years

Mycenae, Greece, July 27, 1965

I did not choose the name Cassandra and, when it was first wished on me exactly thirty years ago, I had to look myself up in the encyclopaedia to find out who I was.

I was a bit surprised to discover that I had changed my sex; was the daughter of the King of Troy; that I could foretell in the stars when the news was going to be bad; that a chap called Apollo had made many a pass at me; that nobody believed me when I spoke the unpleasant truth and that I was going to come to a sticky end by being efficiently murdered by Clytaemnestra the wife of the mighty King Agamemnon.

So I went and had a beer to pull myself round.

Incidentally, talking about a sticky end, a good many years ago when the late Sir John Simon in the House of Commons objected to what I wrote in this newspaper about the conduct of the war, he predicted that, like my namesake, I would come unstuck in a big way.

That unlovable lawyer may yet be right, but it's been a very enjoyable Greek tragedy so far.

On further research I learned that I had been born about 3,500 years ago and that I was telling anybody who wanted to listen (which they didn't) all the bad news in advance from the great fortress town of Mycenae which is about 100 miles from Athens.

Not unnaturally I have long wanted to visit the old home town and so here I am.

It was probably at Mycenae that I told the Trojans that the Greeks were up to no good and that they would build a wooden horse and conceal themselves inside it and that they would sack Troy.

I got the usual brush-off – and the Greeks got Troy.

What remains of Mycenae today are the ruins of a great Acropolis standing high above the plain of Argolid. The stones of the ancient walls of the city and gigantic royal tombs weigh up to a hundred and twenty tons each and, as with Stonehenge and the Pyramids, no one quite knows how they were levered into position.

At the entrance to the city gate there are bas-reliefs of two huge lions and when I asked the slick question as to how it was the Greeks knew about lions since obviously there were no lions in Greece, I got the ball back over the net in double quick time being told that the Greeks saw them in Egypt and almost certainly brought a few back home to keep the kids amused.

So it was here in this wild, splendid, mountainous scenery in the South-West of Greece that I made my ancient prophecies.

So it was here in this great hill-top fortress with its amphitheatre, its royal tombs, its bull-ring, its treasure houses, its granary, its underground cisterns and its magnificent palace that I foretold the catastrophes of the future that no one would listen to. I was a voice crying in the wilderness of on-coming disaster that nobody would believe.

Damn it, they don't believe me today.

The sun blazed out of the matchless blue sky, the oleanders, white and pink, flaunted and swayed in the hot wind, cicadas chattered and buzzed the Greek chorus of the insect world. The mountains all around shimmered in the heat haze and Cassandra Mark II, of the *Daily Mirror,* heard the heart-beat of history and I prophesied to myself that if I walked a step farther up the rocky slopes of Mycenae I'd have to get me a new pair of feet.

My old home town fairly buzzed with tourists. They poured out of their Mercedes-Benz motor coaches. They swarmed all over the place, they were escorted by guides, they took endless snapshots, they consulted maps and they chattered as they goggled.

In Cassandra's time things were tougher. The ancient Greeks loved giving each other a hard time.

They gave me a hard time.

In the Iliad there is an account of what finally happened to me which would have greatly pleased Sir John Simon.

When Odysseus reached the country of the Phaeacians he told them of his descent into Hades where he met the ghost of Agamemnon who was the boss man of Mycenae. The spirit of Agamemnon moved him to deep pity. Odysseus begged him to say how he died, and the great king told him that he was killed ingloriously at Mycenae as he sat at table, butchered as one kills an ox.

'It was Aegisthus,' he said, 'with the aid of my accursed wife. He invited me to his house and as I feasted he killed me. My soldiers and bodyguard, too. You have seen many die in single combat or in battle, but never one who died as we did, by the wine bowl and the loaded tables in a hall where the floor flowed with blood.

'Cassandra's death shriek rang in my ears as she fell, Clytaemnestra slew her over my body. I tried to lift up my hands for her, but they fell back. She was dead as I lay dying.'

The recollection of my coming unstuck 3,500 years ago near the place where I was standing in the blazing sun seemed to call for a reassuring drink, and I told the driver to pull up at the nearest taverna.

I asked the landlord to recommend a good rich red wine to soothe the memories of my gory end.

I think it was appropriate that he produced a bottle of excellent Greek wine called 'The Blood of Hercules'.

Love in Leningrad

Leningrad, May 11, 1960

I shall tell you about love in the city named after Vladimir Ilyich Lenin.

There are almost no church weddings in the Soviet Union. Marriages are legalised in what are called 'Zags'. Zags are roughly the equivalent of our register offices, except, perhaps, that they have captured even a bit more of the 'Cripes-you're-going-to-cop-it-for-keeps' atmosphere.

The young folks in Russia got a bit fed up with gateways to matrimonial bliss looking like a cross between a Post Office and the annexe to a police court.

One pair of love birds about to step on the same perch in a Zags at Kiev were so displeased with the place that they flew up here to Leningrad where they order things much better.

In Leningrad a year ago they had the idea of the 'Wedding Palace'.

It was an immediate success. The boys and girls are now being hooked there at the rate of seventy to eighty a day, at fifteen roubles (or thirty bob) a woo.

The Palace itself is a large building in the best Italian baroque style. It is quite a place.

As I walked in the commissionaire greeted me with great cordiality. It is not every day that I am mistaken for a handsome young bridegroom.

I went into the foyer, an impressive, massive place leading to a wide flight of marble stairs above which hung the inevitable mighty chandelier that is so popular in the USSR.

If there is ever held a World Championship to see who has the best chandeliers, the rest of us might as well give up right away. We can't hold a candle to them, so to speak.

Now watch Josep Shelom and his bride Ludmilla getting married. Each is twenty-one.

Russians seem to get married a lot earlier than we do and of the half-dozen couples I saw in the Wedding Palace none seemed a day older than about twenty-three; most of them looked a good deal less.

There were two waiting rooms. Josep went into the one on the left-hand side with his supporters, looking for all the world like a football team in their best Sunday civvies.

Ludmilla went into the other with her group of girl friends. A gift shop was next door.

Piped-in music was playing. Not the corny aural honey that we hear so much of but thumpety thump stuff that was virile if a shade raucous.

The two parties emerged after a few minutes and the pair were ushered in to the registrar in a large, well furnished room with a carpet.

The registrar was a plump, pleasant lady sitting at a massive desk who took the necessary details with resolute goodwill.

Ludmilla, a nice young thing, managed an occasional blush and Josep exuded manly embarrassment – but was obviously very well pleased with it all.

From there we marched into a huge ante-room on the third floor. All present were dressed in decorous provincial style, second class.

The bride held a simple bouquet of lilac and we all sat rather awkwardly on chairs designed to remind us of the harder outlines of life.

Overhead were, of course, the inevitable chandeliers – four real sparkling whackers.

The boys – you could hardly call them grown men – made suitable forced jokes. The girls were girlish. The canned band played on.

A vast door opened and Josep disappeared by himself. He returned in a couple of minutes. Ludmilla went in and was back in no time.

They had been signing the marriage certificate in the presence of the wedding committee – a tough and most amiable chairman who was the equivalent of a county councillor, and two substantial ladies of the no-nonsense variety.

After a slight pause we bustled into the central chamber. A truly enormous room with chandeliers that must have needed a crane to lift them.

The general decor was elegant and of the late Tsarist period, which perhaps was not very surprising for Peter the Great lived only a couple of minutes away by droshki in the Hermitage Palace just down the road.

At the far end of the room sat the committee on a raised platform, and behind them was a big white bust of Lenin looking benignly on. He had seen some sharpish things in his time, but now the gaze was magnanimous and fatherly.

In the centre of the room, facing the tribunal and standing up, were the love birds.

We formed a military square round them. Loudspeakers tooted jauntily in the distance.

The chairman addressed Josep and Ludmilla like a favourite uncle, adjured them to be good citizens of the Soviet Union, wished them luck, good health, all happiness and added his own personal avuncular blessing.

We clapped. One of the officiating matrons stepped down from the tribunal and handed the marriage certificate, handsomely bound, to Josep.

Then, after shaking hands with both the newly-wedded, she suggested with just a touch of authority that it was about time the husband kissed his very new young wife.

We cheered.

He did.

We clapped.

And the matron, smiling her slightly formidable smile, said that he might as well have another kiss while he was about it, for Ludmilla and her kisses were his. All his.

We cheered and then filed into the Celebration Room at some speed, for the following couple about to be married were close behind us.

The production line of love must not be stopped and there must be no slowing down of those heaven-bent for the sweet bed of matrimonial roses – thorns and all.

Josep and Ludmilla drank a little champagne and their friends raised their glasses. The radio honked its tinny blessing.

Josep gave his bride an apple in accordance with Russian tradition and they ate it together.

You will remember that in an earlier encounter it was Eve who gave Adam the apple, but like so many things in this prodigious land they have turned things round.

Josep hugged Ludmilla and Ludmilla hugged Joe – and they were gone.

The canned band played on.

A Navy lark on my ship

Singapore Naval Base, December 23, 1961

Out here in this sweaty and booming town there is one of Her Majesty's ships by the name of *Cassandra.* Also out here there is one of Her Majesty's subjects – again under the name of Cassandra.

Last night both parties went into joint action to celebrate the advent of Christmas.

I came here at the invitation of Commander Spencer Drummond to make sure that all who sail under the flag and name of the original Greek prophetess of woe and disaster should have a thundering good time as the Eve of Christmas approaches. In short, we did.

Just about 200 Cassandrites – I think it may have been two or three pintfuls more – assembled here in the Armada Club at the Naval Base.

Christmas at home in Britain is, by iron tradition, a matter of snow, of holly, of red berries, of old Santa with his beard and cloak and loaded sack. Also Good King Wenceslas with his page and the white stuff deep and crisp and even all around.

Out here just 70 miles north of the Equator? No snow. No holly. No red berries. And only the damp enfolding heat – about 84 degrees right at this moment.

But in company with all the lads of HMS *Cassandra* we did old Santa proud.

This ship, the ship you taxpayers bought and still maintain, this ship that My Lords of the Admiralty run – and damn you, MY ship – has been out here in the Far East for more than two years now.

There was a break recently when our ship, their ship, your ship, MY ship had to belt off at about 23 knots to look after the trouble that suddenly flared up off Kuwait.

When it was cold there on board HMS *Cassandra* in those Arabian waters, the temperature lurked around 105 degrees. When it was hot – well, it was as hot as hell.

Last night here in Singapore, as the evening baked on, it got a bit warm, too.

At 7.30 sharp in this most excellent NAAFI club the lads marched into my *Cassandra* party looking suspiciously innocent and polite.

When I greeted them they had – or most of them had – that faint expression of infant charm and sweetness and light that usually ends with us all stamping on the table bawling *Sweet Adeline, Frankie and Johnnie* and arguing that if there are any coppers around here, ask 'em up and we'll tell them exactly what to do.

There were hula-hula girls to arouse our most gallant instincts.

A vast cake built by confectioners who must have been brought up in a community of giants, with appetites to match.

American turkey – damn these Yanks, they seem to be everywhere.

York ham – that's better, me lads.

Spring chicken. Sirloin of beef. Fresh lobster – I particularly liked the chap who wanted the casing instead of the innards.

Mixed pickles. Smoked salmon.

Black pearly caviar – damn these Russians, they seem to be everywhere.

Anchovy eggs. Sausage rolls. Sardine fingers.

And a Very Merry Christmas to you all.

The crew of Her Majesty's ship *Cassandra,* your Cassandra, MY Cassandra, is in excellent good heart.

As the proceedings rose to their defiant and jubilant climax I managed to say a few words to the ship's company. I record with exhausted pleasure that the mightiest roar of the whole thunderous evening broke all records when I proposed the toast of the wives, the sweethearts, the mums, the dads and the nippers at home.

Just off the Equator, and very far from the snowline, I wish all of you who have heard of the name of Cassandra, whether it has to do with ships, sealing wax, cabbages, kings, or my particular daily trouble in the public prints, a very happy and most joyful Christmas.

The perfect host

Fort St John, British Columbia, May 25, 1964

You know there is a great deal of civility in this Commonwealth of ours – especially in Australia and Canada.

The other day when I was in a Sydney bar a gigantic Aussie ambled up to me and with a genial grin said: 'Hey, Pommie! Wanna fight?'

I said I could do without it.

He said: 'Some Pommies seem kinda lost without a fight and I only wanted to oblige. Good-on-yer-mate.'

I call that real charm with just a hint of the courtly elegance of Old Vienna about it.

And now there is this flaming business about the oil well.

The oil well in the North-West of British Columbia – a rich and lovely part of Canada not all that far from the Yukon.

I know a man who owns an oil well up there and if you think I'm swanking, you're dead right.

This gentleman said to me: 'I have an oil well. I would be happy to set fire to it for your relaxation should you so desire it.'

The old incendiary in me blazed up at this and I said that nothing would enchant me more.

I felt sure that a blazing oil well and I would get on like a house on fire.

We went to the middle of a field out of which emerged a pipe-line, some tanks and a wheel-valve. In the middle of the field was what appeared to be a very large bomb crater.

Someone turned the valve and then with a roar that was louder than a quartet of jet engines, the well caught fire and a cauldron of yellow and orange flame higher than a five storey house sprang to life. It thundered and it billowed.

A pall of thick black smoke almost blotted the sunlight, out. The heat made you turn your face away from the writhing wreathing flames.

In fact, so successful was the demonstration that the next field caught fire – which was not the idea at all.

The technician who had started the magnificent blaze hastily reversed the process and started beating out the grass and bushes that were by now well alight.

As I said, these Commonwealth chaps really do set themselves out to please.

After the courtesy of the oil well, I went to see the Honourable W A C Bennett who is the Premier of British Columbia.

We talked for an hour and I ended up with his blessing and a presentation pair of gold cuff links.

There must be something about Australia and Canada that can show you an oil well on fire, present you with gold cuff links, and offer you a thick ear free of charge in a dockside bar – all within a matter of a few days.

Canada's endless forests stretch from horizon to horizon. Forests and lakes and lakes and forests. Tens of thousands of lonely timberlands. Places where men have never been.

The bounty of Canada has hardly been touched and it is an empty place compared with our huddled and teeming island with 52,000,000 crammed in an area less than British Columbia.

The mineral wealth of this one province alone includes zinc, lead, copper, iron, silver, gold, cadmium, bismuth, antimony, nickel, selenium, tungsten, barite, silica and molybdenum.

In Ontario near the town of Timmins, there has just started a silver and copper strike that may well bring back the memories of the great gold rush hi the Klondike at the back end of last century.

Last November, the Texas Gulf Sulphur Company was doing test drilling in the spruce forests near Timmins when they struck the largest deposits of silver ore ever uncovered – a hundred million tons of it.

At first the company tried to keep it quiet, but the sweet smell of a billion dollars got into the nostrils of the prospectors and the great stampede is on.

People are staking their claims and from borrowed capital of a few thousand dollars they have sold their rights for millions of dollars.

The geologists, the speculators and the gamblers are in on it and a bonanza for Canada and Canadians is at hand.

In British Columbia, in addition to precious minerals, they have coal, sulphur, clay, limestone and sand. There is unlimited lumber and vast new hydro-electric power schemes.

There are abundant fish in the lakes, the rivers and the sea-salmon, halibut, sole, cod, herring, crab, oysters, smelts and clams.

On the land there is natural gas and oil, beef, grain, apples, peaches, grapes, apricots, cherries and pears.

In the great prairies of Saskatchewan and Alberta there is wheat stretching endlessly on land as flat as an ocean on a calm day.

Nothing but corn and the towering grain elevators.

This is an abundant land.

A gentleman from Whitehall has recently called the Commonwealth a ‘farce’.

That is his own view but I was astonished at the strength and the warmth that these Canadians still feel towards the British.

They are not flannelling. They actually like us. To this there is one notable exception – the French Canadians. Their regard for the British is about as warm as de Gaulle’s, and it is possible that the strong separatist movement in Quebec gains inspiration from that stubborn old man’s chauvinist views.

Not only do the French Canadians not care for the British but they are bitter and hostile towards the ‘Canadian’ Canadians who, they claim, treat them as second-class citizens.

The land of the maple leaf is not all milk and honey, and for those who read mystic signs in flags and banners it may be of interest that the old red Canadian flag with the Union Jack on it may be replaced by a white flag with three maple leaves – and no Union Jack.

With malice to none

April 3, 1957

or
HOW TO SUCCEED IN BUSINESS
WITHOUT ACTUALLY LYING

First of all you make sure that you know the Christian names of everybody you meet – or are likely to meet. You then proceed to address them by their Christian names within a few seconds of having first met them. This gives a fine sense of false bonhomie which is much appreciated by high-powered executives who have been using this phoney trick for years and are flattered by the speed with which you recognise the idea.

It is best however to get their names dead right for I once saw a very ugly scene blow up when the chairman of a steel works whose Christian name was Lancelot had been wrongly called Alf 27 times in the first quarter of an hour.

Next it is essential to talk in a strange, flashy language that will impress all within earshot. Advertising agency men will appreciate the force of what I am saying. Ideas must appear to bubble out of you and as most of them will be a compound of hokum hashed up with balderdash they must be protected from any close examination which will reveal them for what they are worth.

Which is nix.

When you unveil The Big Idea you introduce it briskly thus: 'Well, fellers, let's get the Skull Session on the road.'

Translation: 'Here comes a flight of the highest intellectual thought – interrupt if you dare.'

You then reveal some microscopically small idea, hackneyed and jaded beyond compare, for selling boot polish in Runcorn. You guard against being exposed to sensible criticism by inviting all to join with you by saying: 'Let's run this one up the flagstaff and see if anyone salutes.'

Translation: 'This is a fine idea but we'll wait to see if anybody is fool enough to agree.'

If The Big Idea needs even greater protection from common sense the fashionable phrase which knocks 'em cold is: 'Let's throw this one on the floor and walk around it for a while.'

Translation: 'Let's all discuss my brilliant suggestion and for Pete's sake give me a few more ideas that will not make mine sound such blazing claptrap.'

If The Big Idea is such obviously arrant rubbish that it has to be shelved at once the racy genial comment is: 'Let's throw a blanket over this one and keep it warm.'

Translation: 'You guys may think it's drivel now but maybe tomorrow you'll change your minds when I've had time to plug a few of the holes in this colander of utter idiocy.'

If The Big Idea is so bad that it cannot be comprehended in any way you defend it with a bland smile: 'Okay, fellers, okay! Sure we'll play it by ear. Then maybe when you've finished ad-libbing, we'll follow it down to the grass roots.'

Translation: 'You have no flak but once you get the hang of my ballyhoo we'll examine it coldly and scientifically right to the basic principles of my brilliant inspiration.'

See you in the Board Room, boys.

July 20, 1961

It has sometimes been said of me that I am hostile to the advertising profession.

I am not.

I am deeply in love with it. Day after day they make me collapse with helpless laughter and they fill me with a joy that is unrefined.

Yesterday the official Government Milkman issued a huge half-page advertisement in the papers that was a riot of improbable fun and made me guffaw till the cows came home. Listen:

> We had been married a fortnight. John went off on one of those reunion things. My girl friend came round for the evening. Suddenly the telephone rang. It was John of course. Wanted to know if he could bring the boys back home to see the bride.
>
> "How many?" I asked weakly.
>
> "Twelve," he said. "All right", I said severely, "but all you'll get is a nice hot drink."
>
> In ten minutes they were here – three taxi loads – and I was out of milk. So there was a great emptying of pockets and a great searching for sixpences. Then John came back with an armful of pintas, in cartons.

Actually we drank it straight. Cold and delicious. We had a wonderful evening. (My friend is now engaged.)

As Groucho Marx used to say: 'A likely story!'

August 4, 1960

When I was in New York last week I saw a notice in a strange, seedy shop at the top of Sixth Avenue that appealed to me. There was nothing in the window except a large, stuffed pike lying on a pile of grimy wood shavings.

On top of it lay a faded notice. It said: CUSTOMERS WANTED. NO EXPERIENCE NECESSARY.

August 19, 1958

Here is a circular letter from a firm of furnishers in the South. At the top of this cloying communication there is a florid colour illustration of a spray of roses, a couple of tulips and a carnation. Then follows this oily, up chucking letter :

Good Morning, Madam!

May I introduce myself? I am the Head Office Supervisor for the Area and I am visiting the above Branch today; and going through the Branch Register of exceptionally good settled customers I came upon your name and address.

Pause while the oily flattery is meant to soak in.

Yours was such a valuable account that I would have dearly liked to present you with a bouquet, but as this is not possible, I hope you will agree that the heading of this letter expresses the same feelings.

No it doesn't. The paper reproduction might cost you a tenth of a farthing. The real thing would cost you ten bob. Keep counting your change pal.

It is some considerable time since we had the favour of a further order from you and I am just wondering why.

Couldn't be them greasy compliments could it?

Did you have any cause for complaint? If so please let me know.

Meantime I am desperately anxious to open a further account for you at this Branch.

Keep being desperate.

Do please come along at once. I have instructed our Manager to receive you and to serve you personally.

Sure, sure. But just wait a moment, Bouquet Boy, while we are all sick together in hearty unison.

August 8, 1957

The other day I recounted how, when I was about to start writing a piece about the H-bomb, my typewriter packed up at the critical moment and I was left feeling as if I had had my hands cut off.

Soon after the item appeared in the paper a bright and breezy voice rang me up and said that he was the sales representative of a certain typewriter firm (I forbear to mention the name) and that he was sorry to have read of my plight. Now could he sell me a really good machine that would never let me down.

'Who do you represent?'

'The — Company.'

'It was your brand of machine that jammed solid.'

'Christmas! I guess I'd better get off the line.'

'I guess you better had.'

'Mornin'.'

'Mornin'.'

August 5, 1958

I rather like the warning notice written up in a pub about the dangers of alcoholic loquacity. It has a nice technical note that may be accounted for by the fact that the boozer is next to a garage. It read:

PLEASE MAKE SURE THAT BRAIN IS ENGAGED BEFORE OPERATING MOUTH.

Nothing by halves

Chicago, March 9, 1959

This is a rough, tough old town. Compared with it, New York seems almost prim and shy.

Seen from the air, Chicago is a great blotch of railway sidings, water towers and factories, spread endlessly under a smudgy pall of smoke; from the safety of terra firma it is a maelstrom of violent contrast.

Nothing is done by halves. In the vast hotel where I am staying (typically it has to be the largest on earth) there is the biggest collection of nuns I have ever seen. There must be several hundred of them attending a religious convention organized by the Catholic Libraries Association.

Less than 200 yards away from where these sombre gowned and hooded ladies are holding their spiritual deliberations, there are the burlesque shows, strip-tease acts, and other worldly relaxations.

In the interests of social investigation I took this innocent column of mine along to see the gals.

We paused for one moment outside in the street in the glare of the flashing lights, but a barker, bellowing of the delights within, shanghaied us.

As in all American bars nearly total darkness prevailed. The show was about to start, and a noise like a musical air raid was going on. There was a mighty television set glaring down on us with the volume control full on, fighting a battle to death with a juke box.

My money was on the juke box, for although the telly never stopped screaming, it went completely out of focus now and again when it got savaged by a particularly vicious and ear-splitting chord from the juke box. An automatic machine for toasting sandwiches, full of volts and lights and sparks and cheese, chattered away in front of us. And just to add to that nightmare quality that I treasure so much, somebody had placed a huge illuminated tankful of goldfish on top of a piano that was the only silent thing in the whole place.

Then, with a roar like a guided missile taking off, a loudspeaker announced that 'Boy, we're going to see sumpin!'

An immense girl, who would have been quite at home lifting heavy weights or working in a foundry, stood in a spotlight and with an expression of complete indifference removed 95 per cent – or maybe it was 97 per cent – of her clothing.

By this time the column and I, who are a pretty old-fashioned pair, began to feel just a shade apprehensive. But we stuck to our bar stools and in no time were joined by a business-like young lady who said all in one word 'Honeywouldyouliketobuymeadrink?'

Honey was considering this proposition, but I was brushed aside as she said to the barman 'Double Scotch and soda and a packet of cigarettes.' The barman, a swarthy man with the expression of a clenched fist, slapped down the drink (almost certainly coloured water), named a price that would have made Rockefeller blink and thrust his hand out for the money. Being peace-lovers, we paid.

Said the hostess, 'Guess you come from Texas?'

'No.'

'Milwaukee?'

'No.'

'St Louis?'

'No.'

'Des Moines?'

'No.'

'Then where were you raised, honey?'
'London, England.'
'Gee, I would sure like to see that Eiffel Tower of yours.'
After that we made what is called a 'tactical withdrawal' and slid out into the night.
The whole street was in action. Lights ablaze; pin tables jammed with customers; a tattooist doing a roaring trade; a hotel offering '300 clean beds for only 65 cents a night, men only.'
Next to it was a joke shop selling artificial eyes to stick in the middle of the forehead by means of a rubber sucker, to give your friends a nasty turn. They were being displayed next to a tray full of crucifixes.
We turned for home. One great sign kept flashing GIRLS, GIRLS, GIRLS.
Another red neon Sign of the Cross bore the words SURRENDER TO CHRIST. Mother's prayers are always following you.
The battle between Heaven and Hell is being waged with zest and lust and no half measures in this uninhibited town.

Young man in an old rocking chair

Washington, October 30, 1961

I have been talking alone in the White House with President Kennedy of the United States. The procedure of admittance to this lovely building in the heart of Washington was slightly odd. At the gate on Pennsylvania Avenue the guard, a most genial fellow, asked me to produce some evidence that I was me and that me was I – such as a driving licence, a passport, a letter, a hotel bill – anything.
I had nothing.
I might have been a clean-shaven Castro for all they knew.
He grinned affably and said: 'Better go on up to the House and try your luck.'
I said: 'It will be too bad if I have to open fire to prove the cordial spirit of Anglo-American friendship.'
He replied in a mock English accent: 'That wouldn't be cricket, old chappie.'
The President lives on the second floor of the White House. Outside his oval-shaped study there is a spacious book-lined hall. Around the walls there are elegant paintings of Red Indian life.

The books interested me. A man's library, if he uses it, is often a quick guide to his character.

History, judging by the volumes, was Mr Kennedy's main theme.

I noticed *Their Finest Hour* by Winston Churchill and *The Rise and Fall of the Third Reich* by William Shirer. I couldn't help recalling that the President's father, Joseph Kennedy – when he was American Ambassador at the Court of St James in 1939 – had predicted the decline and fall of the British people at the hands of Adolf Hitler.

For good topical value on the book shelves there was also *On the Beach* by Nevil Shute, which described a dying world after the impact of an atomic war, the *Encyclopaedia Britannica* (more trans-Atlantic co-operation), and a book enigmatically entitled, *Ladies of the White House.*

The President looks astonishingly young – even younger than his forty-four years.

The last time I saw him was about twelve months ago in the middle of his election campaign when I accompanied him on his tour. Once he was surrounded by thousands of screaming teenagers in the main square in Scranton, Pennsylvania, and I thought at the time that popularity with juveniles, in the Elvis Presley manner, might not be enough to cope with Nikita Krushchev.

Now there is no doubt that this most pleasant man carries the greatest burden in the world. The responsibilities of this youthful Atlas are greater than Krushchev's – for the President has to serve and to please a free people and has anything but a free hand.

I asked him whether he thought that tensions – especially over Berlin – and the possibility of war had steeply increased.

He said that it was not necessarily so – and at once turned to the dangers of an all-out conflict in South Vietnam, where many Washington officials think it may be necessary to send American soldiers at any moment, to meet the increasingly aggressive tactics of the Communist troops.

All the time he spoke the President sat vigorously swinging to and fro in his now famous rocking chair.

It is curious how the Americans like these gimmicks. With Truman it was inscribed pens that he used to give away bearing the words 'Stolen from the President of the United States'. With Eisenhower it was golf. With Kennedy it is an old-fashioned rocking chair and its association with wise old Uncle Sam or Abraham Lincoln having forty winks in the best parlour.

Mr Kennedy seemed very conscious of the world-wide liabilities and responsibilities of the United States to hostile pressure from the Soviet Union at many points.

On the question of Berlin there is no doubt that the ultimate line has been firmly drawn – and that Krushchev knows it.

On this point I talked earlier to Mr Charles Bohlen who was formerly ambassador in Moscow and is now a special adviser on Russia to the President, and also to Mr Dean Acheson, a former Secretary of State.

They believe that Krushchev, in the last resort, is not a gambler.

But he has nothing like the authority of Stalin. There are comrades to be appeased. Soviet militarists who like the feel of their own muscles. Technicians who, in the nuclear field, may have been pressing the Russian leader extremely hard to continue with their research in an attempt to get far ahead of the Americans in atomic war techniques.

Another difficulty that the President has to face is the fact that Krushchev is as fanatically devoted to the Lenin-Marxist theory as the Pope is to Christianity, and that in the end he may pursue his ugly faith into the holocaust of war.

The list of Mr Kennedy's problems is endless.

I tried to find out what, in the agonising dilemma of Berlin, the United States has to give away. THE ANSWER is NOTHING.

The President cannot bargain. As a gesture which would impress nobody the President might recognise the Oder-Neisse line – the present boundary between East Germany and Poland. Krushchev and the Poles couldn't care less. They have already drawn the Oder-Neisse line and the endorsement of it by Washington would just be a joke. As for the recognition of East Germany by the United States, it just isn't on.

I questioned Mr Arthur Schlesinger, who is a special adviser to the President, on this subject. He could see no concessions that could be made. The President might make minor adjustments here and there, including a pledge to withhold atomic weapons from the German Army, but that would not set the Kremlin on fire.

The line of no retreat is officially drawn outside the Brandenburg Gate in Berlin, and Washington in its present mood will yield no further.

Yet the local shilly-shallying in Berlin and the alternating policies of rigidity one day and flexibility the next are confusing.

From people everywhere – and that includes officials inside the White House – I got the sharp impression that President Kennedy is not directly in control of the day-to-day situation in the divided city and that some military figure could easily make the fatal blunder.

Another field of confusion which Mr Kennedy must clear up very soon is the question of fallout shelters. He has already made complete plans for a shadow government to take over if Washington should be wiped out, and there are deputies, whose names are being kept secret, for every major job.

But the question of deciding whether the general population should make arrangements for some place to hide has not been settled.

Again the President is in a dilemma.

If he agrees to the building of communal shelters then the Russians may well feel that the United States regards war as inevitable and the temptation to get the cataclysmic blow in without warning may increase. Secondly, the provision of shelters may make Americans feel that H-Bombs are not so destructive as they originally thought they were.

The White House is under no such delusion. The President's popularity is increasing here every day. The main reason – which I well understand after talking to him privately – is sympathy for him. Sympathy that so young a man should bear such a prodigious burden. Sympathy that such an attractive and intellectually sensitive figure should be confronted with such hideous problems. Sympathy with an idealist confronted with the greatest danger that mankind has ever known.

But the harsh fact remains that the realities of brutal power politics cannot be erased by sympathy, and that an older and more experienced man might be a better occupant of the lonely place in the White House.

Two years later Cassandra re-visited Washington – in sadder circumstances

The end of the road

December 16, 1963

I said to the taxi-driver: 'The Lincoln Museum'.

He looked blank.

'You know, the house where Abraham Lincoln was shot.'

He looked blank.

'The old Ford's Theatre where the President was assassinated...'

He looked blank.

So I navigated to Tenth Street between E and F Streets right in the heart of Washington and we made it.

Thus do fame and tragedy fade – at least in the minds of Washington taxi-drivers.

The old theatre building still stands and the ground floor is the Lincoln Museum, which contains letters and documents of the great President, paintings, photographs, engravings, statuary and the Derringer pistol with which the actor John Wilkes Booth murdered him.

The museum was empty when I went in. At the far end is a large model of the theatre as it was on the night of April 14, 1865.

You press a button and a loud-speaker booms out the melancholy tale.

How the President and his wife went to see Tom Taylor's celebrated comedy *Our American Cousin;* how in the third act the assassin crept into Lincoln's box, barred the door behind him; how he fired his gun and put a bullet into his victim that entered above the left ear and lodged behind the right eye; how Booth leapt from the box, crashed on the stage twelve feet below him, smashed his ankle and shouted 'Ever thus to tyrants!' and managed, in spite of his injuries, to escape on horseback; how Mrs Lincoln was overcome with grief and how Booth was shot dead twelve days later by an avenger.

I left the museum with the ghastly parallel of Dallas inevitably in my mind. A gun. A head wound. An escaping assassin. The President's wife right beside him and the killer himself soon struck dead. A nation's tears.

Guns down the years...

Next a taxi to Number Nine Pennsylvania Avenue – the US Department of Justice. The FBI – very much in the news now since the death of John Fitzgerald Kennedy and the kidnapping of the son of Sinatra – showed me something of their unending war against crime.

Their forensic and scientific skill is unmatched in the world and it is as well, for few if any nation can match the United States when it comes to the black arts of violence.

I saw their armoury of captured firearms ranging from dinky and deadly little pistols to the notorious Thompson sub-machine gun that was the chosen instrument of the gangster wars of Chicago at their worst.

At the conclusion of this lethal tour I was taken down into the basement to a range where an FBI man gave me a demonstration of revolver shooting and how to handle a machine gun.

The target was a life-sized paper cut-out of a man at a distance of about twenty-five yards. The FBI marksman grouped six pistol shots in the heart area – all scored within a space not more than two inches in diameter.

One short blast from the machine gun (twenty bullets) was sprayed over an area about the size of a soup plate round the stomach and the heart.

At the end I was presented with this grisly riddled target as a souvenir.

Guns again. Guns...

Now on to Arlington Cemetery. Not far from the White House where America buries those who have honourably borne arms.

It was dusk. The great flood-lit dome of the Capitol could be seen in the distance and the enormous finger of the Washington Monument near by pointed to the darkening sky.

I walked along a winding road and then up a muddy, canvas-covered path with guide ropes on stanchions to a little white palisade.

There were the flowers and three wreaths. On the mound of cypress was the small flame that will burn as long as there are Americans to grieve over John Kennedy.

There, too, was the cap he wore when he was an officer of the United States Navy. Beside him are the two little headstones for his children who died before him.

The four Guards of Honour stood tall and silent and night put her dark arms closer around the scene.

As with Lincoln, the signpost to the end of the road was the gun.

Bye-bye blues…

New York, December 11, 1958

Sleep is an industry. Sleep is a scientific, technical process. Sleep is Big Business.

At the Sleep-center (spelt like that) at number 9 East 54th Street in New York City, there are tons of equipment sold at fancy prices to help you go to sleep.

I shall now describe only a small fraction of the advertised devices and furnishings that are required to help you drop off in America in the insomnolent year of 1958.

First of all you have to have a 'Tranquillizer Bath Kit – drop a spoonful of our sandman's solution into the tub. Kit contains bath solution, bath thermometer and bath pillow'.

When you have emerged and dried yourself and got into your pyjamas you switch on the 'Snug a Bed-Warmer' and also your 'Luxtrol Control Dial' which 'instantly dims or brightens the light in the bedroom.'

Next you turn on 'The World's Most Soporific Music that will delightfully help overworked minds', being careful to make sure that your 'Escort Alarm' is beside you: 'simply press button and its instant siren shriek startles the intruder into making a hurried retreat'.

Before you put on your 'Eloquent Sleep Shade – soothing black sleep shades, down-padded and adjustable with message ("But I DO love you") which lets your lids and lashes move freely' you must have a glance at a book called *You Must Relax* by the 'Eminent Scientist Dr Edmund

Jacobson who will teach you to learn the natural art of relaxation so that you fall asleep and stay asleep'.

It is also a good idea to have a final cigarette 'Using our Robot Cigarette Holder. The smoker puffs serenely through a cooling long tube.'

In order to get safely to bye-byes after this, you must use 'NODS.'

'NODS' are 'ear-stops made of synthetic wax and Goodyear Airform Latex. They are malleable and shaped to fit any ear. They seal ear-opening comfortably and shut out the noises that ruin sleep.'

It is now time in the run-up towards slumberland to take a few more precautions.

On the radiogram you must put on a record called: *The Psychology of Love-Making* which is a 'frank, perceptive recorded discussion by Dr Theodore Reik. Thoughtful, critical wisdom freely expressed about conjugal relations that favour happy marriages. LP record, two sides, high-fidelity, with printed text'.

And keep that high-fidelity spinning, Blondie – or else.

Now to deal with the Old Man.

The brute is getting a bit restive but what, according to the Sleep-center, he really needs is a Carnam Head Warmer; 'Pamper his sensitive pate. If his sparsely thatched pate is sensitive to night chills get our glamorizing Carnam Head Warmer. Light, warm and comfortable. Adjustable chin bands. Dark blue.'

Move on quietly to the next problem about what happens when the brute subsides into swinish sleep:

'PREVENT SNORING. Attach our Anti-Snore Ball to his pajama coat. This discourages sleeping-on-back, a frequent cause of snoring.'

There is now nothing left to you but to fall flat on your soporific face and give one final blast of protest against the Sleep-center of 9 East 54th Street, New York City.

Nothing easier!

But, as a last precaution, you reach for their 'Horn of Nature, price one dollar ninety-five cents.

'CALL OF THE WILD. Express your mood with a genuine imported Horn of Nature. Blow it peremptorily for attention; plaintively for forgiveness; tenderly for affection. Illustrated, sophisticated gift box with directions for effect mood-sounding.'

No wonder the damn Yankee girls get bored.

Major Slaughter

Plattsburg, New York State, May 27, 1964

The spring is bursting out all over around Lake Champlain in this lovely part of America. The lilac sprays are heavy on the bough, the white-flowered dogwood is ablaze, and I am driving into a forest to see five men in a hole who could wipe Moscow off the face of the earth in a trice.

That's not quite accurate – in about forty minutes.

Here around Plattsburg is a 'complex' (how Americans love their technical jargon) of Atlas missiles buried in the earth under hundreds of tons of concrete hidden in forests. The difference between my inaccurate 'trice' and the true fact is the time it takes to launch this vast nuclear rocket (about 15 minutes) and the time it would take to travel from Plattsburg to Moscow – about 25 minutes.

The procedure of being admitted to one of these tombs is bizarre. There is a high heavy-duty wire fence. Inside is an armed sentry. Credentials are passed through the wire and after inspection, the sentry unlocks the gate.

A loudspeaker suddenly bawls: 'Smile please… say cheese!'

My conducting officer grins and I ask him: 'What is the idea?'

'You are being observed below ground by television,' he says, 'and the boys must have their fun.'

We enter an armoured shelter alongside the enormous horizontal concrete doors that open to release the missile. Huge steel doors like the vast vault gates that guard bullion swing open and we enter a lift and go down 50 feet.

More steel doors are swung open and then clang locked behind us. We enter a control room with electronic consoles, with dials and flashing lights and hard-covered manuals enclosed within red covers and printed with heavy black type which reads: CLASSIFIED – which is American for MOST SECRET.

Five members of Strategic Air Command are present in this Command Post. To the back of them, above them and below them, is the vast bulk of the Atlas missile. Its exterior envelope is paper-thin and, were it not sustained with internal gas pressures and liquid oxygen fuel, it would collapse under its own weight.

The whole structure is sprung on springs. The crew, who do a twice-round-the-clock continuous shift, are alone with this brute for one day out of every three. Relief crews take over every twenty-four hours.

I have seen some sad jobs in my life, but sitting in the subterranean nest of this great flying egg, which, given the correct global suicidal conditions, could slaughter a million Muscovites in Moscow in less time than it takes to make a bowl of soup, must be the saddest task in the world.

There they sit far below the flowered sunlight of the forest with the hurtling senseless requiem of all mankind housed in the darkness of its lonely hole.

The warhead of the Atlas is under constant scrutiny of the crew, who keep it under observation with closed-circuit television. I saw the business end of this thing on the screen of the cathode-ray tube.

I am not allowed to tell you either the shape or the size of the nuclear charge of the Atlas. And when I asked a few questions about it they gave me answers strongly reminiscent of another secret I once tried to probe for an American friend who was thinking of buying a very large new Rolls-Royce motor car.

He was most anxious to discover the brake-horse-power of the Rolls.

The R-R boys in Derby have always guarded this information very closely and, when the potential customer from California cabled them on my advice and asked them for the actual figure they sent him a beautifully laconic telegram.

It read: SUFFICIENT.

The size, the shape and the design of the hydrogen bomb perched on Atlas is sufficient – sufficient for all the tears in the world.

There are parts of this mournful cave where no man is allowed on his own. They are called NO LONE ZONES and the idea behind this is that the chances of one man going mad are less if there are two.

Nobody is ever armed in this deadly area in case a murderer amok should reduce the population by 50 per cent and get the Atlas – they call it 'The Gooney Bird' – off the American ground and overhead above Gorki Street in Moscow.

One final poetic touch.

Men in missile sites wear hats with their names inscribed prominently on them. The major in charge at this particular site near Plattsburg dutifully wore his name above his brow.

It was Major Slaughter.

Flight 481

Air-borne, Hawaii to San Francisco, July 23, 1957

The romantic scene is set. Your correspondent is seated in a Pan-American Stratocruiser eastbound from Hawaii. Next to him, heavily veiled, with a determinedly floral hat, was one of the slightly over middle-aged girls who rule all America. We sat in silence for an hour or so, as the evening Pacific sun went down. Martinis were served.

Then she turned to me with a gritty voice and said: 'These hemlocks sure dissolve your front molars.'

I said they sure did.

She said: 'Where from?'

I said: 'London, Eng. Where did you bust out of?'

She said: 'It's a long story Mister. But I'm on my way home from Istanbul. Been there a couple of years. Going to meet my kids again. Colin, aged twenty-one. Sue, nineteen.'

Says I. 'Glad to be going back home again?'

Says she: 'Maybe yes. Maybe no. And just maybe. I am a widow.'

Now when you are in an aeroplane, and especially in an aeroplane over long stretches of open water, you have, if you are sensible about these matters, an alarmingly frank style of conversation. You know that you may never arrive. But, better still, you know that on these encounters you are fairly sure of never meeting your chance acquaintances again. So you open up.

Me: 'Why are you uneasy about meeting the kids at San Francisco?'

'Guess it's Mr Schlesinger.'

'Who is he? A young man? An old man? A rich man? A poor man? A smart geezer?'

'He is elderly and gentle.'

'Are you in love with him?'

'Jeeze no.'

'Is he rich?'

'No.'

'Have you got it more than he has?'

'I make forty thousand bucks a year out of my investments. Mr Schlesinger makes a great deal less. The kids at San Francisco will not like him. He is sixty-five.'

'How old are you?'

'Fifty-seven, but he writes interesting love letters. Would you like to see some?'

The All-American Woman, attractive and contemplative, produced a hard-backed typewritten file crammed with Mr Schlesinger's love letters. She displayed them like the managing director of a successful correspondence course. There were at least fifty. 'He's better on the closing paragraphs,' she explained with a mellow sort of compassion. 'Read this.'

I did.

'Thus, my dearest, you and I together in the ripening close of life will go hand-in-hand into the sunset of our accomplished years.'

'D'ya like that?'

'Indeed I do.'

'Then listen: "The fruit hangs low and heavy on the hanging vine. You and I, O my darling, will pluck it together." Kinda cute, hey?'

'Did Mr S. write many pieces like this?'

'Couldn't stop him. Listen to this: "The sunset of our years blooms with an autumn sheen. We will walk into its beams with the soft tread of those who have dwelt in the vineyard before."

'All righty?'

'All righty!'

O-My-Darling folded the file again with a decisive snap and said:

'Time we got on the perch, Bud.'

'Sure is, Mellow Leaf.'

The next morning at San Francisco International Airport I saw her with Colin and Sue. The boy in his jeans and sweet Sue, pert and abominable as only young American girls can be, fussed round their mother.

She came across to me with the flower hat slightly askew, the veil bobbing fiercely, and said out of the corner of her mouth: 'Mister, were you right! Have these kids got the skids under Schlesinger! Lawdgawda mighty!'

Like an oil painting from Hell

Christmas Island, in the Pacific, June 3, 1957

At forty-nine minutes past ten on the 31st day of May in the Year of Our Lord 1957, in the neighbourhood of Christmas Island, named after Him, the British people exploded their second hydrogen bomb.

It was a dress rehearsal for the death of the world.

Standing on the rolling deck of HMS *Alert* and clad in white protective clothing with hoods and goggles, we, the observers, looked like grotesque mourners.

High overhead, at a height of what was probably eight miles, a Valiant bomber painted all white sped at over 600 miles an hour to the firing point.

In its sleek belly was the bomb known to one and all on Christmas Island as 'The Beast', but politely referred to by the scientific director in charge as 'a nuclear device'.

We were thirty-five miles from where The Beast was due to explode after being spewed out from the bomber – quite near enough in view of the fact that the power of the bomb was equal to several million tons of TNT.

I waited with feelings of excitement, awe and a faint sense of horror.

The ship's loudspeakers broke into an iron, throaty roar as a giant voice began to count downward to Moment Zero.

Forty, thirty-nine, thirty-eight, thirty-seven…

It was like the footsteps that lead to the execution shed. We had our backs turned away from the bursting point…

Eighteen, seventeen, sixteen…

We were invited to cover our closed eyes with our hands. The Beast was plummeting down in a great deadly arc…

Five, four, three, two, one... FIRE!

Through closed eyes, through dark glasses and with my hands still covering my face, I saw the flash.

Brighter than the sun, hotter than the sun, and ripped out of the secrets of the heart of the Universe.

Still with our backs to the burst, we remained there for another fifteen seconds before we were allowed to turn round and open our eyes.

AND THERE IT HUNG BEFORE US, A BOILING RED AND YELLOW SUN LOW ABOVE THE HORIZON. IT WAS AN OIL PAINTING FROM HELL. BEAUTIFUL AND DREADFUL. MAGNIFICENT AND EVIL.

The golden, whirling ball changed colour… from orange and grey... to a light muddy purple.

It then re-formed and became a bloated top-heavy Christmas pudding, with a greyish, whitish sauce streaming out of the top and spilling down at the sides like a filthy lava.

The shock waves could be seen feathering out in scimitar shape, and the grunt and thump of the blast hit us – not sharply but as a dinghy nudges when it hits the shore.

The men around me were too quiet, and in a blasphemous way it reminded me of the silence that was once so poignant a memory of Armistice Day on November 11.

We were watching something also connected with death on a prodigious scale – death, however, that does not lie in the past, but death that is waiting in the future.

The vast shape, now increasing with size every moment, rose upward and turned white with a reddish glow in the interior. A thin, snake-like stem appeared at its base, as steam and water were sucked up from the sea below.

The horrible pudding in the sky became a diseased cauliflower and then changed into the familiar mushroom.

Mr W J Cook – the brilliant scientific director who is not only the stage manager and producer but also the part author of this grim and terrifying performance – was at great lengths to emphasize the safety of the nuclear device from the point of view of 'fall out'.

In his precise and academic manner he became almost enthusiastic about the odds of anyone in the Pacific and in Australia and Japan and the United States suffering any after-effects from this almost – as it seemed – hygienic weapon.

But, with my hands over my eyes, wrapped from head to foot in protective clothing and wearing a device to detect excessive radiation, I couldn't help thinking of the real power of The Beast.

The flash, crash and roar of the hydrogen bomb set off in the most remote and desolate part of the world is a source of wonderment and, indeed, of pride to some people like Lord Cherwell. But, when released over cities where it would obliterate millions of men, women and children in a trice, it is a wicked, an evil thing.

Senseless and Superb

Falmouth, Cornwall, August 18, 1965

Of all the senseless physical operations from pole-squatting to peanut-pushing and to non-stop dancing, the latest exploit of Robert Manry sailing single-handed from Falmouth, Massachusetts, to Falmouth, Cornwall, seems to me to be the daftest.

His boat Tinkerbelle measured just about the length of two full-sized Manrys laid end to end.

Bob Manry suffered hallucinations, but not loss of shaves; he endured visions of torpedoes which turned out to be dolphins; and he suffered yearnings about his wife which can occur to anybody from a bedsitter in Wandsworth to a penthouse on Fifth Avenue in New York.

He grew a moustache to please his loved one because she said it made him look more English, and he fell overboard six times only to scramble aboard again by a carefully hitched lifeline.

He could have crossed the Atlantic about 300 times by jet aircraft since he first left Massachusetts and nearly nineteen times by steamship.

The whole operation, assessed in cold blood, was stupid, foolish and vain.

But why are we standing here by the quayside at Falmouth (Eng.) cheering ourselves hoarse at the arrival of this curious Yankee fellow?

Why do our hearts rise at this furry amateur matelot who has done the impossible and arrived with a laugh and a smile?

I will tell you why.

I am rooting for this chump who has risked his life and those of his possible rescuers who were not called upon to bring him back from the grey grim walls of the Atlantic because boldness, bravery and folly can still overcome the frigid equation of good sense.

This of course is the old story of 'I will now attempt the impossible – the unattainable will be achieved five minutes later.'

We newspaper people take a particular pride in Bob Manry.

He belongs to us.

Robert Manry is a reporter who worked for *The Cleveland Plain Dealer* as a sub-editor and when he had suddenly left his desk he wrote a letter to his boss saying that he might be away for a little longer than his allotted office time of three weeks' official holiday. He would like to apply for a further month's unpaid leave.

I doubt whether this proposal was received with cheers on what the Americans call the City Desk but by this time Bob was swallowing the anchor in a big way.

He got aboard his maritime floating splinter and was off – East, East, East.

Nobody cheered much because nobody knew – apart from *The Cleveland Plain Dealer* who recognised that they were minus one sub-editor and the grey North Atlantic was plus one sub-editor who could be drowned at the curl of one of a billion rollers.

So our boy, our kiddie, our chum doing the craziest, crackiest, self-imposed assignment of all, was afloat.

There's a rather specious tradition in newspaper offices that if you cannot find a good story go out and make one and be the only man who knows the whole truth of it.

Bob Manry did it.

Then there's that other eternal drizzle of criticism that when newspaper people report stories they either intrude on the course of events or the facts don't quite match up.

I give you THE REPORTER FROM THE CLEVELAND PLAIN DEALER.

He intruded on the North Atlantic.

He knocked on the doors of storm and spume and the hail and sleet.
He asked questions from the stars and the scud and the spray.
And he cannot be denied the accuracy of what he did, why he did it, and the reason why in his absurd craft he joins Vasco da Gama, Columbus and Captain Cook. Welcome, dear Bob.

Now there is only one

Spandau, Berlin, September 30, 1966

One overcast morning in Berlin more than seventeen years ago – it was March 16, 1949 – a small Volkswagen motor-car drew up outside the main gate of Spandau Prison in West Berlin.

The cheerful occupant (the smile was about to fade from his ruddy countenance) popped a Contax camera out and took a picture of the sombre, red-bricked gaol with its twin entrance turrets and its massively heavily-barred gates.

In a trice bedlam – organized bedlam – broke loose. Whistles blew. Voices bellowed: 'Halte!' And white-helmeted guards raced out, shouting.

They hurled open the door of the car, grabbed the photographer, seized his camera and, in a matter of seconds, rushed him into the main guardroom – which is first on the left up some stone steps when you've been slung through the main gate.

Those detained against their will that day in the Allied Prison Berlin Spandau, Wilhelm Strasse, 23, suddenly increased. There were on that grey morning long ago: Grand Admiral Doenitz, Deputy Fuehrer Rudolf Hess, Hitler Youth Leader Baldur von Schirach, Reichsbank Minister Walther Punk, Grand Admiral Erich Raeder, Minister of War Production Albert Speer, Foreign Minister and Protector of Bohemia and Moravia Baron Konstantin von Neurath.

AND ME.

It was a daft thing to do.

There are notices forbidding entrance and the taking of photographs. The guards on the watchtowers have orders to shoot and the whole hideous circular structure is surrounded by a high-voltage electric fence.

The Americans – who fortunately at the time were doing their monthly rota of duty and not the Russians – were suitably rude, and after week-kneed protests from me ending in my passport being taken away, the British Colonel was informed. In those days our military divided everything in life and our behaviour towards it into two classes: 'Good Show and Tickety-boo!' and 'Not Good Show and Not Tickety-boo.'

The Colonel told me that things were a damn bad show and distinctly non-ticket-boo. But he got my release and my camera back – minus the film, of course – and inside three hours I was free.

Today I stood outside Spandau again. Neurath, Raeder and Funk are dead. Doenitz is alive and remarkably chirpy, living near Hamburg, after having served his ten years.

And now within a few hours Baldur von Schirach and Albert Speer, having been entombed for some 2,000 days and nights, are about to be released.

Only Deputy Fuehrer Rudolf Hess, the crazed husk of a man now in his 73rd year, will be left to die alone in Spandau. There is no release for him.

He has now been under lock and key since the night of May 10,1941, twenty-five endless years ago, when he climbed into his Messerschmitt and flew to Scotland on his hare-brained romantic scheme to see the Duke of Hamilton and impose peace on Great Britain. Schirach and Speer, by the time you read these words, will have spent their last night in Spandau. They will emerge to a baffling new world they have never seen.

Their names are forgotten, and most of the younger people in Germany have never heard of them.

There will be at least 100 cameramen outside the Spandau gates, and it is highly unlikely that any of them will be arrested for non-tickety-boo behaviour.

The Telly will be there (neither Speer nor Schirach has ever seen it) and nobody will give the Hitler salute.

At the stroke of midnight Speer and Schirach, met by their relatives in two cars, will emerge from the inner courtyard.

It will be twenty years to the day, almost to the hour, since they were sentenced at Nuremberg.

Speer, the least repulsive and easily the most intelligent of the seven convicts of Spandau, will drive about a mile to the nearby Gerbus Hotel in the fashionable Grunewald district.

For one-third of his life he has been unable to move more than 40 yards from his cell, measuring only 8ft long by 5ft wide. It is furnished with an army cot-type bed, a rough wooden chair, a tiny table and a lavatory basin.

For two decades that has been the entire world of Number Five Spandau, for Speer, in common with the others, is not even granted the identity of his own name. At one minute past midnight tonight one-time brilliant Minister of War Production will be on his way to a suite in a luxury hotel with the complete freedom of Western Germany and a welcome in such other countries as may care to admit him.

Both he and Schirach may be rich men, for the figure of half a million marks in fees from a German magazine has been mentioned. Speer will join his brave and affectionate wife and their six children in a more than comfortable home in Heidelberg.

Few men in the history of the world have faced such a sudden transition and will undergo such an emotional storm as Speer.

He has been plunged from the flaunting, ruthless heights of Nazi power to twenty years' entombment and is now back to freedom, comfort and a completely new world that he has never seen.

As with Speer so with Schirach. True his wife has deserted him, and his health, and especially his eyesight, has been bad.

But his son Klaus, now aged 31, a successful lawyer, is expected to meet him, and there are said to be ample family funds available.

Rudolf Hess, silent, solitary and half mad, alone remains. What is he thinking of today when his lucky companions Speer and Schirach will vanish from his life for ever?

He is finally and completely on his own.

The Russians, it is said, will never free him and even if they were inclined to do so they are highly unwilling to surrender this pitiable symbol of four-Power authority in Berlin.

So far it has cost Great Britain £147,000 to keep the original seven men of Spandau. The United States, Russia, France and West Germany have also paid their share.

Now it is estimated that Hess will cost the best part of £100,000 a year to keep in solitary confinement which, it should be noted, was not described in his sentence in Nuremberg.

Allied justice could easily be going astray here.

If things go on as they are Hess will be attended by a military governor, twenty-eight soldiers, five warders, a varying number of doctors and several cooks.

Different Government departments in London, Washington, Moscow, Paris and Bonn will administer his endless misery.

Never has one ageing demented criminal, chained by life to exist in melancholy torment, had such a retinue in a jail built to hold 500 prisoners.

Commonsense, let alone charity and a feeling for economic housekeeping, cries out that what remains of the man should be left to die outside of the bars.

The price of his evil can never be repaid, for he now has nothing left in expiation.

Britain, the U.S. and France are known to be willing to be rid of their wretched captive.

Can it be that the thirst of Soviet vengeance is not slaked?

Details have come through of the final poignant moments when Prisoner Number Seven, as he is known, said goodbye to Schirach and Speer on the day they left and the aged battered creature was left to die in solitary confinement.

He walked in the prison yard on that last afternoon with Schirach, who tried to cheer him up. Speer took a long look at his flowers in the prison garden. Hess listened quietly to it all but said nothing and gave no indication that he had heard the kindly but futile words of encouragement for the empty future and the desolation that lie ahead.

At five o'clock he had a meal, and as was the rule for all three prisoners he put his tray with his plates and his cup in the corridor outside his door.

Then he asked for the chief warder and requested that as a favour the light in the little cell that had been his living tomb for twenty years might be switched off at 5.45 instead of 6.45 p.m. He shuffled in.

They switched it off and the old man was left alone in the dark.

There is still a tiny place for pity.

A fee of fourpence

Munich, September 24, 1962

The name is Stipolitzky – Herr Josef Stipolitzky – and he does a few odd jobs round the Hofbrauhaus here in Munich, which is one of the great roaring pubs of the world.

When I first spotted him looking like a Bavarian edition of Moses with the twinkling wise old eyes of Bernard Shaw, he was bareheaded, and I asked him if he would mind having his picture taken.

He considered this proposition gravely for several moments and said: 'You cannot photograph me without my hat and you cannot photograph me and my hat without my pipe. Do you wish to photograph my pipe, my hat and me?'

I said that I was more than agreeable. He replied that he was honoured but that there was a difficulty, a technicality, an obstacle, a barrier.

'And what might that be?' says I. 'It is an embarrassment,' says he, 'a matter that I can refer to only with the greatest trepidation; a subject that gentlemen such as ourselves would prefer not to mention; a delicacy that really ought not to occur in civilised society.'

'Pray do not disturb yourself,' said I joining him in the stately conversational minuet. 'Please let me know your difficulty. I shall do my utmost to remove it.'

He looked at me with a venerable gaze and sighed; 'It is the money. I shall have to charge you. There is a fee. You will forgive an old man but life has its harsh necessities.'

Photographic models the world over are entitled to their fees, and ten or twenty guineas is not an unusual sum.

Here Methuselah Stipolitzky came straight to the point. 'I must ask you,' he said, 'with the greatest regret, to pay me the sum of twenty pfennigs (about fourpence). I am distressed about this seemingly mercenary request but you are young and I know you will understand the problems of age.'

The money changed hands – plus a bit extra – and Josef Stipolitzky, ripe with time and mellowed with years, smiled into the lens.

How to catch a viper

Newala, Tanganyika, April 20, 1961

Mr Constantine John Philip Ionides rose to greet me. The name is like a roll of muffled drums and, in accordance with a pet and quite untenable theory of mine that people tend to look like their names, Mr CJPI is a splendid looking bloke.

Lean as a young goat, brown as old, soft, polished leather, with a pair of bright disbelieving eyes, white of mane and dressed like an elegant jumble sale, he betrayed not the slightest surprise that a complete stranger from 6,000 miles away should walk in on him and ask to be instructed in the art of snake catching.

Mr Ionides lives at Newala, in the Southern Province of Tanganyika, on the top of a great plateau with what surely must be one of the very finest views in the world; a panorama of 2,000 square miles of bush in front of him ending with the mountains of Portuguese East Africa 60 miles away on the sky line.

His chief fame is that of the greatest snake catcher in the world, but his true reputation rests on the fact that he is an outstanding naturalist.

He was seated in a deck chair in a room of wonderful confusion in which mounds of books (some of them very recent publications) and crates of beer dominated any other furnishings. That Mr Ionides, (regrettably, to my mind, known as Old Iodine to his younger disciples) has a contempt for the passing of time was made clear to me by the fact that the calendar on the wall claimed that the date was Friday, July 24, 1959.

Mr Ionides immediately poured me out a drink and apologised for not joining me, saying that in the course of many years of trial and experiment he had found that, on the whole, it was better not to drink before setting out to pursue black and green mambas, water cobras, puff adders and gaboon vipers.

I couldn't help thinking: 'If you drink don't snake-catch. If you snake-catch don't drink.'

He also said that he regretted not to be able to show me anything, as his latest catch had been dispatched to the United States and he was bankrupt of snakes with the exception of a quite negligible python.

This writhing exhibit he produced with the air of a man displaying a rather indifferent painting.

He then engaged me with a scholarly debate on Gibbon's *Decline and Fall of the Roman Empire* – which he reads regularly as a generating plant to recharge his learned mind – when a commotion outside the bungalow indicated the arrival of excited and jubilant natives.

'You are lucky,' said Mr Ionides, 'they've found something. Care to come along?'

He rose, took a collection of poles that was propped up against one wall and somehow reminded me of ski-ing equipment, summoned his head darkie assistant, who wears a secretarial pencil in his frizzy hair, and in no time about fifteen of us were packed in a Land Rover complete with snake boxes.

We drove five miles along an atrocious road and then steered into the bush.

What was a track became a path, what was a path became a tangled sense of direction.

At times we got stuck, but our African crew, armed with axes, spades and crowbars, dug up the roots of small trees and slashed the vegetation to let the snake express through.

Finally we fought our way to a collection of rush-roofed houses in a tiny clearing and dismounted. 'We walk from now on,' said Ionides.

He was received by the native villagers with evident respect and soon about fifty chattering darkies, with large numbers of delighted children, followed us as we set out.

The Snake Man explained that his reputation, especially among the Africans with whom he had lived for thirty-six years, was greatly exaggerated.

They had an undue horror of snakes and catching them – 'It is quite simple really… if you know how.'

I mentally underlined the last four words and agreed heartily with the Africans.

Quite suddenly we stopped, and a snake sentry who had been posted to watch the brute we were after pointed to a bush. The poles and forked rods and a pair of iron tongs were laid near by. Ionides took command.

Very gently he parted the undergrowth and after a moment invited me to come closer.

At first I could see nothing, then I saw the thing – almost invisible in its natural camouflage and curled up rather like a coloured, coiled rope.

'A gaboon viper,' said Ionides with satisfaction. He then produced the tongs and said: 'He is probably rather drowsy so we will tap him gently on the head to see if anyone is at home. Tactics vary with drowsiness – or lack of it.'

He knocked on the nut of the serpent . . . and it was evidently at bye-byes.

The audience was pretty tense. Ionides was as relaxed as a conjurer who has been producing rabbits out of a hat all his life.

'The gaboon viper,' he announced, 'is almost designed to be caught. The head is very large and if you take it neatly behind the jaws, well, there's nothing he can do about it.'

With a quick dart of the hands that I thought he must have learned from the dart of snakes, he seized the viper in the manner prescribed, held it aloft and gently waved the deadly reptile with a faint gesture of triumph.

The natives chattered with a mixture of pleasurable fright and awe and the secretary with the pencil in his hair approached as if to take a letter.

Instead he brought a box and in a trice the viper was inside ready to be sent to Miami where its venom will be 'milked' for medical purposes.

Ionides said that snakes were gravely misunderstood creatures. Like Greta Garbo their only wish is to be left alone. If they do become troublesome while held in the hands, some species can easily be discouraged from causing a breach of the peace if you hold them by the tail.

'Just jiggle them up and down like a Yo-Yo,' said the Master with a sparkle in his eye. 'They don't like that at all... would you?'

We caught yet another viper within half an hour and were soon jolting and crashing our way back through the jungly scrub. From nowhere appeared an ebony head above a bush and a native begged for a lift in the Land Rover.

'Aaah... the folly of mankind!' sighed Constantine John Philip Ionides.

'A car obviously loaded to the gunwales with men and serpents yet he asks to come aboard.'

A man very much after my own heart is J P Ionides – snakes and all.

I find the Australians guilty of being friendly, forthright and thirsty!

Sydney, Australia, April 20, 1964

I have this day seen and heard a kookaburra, which, if you don't know, is an Australian bird of friendly disposition, trodden on a quince, sailed in a motor-boat, made friends with a cat called Golly, stood in the shade of a eucalyptus tree, had a couple of schooners of the local beer, watched the surf-riders coming in on the Pacific breakers, got slightly sunburned and learned to say 'Goodonyermate,' which is Australian for 'That's fine, chum.'

This local knowledge of the natives, which is a compound of birds, quinces, motor-boats, cats, eucalyptus trees, beer, salt water, sun and foreign languages, is my authority for passing judgment on *Homo Australiensis* – or the Australian Man.

Not that I need to hear the evidence before passing judgment. I don't even need to pass judgment.

I just pass sentence without either of these formalities.

I find the Australian Man guilty of being friendly, forthright, free of snobbery, thirsty (very), opinionated, loyal (more of this later) and heavily addicted to cussing.

The Australian Man includes the Australian Woman – even down to the cussing.

The cussing is not ill-tempered. It is more often a term of endearment or even affection.

'You-ole-Bastard-yer' properly applied in the Australian sense often means 'My dear Sir, I find you of a most agreeable disposition. Let us go and sup ale together or rob a bank or something so that we may enjoy each other's company.'

Then there is the word 'bloody', which I suspect in Australian is spelt 'bluddy'.

They are great bloodiers in Sydney and Melbourne where the language is made to bleed grievously at every sentence. I met a wonderful chap called Clancy who is a mate or cobber of mine.

He is a magnificent champion bloodier and a real delight for an experienced cusser like myself to listen to.

He doesn't actually slit the words open to make the claret flow but he surrounds the non-cuss words. Hems them in, so to speak, and also bloodies from above and below.

The only faint drawback to this – and it is but a quibble – is that a normal sentence of, say, twenty words becomes 120 words long which certainly adds to the colour of speech if not to the brevity.

Almost before I had trodden on the first quince on my arrival in this country I was asked what I thought of the Australian accent. I told the chap who asked me that with the exception of Italian, it was the most mellifluous sound ever to escape the human tongue.

He looked at me darkly and repeated the question. In the interests of avoiding a full-scale war between the United Kingdom and Australia I repeated this preposterous assertion.

The dark looks grew blacker and, if I'd been a sheep, I think he'd have sheared me on the spot just for the Osstralian, Orsetralian or Owstralian hell of it. So, in the interests of my personal safety, I came clean.

I said that to cultured ear-'oles such as mine the accent was a thin nasal Cockney twang spoken to the accompaniment of someone filing cork and attending to a defective foghorn.

This mollified him somewhat, but before he could corner me and ask me if I wanted to know what the Oss, Orse, or Owstrawlians thought of the English Oxford accent, I told him that it was a thin, mincing, affected, snivelling, contemptible sound emitted by persons whom I suspected of deviations of sexual aim.

'Goodonyermate,' he said.

After we'd settled that problem, I was asked by another swaggie – see now I am learning the language – what I thought about the Royal Family. They talk about the British Monarchy with the frequency that we at home talk about our British weather. And, like our deplorable climate, it seems to worry them.

They've got Buck House and all its mysterious wonders on the brain.

Although the last Royal Tour here was considered a rare old blooper this was not the fault of the Queen or Prince Philip, but was a blunder by the clumsy courtiers and Palace officials who snarled the whole trip up.

My liberal views on the Royal Family are well known in Britain, but when I went on to develop my kindly theme (I gave them the short two-hour version instead of the usual five-hour exposition), I could see I wasn't doing so well.

To my proposal that the Monarchy was a lot better and cheaper than, say, the South American Presidential system complete with a costly revolution every other day, I detected the shadow of pain and the cloud of disapproval cross the sunburned Australian face.

This was made no better by my thesis that the game of Kings and Queens gives great pleasure and evokes symptoms of warm happiness somewhat in the manner that Walt Disney does.

The natives here, so sturdy, so independent and so rightly proud of the vast continent, are patriotic and loyal – and touchy about the British Crown and will brook no criticism.

The National Anthem is played after every cinema performance and if Trooping the Colour isn't staged next June in Martin's Place right here in Sydney that is no fault of the Australians.

Sir William Walton is here to conduct concerts and has just made a statement saying that the National Anthem is played far too often and he would ration it down to once a month.

It is not actually known whether Sir William has been thrown to the crocodiles in the Northern Territory or strapped to the biggest kangaroo and driven into the Outback, but he would be well advised to have a care – or rather a truck-load of cares.

But apart from such edgy subjects as these, I find the Australians guilty of openness, of warmth, of cordiality and kindness, and I sentence them to live happy ever after in this remarkable and gigantic land.

A dream comes true

Great Barrier Reef, April 30, 1964

When I was young, I gorged myself on a printed diet of books like *Coral Island, Treasure Island, Blue Lagoon* and *Robinson Crusoe.*

I heard the surf breaking on the coral reef. I shinned up the waving palm and took the coconuts. I was a personal friend of Long John Silver. I ate myself sick with the imaginary loaves of the breadfruit tree, and I saw Man Friday's footprints in the sand.

I could talk about atolls and cays and in my dreams I steered by the Southern Cross.

With the exception of Honolulu, which is as representative of a desert island as Piccadilly Circus is of a bee-loud glade, and Christmas Island, where I saw them rehearsing the nuclear death of the world, I had been nowhere nearer to the real thing than in a seat at the movies... until now.

My dream came true the other day – and right on the Great Barrier Reef. Eighteen miles off the coast of Northern Queensland, I came to Green Island. I knew we were on the right track when the flying fish landed on our ancient and battered little ship *Magnetic.*

The sea glittered and the sun near its zenith in the sky poured down with a light that was almost unbearably brilliant to those who, like myself, come from the soft weeping skies of Britain.

No point of Green Island is ten feet above sea-level and the island itself is founded on coral, which is the limey skeleton of the once-living polpy.

After a few million years the coral built up above the level of the sea and a sandy top-soil formed.

Pause for another heartbeat of eternity.

One day a bird dropped a seed from its mouth or possibly the breeze from the land brought the vegetable spark of life. The seed became a seedling and from the seedling grew a tree. Then, with the silent speed of tropical growth, the green jungle sprang to life.

Green Island – you can walk right round the white, sandy shore to your starting-point in twenty minutes – is a mass of lovely flowering trees entangled with vines and shrubs and ending inevitably with the palms on the water's edge that you see on coloured picture postcards.

It is so like the preconceived idea that when it turns out to be exactly true, you could almost laugh.

This is Hollywood – except that the fantastic scenery is real life. Brightly plumaged birds dressed in the most unlikely colours screech and chatter in the jungle shade, and huge and improbably large butterflies flutter by.

Green Island is part of the Great Barrier Reef – a sight that in its natural wonder is in the same breath-taking class as the Grand Canyon in America.

It stretches for 1,250 miles along Australia's North-East coast. At the spring tides, hundreds of miles of gorgeously coloured reef appear above the blue, ultra-marine and deep purple waves.

To those of us used to the cold greys of Northern seas and the seascapes of the black basaltic rocks, this scene of the colours of the rainbow and the spectrum all in a kaleidoscope together with every pastel shade ever painted, is incredible to the eye.

It can't be true – but it is.

There must be some trick about it – but it is genuine.

When the tide covers the reef you can go out in a glass-bottomed boat and through the clear calm sea observe a watery universe that stuns the mind... The marine life is teeming on a scale that seems to make life on dry land sparse and scattered... In one cubic yard of water you will see a thousand tiny fish.

Fish with neon-bright blue and silver stripes. Fish as bright as marigolds. Fish as red as a flame. Fish greener than the greenest grass. Fish like golden spears. Fish as black as pitch. Fish that are whiter than white. Fish that are flat as pancakes. Fish that are shaped like footballs.

Huge fish the size of torpedoes – not forgetting the ravenous packs of sharks that will slice a man in two in thirty inches of water. Fish with lovely fancy names. The savage Barracudas that account for the remarkably large number of one-legged seagulls. Moray Eels. The Yellow Bellied Sea Snake. Ghost Crabs. Loggerhead Turtles. Swimming Files. Angus Sea Hares. The Giant Clam, four feet across and weighing a quarter of a ton.

The Great Anemone with its attendant Clown Fish. The Anemone's tentacles are fatally poisonous to all other fish but harmless to the escorting Clown Fish which always accompany the Anemone. The tiny Clown Fish will attack much larger fish which try to prey on the Anemone.

This is the watery world of the Mantis Shrimp; the Ass's Ear Shell; the True Bubble Shell; the Black-lip Pearl Oyster; the Strawberry Cockle; the Pistol Prawn; the Serpulid Tube Worm, and the Draughtboard Helmet Shell.

This is the unseen world of a billion wet and watery things.

Britannia rules the waves. But old Father Neptune is the mighty Emperor below the surf and his throne must surely be on the Great Barrier Reef not very far from Green Island.

That little grey home in the south

New Ross, Co. Wexford, June 25, 1963

I am driving a Hillman Minx on my way from Dublin to Wexford. I have seen no shamrocks, leprechauns or harps. But if I had been landed blindfold from a helicopter in the middle of a featureless plain, I would soon know that I was in Ireland.

The reason I can always tell this lovely land is by its surprises. I drove through a small village with a sign bearing the name of Oil – and it is not in Texas. Proceeding south, alert and in full possession of all my faculties and in broad daylight, I saw approaching me a double-decker tram with the alfresco upper storey of the type that was popular in London forty years ago.

There were no tram-lines and there was no overhead electric wire. This enchanting apparition had, in fact, been converted from a tram to a bus complete with steering, pneumatic tyres, a petrol engine and a driver seated in the old tram-driver's pulpit.

No other country that I know of can produce these wonderful throw-away jokes.

A village signposted Oil. A tram without pre-destined grooves. And nobody laughing either.

So it was in New Ross – the nondescript little town in the South which, by order of the White House, is the Founder City of the Kennedy Dynasty.

Three miles from New Ross up a lovely lane is what is called, on a notice board, the 'Kennedy Ancestral Homestead'.

The Little Grey Home in the South is a shed measuring about twenty-five feet by fifteen feet and at least thirteen feet high.

It stands in the concrete yard of a fair-sized farm owned by Mrs Mary Ann Ryan – a good, sensible woman of independent mind who was first of all surprised at the roaring circus that has descended upon her and is now determined not to be overwhelmed by the greatest blitz of blarney that has hit the Republic of Ireland for a long, long time.

The 'Kennedy Ancestral Homestead' is such a depressing shack that the blarney-boys who sell postcards have thatched it and put a heap of peat and two flower beds in front of it.

It is not thatched.

The roof is made of grim green-painted corrugated iron.

There are no flower beds.

There is no peat.

The TV blarney-boys are desperate about this arid hut now used for storing potatoes which could be such a useful picture peg on which to hang The Old Humble White Cabin in the South to the Unhumble Washington White House in the West.

The trouble is, as one exponent of the cathode ray tube said: 'We've got to Irish the place up. Yeats, bee-loud glades, pigs, Sean O'Casey, stout called porther, Mike Coffins and all that. And what have we got? A tin-roofed shack that St Patrick would condemn from a league away.'

The searchers after truth in this most delightful and blarneyful of all occasions are also faced with the fact (that so few of them know) that Mrs Ryan, who is said to be the third cousin of President Kennedy, may not be the third cousin at all.

It doesn't really matter and it adds to the delightful bejesus of it all that jolly Jack Kennedy's father Joe (England-will-be-wiped-off-the face-of-the-earth-by-Hitler) who was Ambassador at the Court of St James just before the war said when he was speaking in the American Embassy in Dublin on July 8, 1938:

'I am sure I cannot be related to all the Kennedys who have written to me. In fact, when I was over in America lately, I asked my sister, who keeps records of family relationships and she did not know of any relations of ours in Ireland.'

All this is spoilsport stuff and I would be the last to try to stem the wonderful golden river of blarney that is cascading through this joyful occasion.

In New Ross they have got the paint pots out. The shops are gay in a spectrum of colour that ranges from acid green to sultry maroon.

Even the gasoline tanks, the size of gasholders, on the banks of the River Barrow have been painted a romantic boudoir turquoise – and anybody who can get that response out of the Irish in County Wexford is indeed the darlin' man.

In the shops in New Ross the flags are out, with Mr Kennedy jut-jawed, young and handsome peering out of the windows. You can get the letter K carved out of blackthorn or a saucer bearing his smiling face.

I looked in one shop in New Ross and noticed that the plate of the President of the United States was concealing another plate which was on sale before his 'imminence' was due to arrive. It was a souvenir to all housewives and bore the following melancholy doggerel:

Bless my little kitchen home,
I love its every nook,
And bless me as I do my work,
With pots and pans and cook.

To obscure, if only for a few hours, this grim memorial to the hot stove and the kitchen sink will have made Jolly Sean O'Kennedy's visit worth while.

The Rose of Tralee

Tralee, Co. Kerry, September 20, 1961

When I first went to Siam, I was delighted and relieved to see a Siamese cat. He was tethered to a stake with a collar round his neck – a practice rightly abominated in the cat world – but the fact that Siamese cats do live in Siam bolstered my faith in the order of things.

So today, in Tralee, I was equally fortified to see a rose.

In fact, there are sprays and clusters of roses round the grey stone houses of this ancient town.

When William Mulchinock wrote *The Rose of Tralee,* more than 100 years ago, he was not referring directly to floral beauty but to the charms of a certain Irish lass. I report to you that the girls here are uncommonly handsome, too. Thus the well-regulated pattern of seeing what you expect is made plain.

I like it that way. Life is too full of surprises: like polar bears in the Congo.

Ireland is laughably like the traditional Ireland of the stage and screen.

Irishmen too have Long Upper Lips. In fact I recommend to those two master cartoonists, Low and Giles, who excel in drawing Irishmen, that they come to Kerry – because I suspect they are getting the length of their Irish upper lips on the short side.

The shamrock DOES grow here.

Ireland, too, is full of donkeys. On a day's drive, with nothing better to do, I counted them. The score was ninety-three as dusk came. The Irish must like donkeys, and they are right to do so.

An Irish ass is anything but an ass. It is a dignified beast of great character.

The reason is, I suspect, that the Irish, who are so deeply religious, remember the fact that the Lord Jesus rode on the back of an ass.

Hence their regard for the animal.

Religion attracts the Irish in the same way as the Godless, baneless activities of Bingo, football pools, and the telly captivate the heathen English.

The other day I was passing through Donegal, Fermanagh, Sligo, Mayo, and Galway. In every village the whole of the able-bodied population was on its way to church. On foot, by bicycle, on donkey-cart, and by automobile, they were setting about their devotions. I should say that in these parts, at any rate, the Irish were more Roman Catholic than the Italians.

When the Mass was over, the whole male population in Galway town seemed to repair to the pub. At one moment the place was empty. The next moment it was jammed to capacity with thirsty worshippers. Scores of thick-set, black-haired, dark-eyed men were jabbering joyfully and drinking determinedly as if all their sins had been washed away.

Outside in the rather superior lounge were two good-looking, animated priests. It always pleases me to see priests with the publicans and sinners.

An amiable priest with a large brandy seems so much better equipped to fight the Devil than a holy man armed only with a cup of tea and a bun.

The Irish in their native land had a profound disregard of time. Time is not money to them. It is the distance between two points in which to enjoy yourself.

I went into a shop at Tuam to buy a postcard.

The local Rose of Tralee, who was behind the counter, was engaged in an animated conversation with a lady customer about how to make a dress.

I stood there a full two minutes waving my postcard and proffering my money. No notice at all was taken. This, I am sure, was not rudeness. It was the placing of first things first – in this case, the cut of the dress taking priority over someone wanting to buy something.

Probably it is better that way.

There is also a simplicity about the whole thing. In the same way that I was glad about the 'Rose of Tralee', I saw a further very uncomplicated thing that was gratifying.

The scene was a field – a piece of bog, rather, surrounded by a stone dyke.

In the middle was a cow. Just one cow. Seated beside it was an old man milking the cow. Just that. It you want milk – just go to the cow. That's all.

Long live St Patrick.

The sword in the scabbard

London, January 25, 1965

The last frail petal of one of the great red roses of old England falls.

And the sword sleeps in the scabbard.

There is sadness at the going of Winston Spencer Churchill, but there is also exaltation at having lived in the tremendous nine decades of his formidable, famous, above all, happy life.

When Queen Victoria died the grief and the mourning for the old lady was thrown over the nation like a compulsory pall and sadness was almost obligatory. With Sir Winston it is different. To have been alive with him was to have dined at the table of history.

He engaged in and later presided in the two great and most terrible military convulsions in history. World War One and World War Two.

He knew the Kaiser, that ludicrous, preposterous and pathetic figure and found compassion for him. He acquitted the Emperor Wilhelm of planning the war and offered in his defence the same plea that was raised for Marshal Bazaine when he was brought to trial for the surrender of Metz: 'This is no traitor. Look at him; he is only a blunderer.'

The golden thread of magnanimity was always there from the beginning to the end; from the Boer war to the Hitler war; from bitter defeat at the polls in 1945 to his dying day.

When the accountancy of these two cataclysmic struggles is finally balanced out, Churchill is unchallengeable as a leader, for not only did he outlive all his contemporaries in the First World War, he overshadowed all of his comrades in the Second World War. Those he has not survived in longevity he has eclipsed in fame and honour.

His main adversaries, Hitler and Mussolini, died in squalid ignominy. His political, treacherous and compulsory ally Joseph Stalin was debased, dishonoured and maybe murdered by his own countrymen.

The Fascist and Nazi regimes were swept away.

The generals have chattered themselves into obscurity and only President de Gaulle, difficult, intransigent and chauvinistic, remains as a major figure on the European scene.

There is, however, for the people of Britain a simpler calculation than all the yardsticks of history about the size of the debt we owe to this man.

Had he not been there in 1940 this nation of ours would most surely have lost the war and the Nazi hegemony would have ruled Europe to this day. When all was logically lost, he won. Europe was at Hitler's feet, the United States would never have come in had the flame died in England, and Japan would have taken care of all Asia.

When the First World War was over Winston Spencer Churchill asked: 'Is this the end? Is it to be merely a chapter in a cruel and senseless story? Will a new generation in their turn be immolated to square the black accounts of Teuton and Gaul? Will our children bleed and gasp again in devastated lands?

'Or will there spring from the very fires of conflict that reconciliation of the three giant combatants, which would unite their genius and secure to each in safety and freedom a share in rebuilding the glory of Europe?'

We know the terrible answers to these questions and we also know the name of the man who tried so famously a second time to redress the balance of right against wrong.

With all the grandeur of his deeds and the sonorous rolling sentences that his speech encompassed, there was always the famous impudent colloquial phrase to capture those who were strangers to Macaulay and Gibbon.

There was the time when Hitler threatened to wring old England's scrawny neck like that of a chicken. Said the descendant of Marlborough: 'Some chicken, some neck!'

And then a few years later when the war was ended, and a well-meaning adviser gently put it to the old man that he should retire at the zenith of his career and not make the error of hanging on too long, Churchill replied: 'I leave when the pub closes.'

Well, the pub has not yet closed but our best and most beloved patron sitting in the chair of St George has gone.

January 28, 1965

Winston Leonard Spencer Churchill lies in state and the greatest funeral in world history is on.

The whole operation is a vast military operation mobilized and prepared like Alamein and Arromanches, which Churchill supervised.

I suspect that the hero of this, the final funeral battle, is also the bold and magnificent author of it all. Everything points to the last choreography by WSC.

When Mark Twain's wonderful Tom Sawyer was given up as being drowned hi the Mississippi and it was not so, Tom crept under a seat in the church to attend his own funeral service.

He listened to every ecstatic word and then, unable to bear the lovely grief any longer, he sprang out of his hiding place, was hailed as the prodigal son and joined heartily inthe singing of *The Old Hundredth* in his own praise.

I am sure that Sir Winston, whose spirit, if not his hand, designed this most splendid occasion, is thinking like Tom Sawyer.

He wanted the bands – seventy-six trombones and all – and I know that a former naval person would have loved and foreseen and authorised the drama of the funeral barge coming up Old Father Thames from the Tower to Waterloo.

When I went to Westminster Hall right on the dot of eleven o'clock yesterday morning I suppose that, like every tombstone of history, I automatically conditioned myself to a mood of the oppression of sadness and the shadow of death.

But no.

First of all there is the stark simplicity of it all. The great crepuscular, religious shadow such as attends the death of Popes, is entirely missing.

The raised coffin is covered by the Union Jack, which is one of the most badly-designed national standards in the world. Many love it in spite of its banality.

The six vast candles around the coffin smoke in the cold air of the famous hall which is remembered for the fierce and terrible trials of William Wallace, Sir Thomas More, Guy Fawkes, Charles the First, Warren Hastings and the deposition of Richard the Second.

At Westminster they knew Winnie.

They knew him like they knew their own fathers. They knew him in peace and war. They knew him for good or evil. They knew the grandeur and the petulance.

They knew the fun and the fury.

They knew the chuckle as well as the frown.

And although the sense of loss is there, the triumph, yes, the happy triumph, of being alive in his time makes this last occasion a proud blast on a trumpet that silences the muffled weeping of strings.

January 31, 1965

I heard no sighs. I saw no tears.

This was grief exultant.

This was sad soft cypress but it was also the triumph and the waving of palms and the shout of hosanna.

Here in St Paul's, Winston Leonard Spencer Churchill finished the long journey of the alpha and the omega. Here in splendour and in pomp and circumstance the last great challenge from Corinthians rang out:

'O death where is thy sting? O grave where is thy victory?'

This was a place of contrasts.

A vast congregation clothed in solemn and almost sullen black against the flaunting colours of the Heralds, the swaggering vermilion of the military, the great gold glittering Mace, the deep and heavily veiled mourning of Lady Churchill and the incongruous absurdity of a coloured foreign potentate wearing a little red and blue and yellow hat that would have looked frivolous at a fun fair.

The Purple Staff Officers and the Household Gentlemen Ushers, all elegance and distinction, went about their business with a wonderful mixture of solicitude and polished pride.

The ceremony was studded with fascinating archaic words like Targeand Crest and Tabard and Remembrancer.

All the other vocabulary of State and Church, Mourning Swords and Minor Canons, Marshals and Archbishops, Pursuivants and Sacristans, Pursebearers and Registrars.

And then, of course, there was the Telly – the ever-persistent, the omnipotent Telly. The great congregation, probably three thousand of us, all watched from inside the Cathedral while the Great Pagan God Telly went about his peering business.

We looked at the procession through dozens of receivers installed in the Nave and the Transepts.

We saw the procession from our front row pews as it left Westminster Hall and arrived at the steps of St Paul's. And then we went on staring at what was going on in front of our very eyes.

The Archbishop of Canterbury, vastly venerable beyond his sixty-one years, walked in stately procession and, within a few yards, about two cricket teams of choirboys twittered and cautiously larked about behind a red curtain.

When they emerged to go to the Choir it was almost a shock to see their youthful mischievous faces in contrast to the graven gravity of the high and the mighty of this land.

Ivan Stepanovich Koniev, Marshal of the Soviet Union, a grey and grim and rocklike man, took his place – and one wondered what HE thought of it all.

What was in the mind of the liberator of Kharkov, the Comrade of Joseph Stalin who so well remembers Winston Churchill's enthusiastic aid and support for anti-Bolshevist attacks on Russia after the armistice in 1918.

President de Gaulle was there, impossibly tall, concrete-faced, remote, aloof and maybe ready to fall back on the ramparts of disdain.

What was HE thinking of Sir Winston Churchill? What were his thoughts about the ally with whom he had so often battled in a cause they both enjoyed? How deeply did HE mourn the Man from Blenheim?

The Queen and Prince Philip and Princess Margaret were there with a massive turnout of what remains of European royalty. But on this occasion, somehow, they were dwarfed by the memory of the man they were mourning.

Winston Churchill was larger than life.

He was also larger than death.

The bearer Guardsmen, tall and true, carried then- grievous burden slowly up the Nave, their broad shoulders strong and their heads pressed close and tight against the coffin.

It seemed to me, here, that they might have been listening for a heart-beat from the dead warrior.

When the coffin had been placed upon the Bier we sang *Who would true valour see,* and schoolboy memories, for me at least, came jostling in.

The odd medieval phraseology of 'No goblin nor foul fiend' contrasted with the bluish unblinking stare of the Telly remorselessly gazing on.

The prayers were offered and all stood to sing *Mine eyes have seen the glory of the coming of the Lord* – a magnificent battle hymn with the deathless words 'I can read his righteous sentence by the dim and flaring lamps' that Churchill himself could have written and which he most surely chose for this occasion. There was *Fight the Good Fight.*

There was *O God, our help in ages past* and, if the choice at times seemed banal, the occasion stifled the doubt.

Someone in the organisation of these proceedings, which had included the great American battle hymn, had a flash of wit and inspiration – if such qualities can be brought to bear upon funerals.

He, or they, had arranged that the Choir should sing the words 'Give rest, O Christ, to thy servant with thy Saints; where sorrow and pain are no more; neither sighing, but life everlasting.'

The words, which were superbly sung, come from the Kieff Melody which is the Russian Contakion for the Departed. I hope that Marshal Koniev appreciated that we were singing a hymn from the Russian Orthodox Church, of which neither Mr Stalin nor he himself was a particularly prominent member.

Could it be...

Could it be that WSC chose it?

The Egg-Man Cometh

The Goose-Egg Man was a faithful and favourite correspondent over many years. Anonymously, the first goose egg arrived in 1953. Thereafter Goosey Gander and her owner sent Cassandra the first egg of the season. The column recorded its gratitude, deploring the fact that it could never name the donor. Then, in 1965, no egg. The Goose-Egg Man had vanished without trace, and Cass sang a little requiem for his passing.

The Egg-Man cometh

February 24, 1953

There has just arrived on my desk a book called *A Shilling Cookery For the People,* by the famous chef Alexis Soyer. It was published in 1855.

I opened it by chance on page 115 and my eye lit on a short paragraph describing how the shepherds in Egypt used to cook their eggs.

'They had a singular manner of cooking eggs without the aid of fire; they placed them in a sling, which they turned so rapidly that the friction of the air heated them to the exact point required.'

Then arrived THE BOX.

It came three days ago and was exactly four and a half inches by four and a half inches by four and a half inches. It was wrapped in brown paper, securely tied and was addressed to me.

Now, I am an old parcel hand. I can look at a parcel and, through many years of cautious de-parcelling, I can tell, without unwrapping it, a friendly parcel from a hostile one.

This latest had a scowl on its brown-paper face so I didn't open it.

I left it on the top of a filing cabinet so that the acid would eat its way through the copper tube and release the spring that set off the detonator to explode the charge. Nowt happened.

So after another probationary period I decided to open the brute.

I took off the brown paper.

So far, so good.

Underneath was a neatly made plywood box. Too neatly made for my liking.

It had french nails on the sides and bottom and four small neat screws on the lid. A bad sign.

Count Stauffenberg, who placed the Hitler bomb on the occasion of the famous attempt on the Fuehrer's life in 1944, would have approved of it.

However, there was no ticking.

I removed the four screws and adopted the Light-blue-touch-paper-and-retire-immediately technique.

No hissing.

I then ordered my elegant secretarial equerry out of the room and, like the heroes who first de-fused the magnetic mines on the South Coast in 1940, I opened the infernal machine.

On the top lay a little unsigned note.

It was written in a homely hand on ruled paper.

The words ran thus:

Dear Cass,
The first egg of the season.
Remembered that you once wrote that you liked a goose egg for your tea. Hope you will accept and like this one.'

It was unsigned.

And underneath, in a nest of torn newspaper, lay a beauty.

She weighed nine ounces, and in small and I think feminine writing on the shell was the recorded date of the birth of the goose egg:

Feb. 18, 1953.

O the lovely silly human race, and how I like its crazy smiling face!

February 21, 1956

I get a goodly shower of abusive letters and they are a source of great strength to me. If the opposition – and the enraged opposition at that – disappeared I should feel utterly lost.

It is very comforting if you write a daily column to know that high up in the gods the old faithfuls are there with the brickbats handy and the rotten eggs poised.

There are also the old faithfuls with the good eggs. Every year during the third or fourth week of February an anonymous egg-man sends me a whopping great goose egg. Yesterday the lovely monster arrived with the following note:

Dear Cass,
Sorry the egg was a day late in making its appearance this year.
I remonstrated with the old girl but the look in her eye plainly told me that if I could do better, well, have a go.
Look after yourself and I hope you enjoy your tea.

Dear Eggman,

I shall indeed enjoy my tea. I shall boil the great white beauty for nine and a half minutes and then relish every sup of it while reading a pile of venomous letters which will add savour to the eggy scene.

Best wishes,

Cassandra.

April 10, 1963

The Ceremony of the Goose Egg is an in-built part of this column. Other columns win applause. I receive goose eggs.

Today, for the eleventh year in succession, I have a tale to tell on the eggy theme.

My life has always been mixed up with eggs – I once made a forty-two-egg omelette near the Leaning Tower of Pisa – and an odd incident occurred many years ago before the war, when I had a hand in running Live Letters.

For some unaccountable reason – I think we must have been slightly deranged – we thought it necessary to see if a clutch of eggs could be hatched out by a human being. So working backwards, we theorized that somebody bedridden and preferably beautiful should be located.

In no time at all we found a lovely girl with a broken leg who lived in Battersea. She agreed to our important sociological experiment.

The fertilised eggs were placed in a cotton wool nest that was put under the sheets with the girl.

In case of a sudden drop in temperature, a thermostatically controlled electric heater came into action and kept the nest at the proper heat of 102-5 degrees Fahrenheit. After the correct period for incubation, twenty-one days, we were gathered at the bedside for the triumphal cheep. But there was no cheep, no faint pecking, no sign of tiny feathered life.

We kept a stiff upper lip but did we have trouble with that gal? She was deeply grieved.

And only a great floral avalanche of roses and repeated boxes of chocolates repaired her broken heart.

Funny things eggs.

And, come to think of it, funny things women, too.

The Egg-Man cometh not

June 22, 1966

Today we will have a little requiem in our heart. Now the clouds mist over the sun in the green meadows and a few raindrops will serve for tears.

For eleven years the Goose Egg-man came by post each spring with his gift neatly laid in a small wooden box. The great white ovoid nestling in the wood shavings was annually presented to me with a brief courtly message of goodwill.

The Goose-Egg-man did this for over a decade and never revealed who he was.

Last year there was no goose egg and the seeds of doubt were sown.

Was Goosey ill? Or, more mournful still, was her boss sick or gone away?

Such prayers as are made for geese and goose eggs, and the owners of these mighty and strident birds, were offered up and we banished our dark thoughts near where the rushes grow by the pond.

But this year ?

We asked Goosey Goosey Gander whither his girl friend had wandered. But there was no reply.

There was quiet in the barnyard, and the wind sighed in the hayricks.

Bring out your soft sad cypress.

Lay on your boughs of dark yew.

The Egg-man cometh no more.

Saints and Sinners

Cassandra pen-painted them all: the saints, the sinners, the famous, the infamous. Portraits in this gallery were either drawn from life or sketched after death in candid obituaries. Purists may quibble that Marilyn Monroe has. no place among the mortal men. Included is a miniature that Cass himself might have chosen: the study of his Uncle Ezekiel, who used to read the *Financial Times* in a hansom cab without wheels in the middle of a Scottish wood.

He put his arm round the heart of the world

June 2, 1963

What splendid rolling names these Popes have had – this great succession of 259 pontiffs who have reigned for nearly 2,000 years...

Celestine, Eugenius, Sixtus, Honorius, Anastasius, Eleutherius, Zephyrinus, Adeodatus – they have the thunder of bells and deep organ music about them.

But there are other names too. Short commonplace names. There are Peter and Paul and John, and the sound of their chime recalls the simplicity of fishermen on the Sea of Galilee.

The first Pope John, and there have been twenty-three of them, was Holy Father way back in the year 523.

Pope John the Twenty-third has been in the Vatican for fewer than five years, but in those years his achievements have been incalculable.

By the bright flame of his deep humanity, his love of mankind, his courage, his piety and his gaiety, too, he has done something that no other Pope has done. He put his arm round the heart of the world.

Five years ago, had you mentioned the name of Angelo Giuseppe Roncalli in England, not one person in ten thousand would have known whom you were talking about. Mention Pope John today and everybody knows who you mean. Angelo Giuseppe Roncalli and Pope John were the same man.

Not only has the ordinary man in the street heard of Pope John but he has an exact and vivid conception of him. The popular portrait is clear.

A kind, good, warm avuncular man. A jolly man. A genial, tubby man. A man without cant or pride.

The stories about him, many true, some false, are endless. Anecdotes, reminiscences, statements, vignettes all add up to the same benign total. An overwhelmingly lovable man.

In these days of public relations, of building 'images' of people, of boosting conceptions, of plugging 'personalities', nothing can compare with this immense spontaneous repertoire of tales about the Pope.

All are in his favour. All are friendly. None has the whisper of ill will or malice. His actions inspire the benevolent (and sometimes fictional) cloud of reports that surround him.

When he visited the Regina Coeli prison in Rome (a very horrible place) there were barred sectors where the worst and most violent prisoners were kept.

It was held inadvisable for the Pope to go too near. The criminal human animals were dangerous.

He said: 'Open up the gates! Don't bar me from them. They are all children of the Lord.'

And he went into their cells where murderers and rapists fell on their knees and asked his blessing.

Such actions are fertile ground for further stories.

It has been the custom because protocol requires it, that the Pope should eat alone.

The Italian papers reported that the Holy Father had confided to a French diplomat at a private audience that he should have his meals by himself – except under the impassive gaze and silent presence of a member of his suite.

'I like eating,' he said, 'but doing it alone cuts my appetite – so I invited my gardener to lunch.'

He is supposed to have recalled that when he first became Pope he still felt as if he was a Cardinal and when asked to deal with some matter, said: 'I'll speak to the Pope about that.' Correcting his error he would say: 'But I AM the Pope. I'll have to take it up with God.'

When he visited the carpentry shop in the Vatican garden, he watched the joiners at work for some time and then said: 'This looks like thirsty work' – and ordered wine all round.

Once, when he was away from the Vatican, his Papal police thrust away the sightseers and those who wanted his blessing.

'Why did you do that?' asked the Pope. 'For security reasons,' replied the officer. Replied His Holiness: 'Security? I wasn't going to hurt them.'

He has received the high and the mighty and the low and the humble. The Archbishop of Canterbury and the barrow-boys from the streets of Rome; Princess Margaret and a travelling circus; Mrs Kennedy and the gondoliers from Venice.

Princes, peasants, wise men and certainly foolish men, of whom there are many, have been received with kindness, with wit, with humility and – I'll bet most of them needed it – with forgiveness.

This welcoming simplicity proved irresistible. Sheer unaffected goodness has limitless power. All this contrasted with the cold reserve of his predecessor, Pope Pius XII, who seemed, to some, to be too detached from the world.

Pope John will be remembered for other things than the worldwide affection he created. He was the architect of the Ecumenical Council which gathered in Rome to examine the whole machinery, doctrinal and administrative, of the Faith.

It was a tremendous undertaking and to inspire it, to promote it and to take part in it, secures his place in Catholic history as a great pontiff.

Vatican City is certainly the greatest religious power-house in the world. There is nothing to compare with its experience as a place of thought and contemplation. Rome understands national politics: it enfolds, and as history shows, can exploit, hideous barbarians like Mussolini and Hitler.

A century can be a day. A bloody revolution a skirmish overnight.

The Roman Catholic Church is rich beyond compare – and yet it thrives in poverty. It knows the inner clockwork of fallibility and the fatal flaws of power.

In this ancient temple of knowledge, of experience, of understanding, of enduring subtleness and intellectual guile, Angelo Guiseppe Roncalli, the son of a Lombardy farmer, also called John, after the Baptist, has triumphed with the palm of peace and love.

The man who buried all his friends – without their consent

March 7, 1953

He died in his bed. That was the last triumphant, exultant trick of Josef Vissarionovich Djugashvili – otherwise Joseph Stalin, the most powerful man in the world.

Mussolini hung by the heels outside a garage in Milan, desecrated and mutilated by an Italian mob. Hitler committed suicide in a back garden.

But this short, chunky super-dictator, who made fools of them both, who completely outwitted Roosevelt, and who was often much too slippery for Winston Churchill, departed from this life between the comfort of the sheets.

No assassin ever succeeded in pulling out a single whisker from his pock-marked face; no gunman ever nicked him with so much as an air-gun pellet. Millions were in their graves before their time because of Joseph Stalin, but he himself lived over three score years and ten, the latter part of it in considerable luxury and absolute security.

He was the political Colossus of our time. Yet no man in history ever trafficked in death like this man.

A quarter of a century ago he was murdering, torturing, beating and imprisoning his fellow countrymen in the early stages of his five-year-plan to collectivize farming. Ten million people were involved in this merciless and bloody operation. Since then, with the aid of a monstrous apparatus of internal spying, he has continued his war against mankind (entirely for their benefit, he claimed) until something like 14,000,000 people were enslaved in his vast network of camps.

Stalin himself remained unscratched. He kept it up to the end and even the manner of his death was probably not distressing to him. He had a stroke and simply became unconscious.

There were doctors around to ease any pain and there were professional mourners and eulogisers to lament his death and extol his deeds.

What was he like, this shoe-maker's son from Gori, in the Caucasus Mountains?

He had eyes that were heavily lidded and dull; a thick, bushy moustache, a prominent nose, and a manufactured smile – one of the best recorded examples of which is in the picture taken when he was with Ribbentrop after signing the notorious Nazi-Soviet pact in August, 1939.

In manner he was dour and attentive. There was no personal magnetism about him such as Hitler wielded. In fact, he hacked and slogged at an argument and never sought to win points with brilliant phrases. He was the dull secretary of the Central Committee of the Party and was regarded as not much more than a faithful plodder. All he wanted was to win. And win he did.

Yalta remains a shattering memorial to his ponderously successful strategy. It won him half Europe in a week.

His main armoury in conversation was lying accusations, taunts and jibes. Winston Churchill was often stung and sometimes deeply wounded by his malevolent crudities.

He accused the British of being afraid of the Germans. He accused the Royal Navy of cowardice and of cynically abandoning merchant vessels in convoy to Murmansk. He accused the British Army of being afraid to take risks.

He hinted that Britain and America were toying with the idea of a separate peace with Germany and indicated that if there was any ratting to be done he would be there first – a point that carried considerable weight with Mr Churchill, who remembered only too well the previous unholy alliance between Moscow and Berlin.

In the end, on the very practical basis that the man who succeeds in retaining the most booty after the battle has won the war, Stalin beat everybody else to a frazzle.

Poland, Hungary, Rumania, Czechoslovakia, Albania, Latvia and Estonia and half Germany were seized in the West. Finland was intimidated and Greece was nearly overthrown.

In the East, the whole of China was brought into the Communist power orbit and three dangerous and promising wars were started in Malaya, French Indo-China and Korea.

The final result was that half the world took orders from the gruff, gritty man in the Kremlin, who had buried all his friends without their consent.

No one ever challenged Stalin for long. Many died suspecting him.

Trotsky was pursued halfway round the earth before he was finally done to death with a meat axe in Mexico. Not one single comrade of his early days remains. Where are Arieoff, Zinoviev, Kamenev, Dybenko, Lunachevski, Yagoda, Bukharin, Rykov, Rakovsky, Smirnov? The list has grown monstrously over the years.

Even the secret police who knew so much and who had been his main instrument of power were themselves butchered in their own prison cellars.

At the same time that this endless horror was securing him limitless power, Stalin was engaged in the process of making himself the God of the Russian peoples. Religion was derided, children were taught that Stalin was their Father, and he had himself proclaimed as the fountainhead of all blessings.

By his express orders countless flattering portraits and complimentary accounts of him were broadcast. Special hymns were written about him. One is entitled, *Live for Ever, Beloved Leader.*

Stronger than steel is thy name,
Brighter than sun is thy glory,
Sweeter than honey is thy word,
Live for ever, beloved Leader.'

The last line has happily not been fulfilled.

His seventy-three hideous years have been enough. In his time he did titanic things and the whole world was his chess board. No tyrant ever planned on such a scale and continents rather than countries were his prey. Probably he was brave. Certainly he was shifty and cruel. His skill in power politics was unsurpassed.

But his purpose was evil and his methods unspeakable. Few men by their death can have given such deep satisfaction to so many.

A priest in the sun

April 17, 1961

Come with me into the sun. The journey is a long one. Nairobi, Mombasa, Tanga, Dar-es-Salaam, Zanzibar, Kilwa and then to Lindi about ten degrees south of the Equator.

Lindi is little more than a village by the sea, a fading little place with broken dreams of grandeur from having once been the appointed port for the groundnuts scheme.

There are massive Gothic graves under the palms to remind you that the Germans once ruled this remote and lonely place.

From Lindi I took a car and set out westwards from the ulterior. For the first fifteen miles the road is just plain bad.

From then on for the next eighty miles it is worse than abominable and next to impossible.

It is a narrow mush of red sand at times less than ten feet wide with vicious ruts.

The jungly scrub would soon overgrow this desperate track if it were not for the sparse traffic that fights its way through; and the leathery fronds, the hanging vines and the matted trees would quickly swallow this extremely bad joke of a road.

In this green and steaming wilderness there are lions, leopards, hyenas, wild boar, baboons, rhinos and – in the swamps – crocodiles.

My driver was a fierce-looking Moslem who spoke English as well as I speak Swahili. Which is not at all.

So we had a chat in complete silence, which broke into sign language as the car started to overheat.

The temperature gauge said DANGER, the smell was like hot cinders mixed with boiling oil and there was steam all over the place as we sizzled to a standstill.

The Moslem grinned and got out and within a few moments long thin men as black as soot wearing practically no clothes emerged and smiled with huge delight.

From nowhere they produced a great iron bowl about a yard wide and led the way to a muddy waterhole guaranteed fit for a hippo.

We baled the sludge up, thrust rather than poured it into the radiator and lurched west.

Masasi is little more than a fair-sized clearing in the scrub with a police station, a garage (O great sign of civilization), a few houses and the hospital and Mission of Mkomaindo.

Here lives a fine and famous man – Doctor Trevor Huddleston, better known as Father Huddleston but now the Bishop of Masasi.

The last time we met in Africa was in the slum satellite of Johannesburg, Sophiatown.

He met me at Masasi, driving his own Land Rover. No other civilian vehicle could cope with this rugged place – you keep the windows shut to stop the branches coming in.

He stepped out, white cassocked, to greet me with his tremendous welcoming smile.

Dr Huddleston practises his faith the hard way. His diocese is larger than Wales, his complement of souls is about 40,000 and his clergy total seventy-five, of whom thirteen are white.

The climate is hot and sticky. There are flies and perhaps more malaria than you will find anywhere else in the world.

Trevor Huddleston is in the middle of the fight. He told me that in some ways it was more like practising Christianity in England a hundred years ago. The problems were right outside your door. Poverty, ignorance, disease.

It struck me with some force that here in Masasi there was precious little time for the polished in-fighting that sometimes goes on in an English cathedral close.

I visited his hospital, which is run by a gifted and devoted woman, Dr Taylor. We toured the wards. It was heroic, but it was also pathetic.

Here were few trivial ailments. Tuberculosis is an active, ravaging scourge – the curse of this remote part of Central Africa.

Malaria is commonplace.

Leprosy is well known.

I saw one bright-eyed girl of about eighteen. The middle part of her face was heavily bandaged, and I asked the cause.

'This unlucky girl,' said Dr Taylor, 'had her nose bitten off by a hyena the other day.'

I tell this tale because that is what life can be like in these primitive parts. Plastic surgery could have worked wonders for this poor girl, but there is precious little plastic surgery in the South Province of Tanganyika.

And one of the reasons is money. The Mission needs money. Desperately so.

Dr Taylor does all the operating herself. I saw the theatre and it looked distinctly rudimentary to me – none of this shining, gleaming stuff with great lights and costly modern equipment.

But the kindness and the care and the love are there all right.

I talked to Dr Huddleston in his house. 'Come,' said he with a smile, 'into my Palace.'

It is a pleasant place of four rooms, one of which is his private chapel. The roof is thatch and the rain sometimes comes in.

The bishop looked at the tropical storms rumbling up from the Portuguese East Africa direction and said, 'I must put the plastic sheet over the desk. That's where the water drops.'

The place is laden with books (which always improve the look of any room) and there is a battery-operated record player which his friends gave him before he left London. The lighting is by oil and of course there is no running water.

But this great priest in the sun is happy.

There is no ecclesiastical pomp and circumstance. There is no retinue.

Only one coloured boy looks after the bishop. Trevor Huddleston is paid no stipend.

The design of his life is blazingly right.

He combines gaiety with massive inner strength, tenderness with toughness, compassion with competence. And here in this immense wilderness no one doubts how greatly he loves the name of the Lord.

The man in the glass cage

Jerusalem, April 12, 1961

The time is six minutes to nine o'clock in the morning. The place is the court-room of the community centre in Jerusalem. A side door opens and Adolf Eichmann walks into his bullet-proof armour-plated glass dock.

So this is the man who, if the charges are proved against him, will be by far the greatest killer in the history of mankind. Compared with him Genghis Khan was a welfare worker.

What does Eichmann look like? The appearance is that of a rather severe country solicitor who might well be on the board of governors of the local hospital.

The lips are thin, the hair is sparse, the nose beaky and the complexion sallow. He wears a dark, neat suit, a white shirt and a spotted tie. There is an air of respectability about him.

Three judges enter and all stand. Eichmann bows very slightly towards Supreme Court Judge Landau, who at once begins to read the tremendous indictment.

In its scale, it is almost incomprehensible. The mind just cannot grasp what is being laid at this man's door.

The scenes of horror cover twenty-one countries reaching from the steppes in Russia to the tiny State of Monaco. The work of this man, this creature, penetrated throughout the whole of Europe with the exception of the British Isles and Spain – and we may count ourselves lucky.

Death was his business and he knew it well.

Adolf – son of Adolf Karl Eichmann, as he is rather ceremoniously styled in this court – is accused of causing the death of six million Jews 'of torture, of starvation, of oppression, of overcrowding, of enslavement, of persecution, of deportation, of causing mental harm, of terrorist methods, of sterilization.'

As the hideous catalogue of evil is read out to him – first in Hebrew, then in German – his face remains completely impassive. There is nothing unusual about him, except that he stands oddly and bends slightly backwards. The accusations take seventy-three minutes to read and translate before his counsel Dr Robert Servatius, rises.

The Doctor is markedly Teutonic in appearance, with a massive head that rises straight from the back of his collar. He speaks slowly and deliberately.

I have the impression that out of Dr Adenauer's Germany has come a strong defender of what most people think is the impossible. At once, he challenges the constitution of the court. This is an excellent, if obvious, tactic. He immediately questions the right of one of the three judges on the grounds of prejudice and lack of authority.

Eichmann himself has obviously not been ill-treated.

He has been scrupulously well cared for, for the overwhelmingly good reason that at this moment he is a most precious human being to Israel – and although they may make him a corpse in a few months' time, they want him alive, alert and well, to play his terrible part in the demonstration that one man in the base and bestial Nazi regime could murder six million of his fellow men.

The Commandant of Jerusalem, Colonel Rossolio, who has been responsible for the custody of Eichmann for a year, told me yesterday that when the prisoner first arrived in Israel he seemed almost relieved that his wanderings and his flight had ended, but that a note of anxiety at the prospect of what might be in store for him became apparent later.

Eichmann was always scrupulously polite and stood to attention when spoken to. There was no tendency towards suicide, as far as his gaolers could see, but they were taking no chances. He was utterly unemotional, had not the slightest trace of humour, and did not ask for spiritual solace.

When the team of psychiatrists had finished with him 'it was,' said Colonel Rossolio, 'they who felt they had gone nuts.'

Eichmann was amenable to his guards, who had been specially chosen as not having been bereaved or connected with the atrocities of the concentration camps.

He was obviously an able man or he would never have been able to run the enormous and monstrous organization that led to genocide. It was a vast machine and could not have been controlled except by an extremely competent man.

The only time Eichmann showed some slight feeling was when he heard

Schubert or Mozart being played on the radio that belonged to his guards.

I can see him as I write these words. A thin, trim man who at this moment is, through his lawyers, complaining that he cannot bring witnesses to Israel to give evidence for him as they would not be given a safe conduct.

There was not much safe conduct for the Jews at the hands of Germany between 1935 and 1945.

Not much safe conduct in the gas ovens.

Not much safe conduct for the women and babies machine-gunned in the communal graves and pits.

It is odd that all the maniacal madness of mankind gone berserk should be symbolized in the physical person of one who would go unnoticed at a church service in Balham.

When saint and sinner meet

May 21, 1954

Who knows how to be hostile ? I do. Who knows how to be suspicious ? I do. Who knows how to be sceptical ? I do.

I can wield these unlovable qualities like a whip. And when the Reverend William Franklin Graham first arrived on this sinful island of ours, I took some pleasure in letting the lash whistle and hiss rather close to his handsome head.

'William Graham,' said I, 'is the smartest, the smoothest, the slickest and the most graceful opponent of iniquity I have ever seen in my life.' I called him 'this Hollywood version of John the Baptist,' and for good or evil value tossed in a few other incivilities.

I now have to report that Billy knows a trick worth two of that for he at once wrote me a short note that burst in my slit trench like a posy of honeysuckle.

> Dear Cassandra,
> I should like to have the privilege of meeting you.
> While your articles about me were not entirely sympathetic, yet they were two of the most cleverly written that I have ever read.
> Sincerely yours
> Billy Graham.

Now I flatter very easily and a kind word has me all over the shop.

But I watched my step. I took careful aim and triggered this one off at him.

Dear Billy Graham,
Thank you for your kind letter. Yes, let us by all means meet.
Will you meet a sinner first on his own ground?
Will you meet someone fairly hell-bent and not averse to a little quiet wickedness ? Someone picking primroses on the path to the everlasting bonfire; someone who is on guarded but at times friendly, terms with strong liquor and who believes that St Thomas the Doubter was the most human of the saints.

First let us meet in an English pub. I know that after your visit to the Elephant and Castle district such places are within your compass. Why should we not meet in a pub called The Baptist's Head or The Mitre or – better still in my case –The Prodigal's Return? You could drink what you choose while I *sin* quietly with a little beer.

Yours sincerely,
Cassandra.

The answer was yes – with the very reasonable proviso that Mr Graham had first to work off a number of existing engagements.

Then silence.

And more silence...

It was a bit too quiet for me so I sent up a Very light to see if I could illuminate the target:

Dear Billy Graham,
Why tarriest thou? (Acts 22, 16).

Yours sincerely,
Cassandra.

Three weeks later, when I was in Washington, I got a message agreeing to the meeting. I cabled back:

BETTER IS A DINNER OF HERBS WHERE LOVE IS THAN A STALLED OX AND HATRED THEREWITH (PROVERBS FIFTEEN VERSE SEVENTEEN) STOP SUGGEST NO HATRED BUT STALLED OX CASSANDRA

Answer: yes –

Place: Sinners' Ground. The Baptist's Head, St John's Lane, EC1 (note how Billy instantly agreed to St John's Lane after being called a Hollywood version of the saint). Agenda: Anything. Everything.

So at last we met.

Let me describe Billy Graham. Let me tell you what I think of this appallingly handsome young man. Let me tell you what I think of the too-good-looking evangelist from North Carolina who has attracted a truly astonishing total of 1,336,500 people to Harringay.

I think that he is a good man.

I think that he also is a simple man.

And goodness and simplicity are a couple of tough customers.

When he came into The Baptist's Head (which neither of us knew before) he was absolutely at home – a teetotaller and an abstainer able to make himself completely at his ease in the spit and sawdust department; which is, in my view, a very difficult thing to do.

Billy Graham looks ill. He has lost a stone in this non-stop merciless campaign that goes on every night at Harringay. How he does it I do not know for I can think of nothing more formidable, nothing more agonising than this immensely successful nightly act which rivals the London Palladium in the pleasure and the entertainment which it gives to the gigantic audiences he has attracted to hear what he says about the Testaments Old and New.

I asked him whether he felt pride at the wonderful success that he had made in Britain which, judging by church attendances, was one of the most irreligious countries in the world. I asked him whether he felt proud 'to be the chosen vessel of the Lord'. The answer was that he did not: that pride was often arrogance and that he himself had no real directive force in what had happened. Normally I would have regarded the reply as one of questionable humility. I don't think that in this case it was.

I asked him whether he realised that after the warmth, the friendliness, the theatricality, and the glamorous display of his meetings at Harringay it would not be a dangerous and terrible anti-climax for his converts to go back to the unromantic austerity of cold chapels and of empty churches run by clergy sick at heart because of their failure to get congregations.

His answer was Matthew (Chapter 13): 'Behold a sower went forth to sow... some seeds fell by the way side... but others fell into good ground and brought forth fruit, some an hundredfold.'

He is prepared, he says, to take the chance. I reminded him that when he first arrived he was not only received with suspicion by the Press (about 200 of us were derisively pleased when his head baritone George Beverly Shea got up and sang unaccompanied 'I'd rather have Jesus than riches or gold'), but he was also greeted with a notable lack of enthusiasm by the Anglican Church. The Bishop of Barking was the only one to come wholeheartedly out in his support.

Yet on Saturday at Wembley, when this roaring and remarkable campaign comes to its almost ecstatic climax, who will be there to give himself what I regard as a belated blessing but the Archbishop of

Canterbury. I put it to Dr Graham that nothing succeeds like success.

He would have none of it.

He was grateful for any support. He didn't mind when it came, how it came, or why it came.

It was the superbly diplomatic answer. It may also have been the true one.

He tries to avoid politics like the plague. He feels that people are politically severed in two by being either Tories or Socialists or, in his own country, Democrats or Republicans, and that to come out with political pronouncements is automatically to alienate about half the population who want their religion kept away from the ballot box.

I would say that this is sheer expediency. Graham does not agree.

But this fact he can carry back to North Carolina with him unquestioned and undisputed. It is that in this country, battered and squeezed as no victorious nation has ever been before and disillusioned almost beyond endurance, he has been welcomed with an exuberance that almost makes us blush behind our precious Anglo-Saxon reserve.

I never thought that friendliness had such a sharp cutting edge. I never thought simplicity could cudgel us sinners so damned hard.

We live and we learn.

Saint on the air

Delhi, October 10, 1947

'Today I am a back number.' Six words uttered against a background of appalling violence in India.

The speaker was Mahatma Gandhi.

The occasion, the nightly prayer meeting at which this extraordinary and saintly man gives his running commentary on world affairs.

The prayer meeting is a remarkable and, to Western eyes, bizarre performance. I saw it in Delhi when Gandhi, the Great Untouchable, the friend of the outcasts and the sweepers, appeared in the lovely garden of one of the richest men in India.

Half an hour before it began, Indian technicians were testing a portable amplifier and three huge loudspeakers garishly inscribed CHICAGO RADIO. On a raised platform 'disciples' were arranging a cushion and a mat for the Master. One of them, an alert young man speaking English with a slight American accent, who would have been quite at home at the Harvard School of Business, told me with satisfaction that the diary of his intimate association with Gandhi, which he had been keeping for years, should interest the publishers.

The crowd were now assembling – little children and old people, boys and girls, beggars and wealthy Indians all gathering to listen – and to worship. At exactly the scheduled time the Mahatma appeared. He was supported by two young and lovely girls who were reputed to be his grandchildren. When you first see him, you at once realise what a perfect chance he is for the cartoonist: a wispy, thick-lipped, be-spectacled creature who happens to be one of the great and good men of history.

He squats on the cushion, closes his eyes and appears to mutter prayers to himself in a rather desultory way. A choir of young girls chant – almost wail – Indian hymns. The Mahatma, who appears to be in a trance of brooding thought, suddenly begins to clap his hands to keep time. A rather deep voice from behind him draws your attention away to a severe European lady in native clothes. Iron grey hair. Fierce eyebrows. Prominent nose. Confident chin. The name is Shrimati Mira Bai – or Miss Madeleine Slade, the daughter of an English Admiral, who has followed Gandhi for twenty-two years.

A member of the congregation, right up in the front by the dais, appears to be whispering to his companion. Miss Slade gets up, tiptoes across and rebukes him. In a curious spasm of mixed terror and respect, and with his hands together in praying fashion, he beseeches her pardon. Soon the singing ceases and the half-naked aged Mahatma pulls up the microphone to his lips. He whispers into it and the amplifiers magnify the words into a clear and tremulous sing-song.

The Saint is on the air. Gandhiji, as they call him – an affectionate diminutive which approximately means 'dearly beloved saint' – is thinking aloud. No subject is barred but no questions are allowed. In the midst of unbridled passion and the fearful war between the Hindus and the Muslims, he preaches forgiveness and the doctrines of brotherly love. It is the Sermon on the Mount again expounded with grief and personal anguish amid one of the most gigantic massacres that Asia has ever seen. His influence is still enormous and the truth of his simple assertions overwhelming but the lonely voice of compassion and goodwill is drowned in the storm of hate.

'Today I am a back number.'

The innocents

Naples, December 3, 1957

This is the story about the scum of the earth. The small scum, the innocent scum, the diseased, the lonely and the lost. On the scale of numbers not many are involved – about 120 souls in all, none of whom is known to you.

They are the human rubbish of Naples, born in misery and sin, and every one of them guilty of the crime of poverty. They are the deadend kids of the most desperate dead-end city in Europe.

There is no town that I know of quite like Naples. It is beautiful and abominable. It is serene and ferocious. It is light-hearted and utterly vile.

When you stand on the heights of the Vomero above the city you survey one of the most beautiful prospects on earth.

When you go fifty yards off the Via Roma, the main street, you enter the vast crescent of crime and filth that encircles dockland and you go into a world of such squalor and degradation that the mind cannot encompass that this is Europe in 1957; that this is the gay Italian people; that this is Christian Democracy in the West.

Seven years ago Father Mario Borelli, a priest born in the slums – he was one of a family of ten children – began a great experiment to reclaim the generation of the innocent and the damned. The poor abandoned kids of Naples.

Borelli and the two priests who help him live from hand to mouth in a bombed-out church in the Square of San Gennaro di Materdei and they never know where the next hundred lire are coming from.

Father Borelli, Father Spada and Father James – the latter an English priest from Norfolk – struggle on with their astonishing fight to keep these boys in spartan cleanliness and self-respect.

Borelli himself, sometimes clad in the rags which he knows so well and which were the garb of his up-bringing, has brought these children in and can speak to them in their own language. He knows the gutter, the bleak horror of the starving city, its crime and its vice.

The House of Urchins has almost no rules. It is run with the freedom of mutual trust – and it works. Their funds are meagre and at times the kitty is almost empty. Yet the miracle continues and the river of support has never yet run entirely dry. They never lose heart, they never despair.

The work goes on. To see these kids sit down to their evening meal is a delight – and a blow to the heart. They are gay as only Italian children can be. They are full of fun and mischief and gratitude to the world that has so shamefully used them.

In a bare room high in the battered church I saw them sitting down to a bowl of soup that in England would be regarded as prison skilly. A big hunk of dry bread and a piece of wrapped cheese completes the meal.

I tasted the soup. By English standards it was greasy – and unappetising.

By their standards – the standards of fierce hunger and bitter poverty – it was delicious. The boys chattered, they laughed and they enjoyed to the full what they ate. They sat on broken chairs around wooden tables over which threadbare cloths had been laid, and ate off tin plates.

But I noticed that each child had a little square of cloth beside him that stood for a serviette and it seemed to me to be a brave little flag of tattered elegance that stood for civility and self-respect.

When the boys of the House of Urchins reach fourteen and are old enough to go to work – if they can get it in this city where there are 200,000 unemployed – they divide their wages into three. One third goes to pay for their keep, one third is put by as savings for later on, and one third they have to spend just how they will.

They help with the cooking, the cleaning and the making of beds. The whole arrangement is on a voluntary basis and Father Borelli's flock are free to leave whenever they will.

They do not choose to do so. They are chained by kindliness and locked in by the love they have never known before.

All around lies the corrupt and semi-starving city of Naples. The hovels in which people live vary from the vast tenements more than a century old – a dozen people sleeping in one room – to unspeakable shacks made of cardboard, corrugated iron and orange boxes.

There is no running water and what is available has to be carried in by a pail from a pump. The people are diseased and verminous. Illegitimacy and nicest are commonplace. Typhoid is more prevalent than the guide books care to mention. The gutters run with filth, and thieving and prostitution are major industries run by cynical receivers and degraded pimps.

Those who deride the Welfare State should come and see the free-for-all and devil-take-the-hindmost State that is south of Italy. The contrasts in Naples itself between flaunting riches and agonising poverty are as great as you will find in Johannesburg with its millionaires' villas and its shocking satellite towns.

Into this sunny hell-hole Father Borelli, and the good priests who help him, are fighting a fight with compassion as their sword and kindness as their shield.

The smile on the faces of the children of the House of Urchins is their flag of victory.

The glint in every man's eye

February 15, 1955

It was 4.53 in the afternoon on Fifth Avenue in New York.

I was in my underpants buying and trying on a pair of new trousers when the telephone rang – and I was breathlessly told that Miss Marilyn Monroe would see me in the Gladstone Hotel between 9 and 10 next morning.

I regained my overpants.

Now over to the Gladstone Hotel at 9.30 in the morning. I went up in the lift, found room 614, pressed the buzzer and waited a moment.

The door was opened by a sad wolf-like character, name of Joe DiMaggio.

Would I come right on in? I would.

And there in bed in a darkened and rather scruffy room in a slightly nondescript hotel lay the golden darling of the sex world.

The famous blonde hair flared out across the pillow. Her pert, pouting face with no make up on and unclear eyes switched on a rather automatic smile – and I knew the kid was ill.

While Joe plunged around in the tiny alcove that American hotels call a kitchen, Marilyn and I got talking.

Had she ever been to England? No.

Would she like to come to England?

Yes, she would love to come to England and especially she would like to appear at the London Palladium. But so far her contract had forbidden it.

She said that she liked the British and in her youth (what's that, you sweet old lady?) she had been brought up with a kind lady from Yorkshire.

I asked her whether she knew any English people in Hollywood.

Yes, she did.

She was a friend of Edith Sitwell and an admirer of Edith Sitwell.

This, I think is one of the finest juxtapositions I have ever heard of. I also think it is a genuine friendship...

On the left we have Marilyn, the girl who, when asked: 'What do you think of sex?' replied: 'I never give it a second thought.'

On the right we have the gothic Edith Sitwell – one of the most formidable, wise, witty, terrifying, antique and seasoned women in the world.

Marilyn likes Edith.

Edith likes Marilyn.

And I believe the pair of them.

I believe that all the locked-up wisdom of the mentally heavy-gunned Edith takes to Marilyn who began her professional life by being photographed in the nude for what is known as an art calendar.

I am pretty sure that Miss Sitwell who has Hollywood very firmly by the throat takes, as they say here, 'real kindly' to Marilyn who has been made but yet may still be destroyed by the international moguls who profit so assiduously by selling the dreams of the movie screen.

I asked Marilyn whether she had ever owned a home of her own. She had not.

Then where did she live?

She lived in hotels and apartments. Why didn't she buy a place of her own? Marilyn smiled a weary smile and said that she had never had the time.

Joe, the silent, wolf-like Joe, still lurked gloomily in the kitchen.

Said Marilyn: 'Would you like a cup of tea?' This is the deepest and most flattering and most kindly thing that the Americans can say to the British. They know that without it we would perish.

As it happens I dislike tea with a deep and abiding loathing, so I said that I would like a long glass of iced water. Marilyn registered the penumbra of disbelief. Mr DiMaggio got busy with the ice box and tap.

Miss Monroe lay sad and sweet and, I thought, for once very firmly removed from her traditional role of the greatest accumulated sex horse-power in the world.

I asked her if she had ever escaped from the repellant maze of the film business... Had she been in Europe? ...No. In Africa? ...No. In Asia? ...No ...but once to Korea where, as I well knew, she had been a wonderful and frantic piece of dream ammunition for the troops.

Marilyn has, in fact, ever since she was a leggy orphan been fighting the eternal and gruelling fight for dough.

And she has been a resounding financial victor.

But for all that when Miss Edith Sitwell says, as she has done, that she likes Miss Monroe, I think that Edith is right.

A very mixed up, mournful and pleasing gal.

Fun at the Dentist's

May 22, 1953

I'm a bit short of sleep and to save anybody else asking me what Senator Joseph McCarthy is like and how do you set about seeing him I'll set it down in black and white. Then will you let me roll over and doze?

This is exactly how you do it.

You fly to New York and then you fly to Washington. You then pick up the telephone book, look up Senator Joseph R. McCarthy and ring him up in the Senate Office Building.

'May I speak to Senator McCarthy please?'

'Who's calling?'

You tell the sweet, suave feminine voice and she says that the Senator is busy. Will you call later?

You will. You do.

This telephonic crane-dance goes on for a couple of days. Will Miss Sweetness please place personally in front of the Senator a message to say that a man has come all the way from Europe to see him. Will she please tell Senator McCarthy to stop wasting my time, to stop wasting his time, to stop wasting his secretary's time, to stop wasting electricity on the telephone system and to tell me to clear off to Europe; which I will do with great speed and pleasure or alternatively will he see me? Just a plain yes or no. Miss Sweetness says sure she'll be glad to tell the Senator, and she'll call me back.

Yes, the Senator will see me and will I please be at his office at mid-day? I get there. He keeps me cooling my heels. At last McCarthy comes out.

Can wickedness have charm? I think it can and in this stocky, dangerous, vastly ambitious man it seems to go hand in hand. Will I ride downtown with him in his car? Yes, but is this one of these squalid gabble-and-run occasions in which he can spare me only two or three minutes in a phoney American schedule-crammed day?

McCarthy grins and says hell no.

He's going to the dentist and would I care to step right in. I told him that indeed I would, but perhaps it would be better to let him know right away that I detested everything that he stood for, that I opposed what he was doing, and that on further acquaintance, I felt almost certain that I would hate his guts. Furthermore, what the blazes was his idea in keeping me waiting in this sweaty town? The Senator for Wisconsin remarked thoughtfully that 'Jeez, this was straight shooting'.

We went into the surgery and McCarthy, still urbane and still slightly boyish, introduced me to Dr Stirling. This was a reporter from England. This was a straight-shooter and Joe personally liked straight-shooters. Would I have an anaesthetic? I said I'd have a double chloroform. The Senator said he'd have one too, and make it Scotch for both of us. McCarthy sat in the chair with his drink in his hand. I sat next to him.

I told the dentist that I dearly hoped he would hurt the Senator and that if he thought this was a joke I was never more serious in my life. McCarthy grinned and said: 'See what I mean, doc?' I asked McCarthy whether he knew that a total blockade of China would mean the downfall of Hong

Kong and did he want to see bits of the Empire drop off like rotten apples?

He made a long rambling reply, the gist of which was that we were sending explosives to China under the guise of fertilisers which were killing American boys but he could sympathise with us if we saw our Empire falling apart.

I asked him what he thought of Cohn and Schine and he said that they were about their lawful business in Europe and what was all the fuss about? I told him that we disliked little snoopers but that if he wished to drive a further wedge between the United States and Great Britain then he should send Cohn and Schine back to England again and he would further damage Anglo-American friendship. More Scotch was served.

The dentist drilled his teeth. The nurse, charming and attractive but also deeply impressed and honoured to have such a distinguished patient, fussed round. McCarthy lay there with his mouth wide open and as he was unable to talk, I asked him if I could tell him a funny story. He nodded. I said that in Milan there is a square which is called the Piazza Loreto. In the Piazza there is a garage.

Outside the garage there is a canopy, and supporting the canopy there is an iron girder. On the morning of the 29th of April, 1945, there was a gentleman attached to the iron girder. He was suspended upside down by a rope. His mouth was very wide open – just like the Senator's – and the similarity, to me, was astonishing.

The name of the man was Benito Mussolini, and I wondered if dictators dead could look like would-be dictators alive.

Joe shut his mouth, and I think what could be called a shadow of pain clouded his face. The dentist looked as if a blockbuster had hit him.

The nurse sagged and appeared dazed. So I gave her what might be called a mirthless wink which, to my astonishment, she returned in an unhappy sort of way. I asked McCarthy to soothe the pair of them.

I said that there should be no cause for distress anywhere as it was clearly understood between Mr McCarthy and myself that this was going to be a frank conversation of the type that formidable and powerful politicians could handle in their stride.

Would the Senator therefore calm the dentist and put the nurse at her ease? Mr McCarthy growled 'Relax'.

Order was not fully restored so I made what I thought was a helpful suggestion and indeed a social gesture. Would the dentist prescribe another anaesthetic and I personally did not care too much for ice with my Scotch?

Drinks were served.

The semi-electrocuted dentist went on with the filling and the nurse continued in her role of an attractive but astonished barmaid.

From the dentist's with all its corrosive jollification, we moved back to the Senate Office Buildings where the Senator indulged in a little verbal mayhem himself denouncing the British for killing American soldiers for the sake of commercial gain. The few odd calculations that I was able to make about blood spilt in two World Wars and treasure piled up in the second which made the United States easily the richest and most powerful nation on earth, made no impression on McCarthy. From the Senate Offices we moved on to a house which he either owned or in which he was welcomed as a most favoured son.

I was now in the role of a violent extraordinary trophy that the Senator had brought home for his friends to see. He remarked that he had never seen anybody like me before and I replied that in his case neither had I, and I hoped that it would never occur again.

A rancorous time was had by all, and after remarking that I hoped his teeth hurt for ever more the fragrant encounter came to an end.

Archbishop Makarios

Athens, January 17, 1958

Today I was received by His Beatitude Archbishop Makarios, the Head of the Church of Cyprus and Ethnarch.

That sounds rather grand. And in a way it was slightly grand, for this turbulent priest, this saint, this sinner, this Rasputin, this St Thomas Aquinas, call him what you will, is a deeply impressive man.

His office is in a modern block of flats just off the main square in the centre of Athens, I was ushered – that is the only word – into a simple tasteful office with a refectory table. The Archbishop rose to greet me with a disarming smile, and at once I found it hard to reconcile his grave and dignified presence with the violence and the cruelty that have attended his passionate cause.

Instantly, it was apparent that I was talking to a subtle, sensitive, and deeply comprehending man.

If the British Government wanted a battle of wits over the problem of the Eastern Mediterranean it could not have selected a more redoubtable opponent.

To have pitted an honest and uncomplex soldier like Sir John Harding, the late Governor of Cyprus, against this skilled and labyrinthine prelate was, in my view, plain cruelty to political children.

Makarios has a sad and gentle smile. He speaks excellent English (he studied at Boston University in the United States for two years) and he told me that in spite of everything he bore no ill will against Sir John Harding.

In fact he liked him personally.

I believe Makarios.

He said that he felt that all along he was dealing with a luckless man who was forced to implement policies of which he was not the author and which were in the long run actually anti-British.

I asked Makarios what he thought of the British Government's action in deporting him to the Seychelles. I used the word 'kidnapping' and he laughed. He said that when he learned of the Government's intention to carry him off to the Indian Ocean he could not believe it.

He could not credit it that a Government which was reputedly the most civilised and sagacious in the world could stoop to such an act of folly which would inevitably rally world opinion against it.

The British have an unfortunate record when they imprison or deport their political opponents. Their victims have a habit of turning up again as Prime Ministers, like Mr Nehru, or Mr de Valera.

I am sure that the Archbishop's status has been greatly improved since the Seychelles incident.

I asked Makarios whether he had been well treated on those lonely islands.

He smiled his slow, melancholy smile, and said that every courtesy had been extended to him. He was, of course, completely cut off from the rest of the world, but in his exile he had grown to like those whose duty it was to keep him there.

In all his answers he gave patient, thoughtful replies that conveyed the impression of a brooding, formidable mind.

Did he think that the climate of opinion in Cyprus and Britain had improved over the past two months?

The Archbishop thought that it might now be more favourable, but the past Tory policy it maintained could offer no hope.

His mind is flexible and adaptable but his ultimate aims are rigid and exact. Yesterday he offered to go to Turkey to discuss the problem, probably knowing that there would be no reply. But at least he went on record showing that he was willing to talk with Greece's ancient enemy.

Given half a chance I believe that Sir Hugh Foot, the new Governor, may be able to do a deal with this extraordinary man.

Here, in Athens, he is a legendary figure.

He is young, 45, handsome, cool and charming. He dresses immaculately in his ecclesiastical garb, and with his beard, his robes, and his massive crucifix, he is the personification of elegant reverence.

I do not think that Makarios is fundamentally anti-British, and at times he seems to bring an odd sort of detachment to the problem. But what is certain is that in the end we will have to deal and negotiate with this meticulous and maybe coldly fanatical man.

In himself, for better or for worse, he has invested the whole problem of Cyprus and Greece.

In the end I think that a meeting between Archbishop Makarios and Sir Hugh Foot is inevitable.

It will be a memorable occasion. Neither side can fail to appreciate the other.

In terms of sheer intellectual horsepower, the Cypriot priest and the British Colonial Civil Servant will at once recognise that both parties are firing on all cylinders.

That they are outstandingly intelligent men brings hope to a problem that has been cursed with stupidity over the past five years.

Hail – and farewell

February 4, 1964

A Georgian monument died yesterday. The name of this structure was Professor Sir Albert Edward Richardson, and although by a delayed accident of birth he was forced to live in the nineteenth and twentieth centuries, his heart was in the eighteenth.

In the age of conformity he did not conform.

In the era of drabness he tossed pots of bright paint in the public's face.

In the times of the dumb and the inarticulate, he spoke out. The Professor was part sage and part buffoon – but the sagacity was greater than the tomfoolery and the going of him darkens the contemporary scene.

Professor Sir Albert loved the Georgian age and he believed that the art of living reached its highest peak in those elegant times. This splendid era of English architecture, this period of the superb design of furniture and silverware, this age of the construction of lovely clocks and fine painting and of inspired music has not been surpassed in British history.

The architecture of post-war Britain, with its sterile and graceless buildings dictated by 'developers' and millionaire 'property tycoons' who have largely destroyed central London, was a main target of his. He had a fine waspish tongue mixed with a rare dash of the vulgar London Palladium wit.

Of the 'developers', he said: 'Men with insect minds on the pavement levels and the ambitions of giants. They have strip-teased the buildings. Nothing is left – not even the ear-rings.' He was right. These vast steel-

and-concrete and glass cubes say nothing – except that the ants inside can be accommodated at such and such a density in so many cubic feet, at such and such a yield on the investment.

No architect worth his sovereigns in Georgian days would design a building without saying: 'I will express myself in this building. I will make it smile. I will try to please those who dwell in it and those who behold it.'

The clockmakers of this period were not content with making the most beautiful clocks the world had ever seen, but on the brass back-plate hidden away from sight they engraved their lovely chasing just for the delightful heaven of it.

Professor Sir Albert shared this view of delight for delight's sake when he said: 'There should be fountains in the streets with Tritons throwing water at each other.'

Where are the fountains in Tottenham Court Road – that ultimate hell of architecture?

He was all for the Royal Navy and the Merchant Marine going to sea again in the nineteen-sixties with carved figure-heads under their bowsprits. The fact that there are no bowsprits and that the Royal Navy, in a nuclear clinch, would be scrap-iron in the skies and scrap-iron at the bottom of the ocean two minutes later, was correctly overlooked by the Professor Sir.

He mixed whisky with his paint and he drew portraits in church. He burnt incense while he worked because he said it gave him inspiration. He designed the facade of the Polytechnic in London's Regent-street and, for that, I would have sentenced him to two years, but I would have opened his cell door the next morning because like me he hated, loathed, despised and scorned the telephone.

He has left his lovely house in Bedfordshire to the National Trust. He loved craftsmanship and laid about him in the penumbra of art criticism by dismissing the practitioners as 'Owls, bats and fleas'.

Then, when pressed to explain what he meant by his provocative remark, he said: 'They are owls because they hoot, bats because they see things upside down, and fleas because they nip.

That particular jest smelt of the midnight oil, and although it may not have been midnight when he took it off the drawing-board, it was by oil that he must have contrived it, for he abhorred electric light (or said he did) and loved to work and eat and drink by the pale light of the oil lantern.

The ex-President of the Royal Academy – for he had commanded that horny-headed body – smoked a churchwarden pipe, dressed in knee-breeches, wore a periwig, liked shoes with silver buckles, was inclined to a cornered hat, and used a sedan chair for transport – presumably as a heated reply to the bubble car. He was a jester and show-off.

He was a magnificent clown, but he was at the barricades fighting for what he regarded as the golden past against the tinsel, tawdry present.

Hail – and farewell.

Old lonely heart

December 8, 1954

I first collided with Gilbert Harding by chance about a year ago in a public restaurant. The bows were stove in after the crash but both vessels were able to proceed under their own steam without assistance.

The language from the bridge was absolutely appalling and continued without cessation until both parties were out of earshot.

The occasion was not accounted a social success.

Mr H is an old and accomplished hand in the acerbity business and, in measuring incivilities with him, I freely concede that he is a very considerable artist in verbal mayhem.

On the return match last Friday he arrived late, hot and not bothered. He apologised fiercely for not being on time and expressed his hearty contempt for those who could not keep appointments with a harsh expert gruffness that had a rather remarkable effect.

I got the impression that somehow I should feel guilty on behalf of all latecomers in spite of the fact that I had been there dead on time and he had been ten minutes late.

I must try this technique sometime. The apology used instantly as a club has great possibilities.

In non-cathode ray tube life Gilbert Harding is a sort of 3D, wide screen, coloured version of what he is on the television. Bigger, rounder, grumpier, deeper-voiced and even more full of his over-brimming fulminating self.

He has a fine line in glares, deep-breathing, sustained bristling, bottled fury, cerebral blood-pressure and all the other signs of the fierce protestant.

Yes he is not a Protestant with a capital P. He is a Roman Catholic and, I suspect, a highly disturbed one at that. I asked how it was that he, rebellious, ebullient and disputatious character that he is, was able to make the act of faith and total surrender that Rome demands. He shrugged his shoulders and said: ‘Doesn’t one always have to give in at the end?’

Harding is like what I used to think a golf ball was when I was a child.

Do you remember the tale that they used to put over us kids? They said never cut a golf ball open. Never try to get under that tough outer skin of guttapercha. You split it open at your peril. Having taken this risk we nippers were then astonished to find miles and miles of thick india rubber which we half unwound but never went too far, for we had been told that right in the heart of the ball there was a dangerous explosive centre that would burst, blowing up what was left of the ball, and wounding those who stood around.

I would never try to unwind Gilbert Harding too far. Too many people including Harding would get hurt, I suspect that at the heart of the man there is intense kindness, and loneliness and bitterness not about other people but about himself.

The great roaring Dr Johnson that delights us on Sunday night is not really true. Nothing so simple. The gruff old teddy bear lives in his own jungle of doubt and self-criticism.

We were talking about his past life in Canada and he went on to mention the city of Toronto, where he had stayed. Of all cities, said Harding, this was the one for which he had the most abiding dislike.

I said to him, 'If you hated it so much why didn't you clear out?'

'Life, sir,' he replied, 'is not so simple as that. You see, although I could always get away from Toronto at any time, I can never get away from Gilbert Harding.'

The man, of course, by usual normal standards, is a gigantic success. He earns an enormous income. I asked him why it was that it is impossible to open a newspaper without seeing his ferocious endorsement of advertisements for shoes, sealing wax and what-have-you.

'Well,' he said, 'I suppose it's because I'm afraid of not being thought a practical man by people who pride themselves on being practical men.'

A somewhat tortuous explanation about money, I thought. Maybe, unlike me, he just doesn't want the stuff.

Of all the radio characters he is in a class of his own.

He is not like the BBC. He is never oleaginous. He is not smug, smooth or smarmy. He is not even urbane.

The radio has produced a set of professional friends of the people who are for ever interviewing the lower middle class and appearing to get on enormously well with them. They are the expert patronisers who mouth limitless homilies in homespun or city-slick accents. They are the do-gooders nudging up to frail old ladies in almshouses. They are the hushed-voice mob who report Royal occasions.

Harding is not among them.

Much of mankind gives him the belly-ache and he is honest enough to feel it, to show it and to express it. He is jovial in a limited sort of way and his audience can sit back and enjoy his dwindling patience, his rising irascibility and his I-wish-to-God-I-were-out-of-hereness.

In *What's My Line?* he is the founder of the act. Without him the prairie oyster would have lost its Worcester Sauce, and the roast beef its horse-radish. It would subside in unbearable archness.

His background is academic, rather absurd and somewhat tormented.

He was born in a workhouse – the Union Workhouse, Hereford, where his mother was the Matron and his father was the Master. He tells a tale how years ago the Mayor visited the Poor Law Institution one Christmas afternoon. The civic dignitaries were late, but when at last they did arrive the Mayor addressed the waiting inmates with these opening words:

'Good afternoon. Me and these other gentlemen 'ere on this platform 'ave come to see that you paupers 'ave 'ad a good Christmass...'

Harding glared with outrage and guffawed with angry amusement.

He won a scholarship to Cambridge, where he did most of the arrogant nonsensical things that undergraduates do, including the almost compulsory escapades with chamber pots. He became a teacher in Cyprus, in France, and was also a 'crammer' in Chancery Lane. He was a policeman in Bradford.

He hated policemaning. My own view is that Constable Harding was about the most inadequate policeman the Law has ever had. He seems to have been both insolent and inadequate.

Harding says with grim satisfaction that, when he left, the Chief Constable of Bradford gave him a parchment to the effect that during his service in that town his conduct had been 'exemplary'.

Gilbert Harding is criticised for his brawls with the public in which he complains, quarrels and kicks the table over as he did when he was invited to Grimsby to have a fish lunch.

He sounded off in an enormous way when they slung sauce over his 'Dover Sole *a la* Gilbert Harding'.

He is thus exposed to the criticism that he is a rough, crude commercial fellow. Rubbish.

These municipal clerks hire him for one reason. He is the Best Tantrum in Town. And when they get it and don't like it they are bad buyers and rotten judges of human nature.

Old Lonely Heart is above all things a kind man. His enemies – and they are many – admit it. His friends proclaim it. He is ill-tempered and immensely good-humoured. He is fierce and he is timid. He is arrogant and he is surprisingly humble. He is crammed with likes and dislikes and loaded with endless assertions and countless doubts. He also has asthma.

He is also not what he seems. Maybe Gilbert Harding can't get away from being Gilbert Harding, but millions rejoice in his uneasy dilemma and wish him to stay chained to himself right where he is.

G.B.S.

November 3, 1950

Shaw is dead. The great dark gates of death that have been locked against him for so long swung open for a moment at dawn yesterday and the lean, derisive Sage looked over his shoulder for a final twinkling trice – and was gone.

G.B.S., who has said most things worth saying in the past century and who has had the world by the ears and the tail for longer than any writer in history, finally learnt the last and most simple of all tricks – how to die. The frozen field-mouse stiff and cold under the hedgerow knew it before him; the fledgling in the cat's paw understood it and the poor, weighted mongrel struggling in the canal beat him to it in having an earlier glimpse of the last sombre secret of how to leave this life.

Only this glittering Jack Frost of a man, whose contemporaries began to die at the turn of the century and who had pierced and exposed most of the follies and foibles of mankind, had not, until the birth of yesterday, achieved that final shattering achievement, the ending of life and, in his case, the ultimate awesome passing of George Bernard Shaw.

The mould is broken. There was none like him before him, none like him when he was alive – and there will be none to match him now he is gone. Shaw in love seems almost grotesque – though there is much evidence that at the time many women did not think it so. How, for instance could a girl in his arms deal with this sort of stuff?:

'When you loved me I gave you the whole sun and stars to play with. I gave you eternity in a single moment, strength of the mountains in one clasp of your arms, and the volume of all the seas in one impulse of your soul. We possessed all the universe together – and you ask me to give you my scanty wages as well!'

Mr Churchill, who knows a golden intellect and a diamond-bright pen when he sees one, has paid his profound respects to G.B.S. But he has also recorded his censure of some of the gaucheries of the Sage in his antics:

'If the truth must be told, our British island has not had much help in its troubles from Mr Bernard Shaw. When nations are fighting for life, when the Palace in which the Jester dwells not uncomfortably is itself assailed, and every one from Prince to groom is fighting on the battlements, the Jester's jokes echo only through deserted halls, and his witticisms and commendations, distributed evenly between friend and foe, jar the ears of hurrying messengers, of mourning women and wounded men. The titter ill accords with the tocsin, or the motley with the bandages.'

GBS died after a fall when reaching out to prune an old and dying bough with his secateurs. The symbolism would not have escaped him. He was almost certainly a happy man for a very long, long time.

But even on that he has the last paradoxical word. Said Mr Shaw: 'A lifetime of happiness? No man could bear it: it would be hell on earth.'

My Uncle Ezekiel

October 25,1963

Uncle Ezekiel was an Aberdonian and, in all Caledonia, stern and wild, there is no fiercer or more canny strain.

Sugar on porridge to Uncle Ezekiel – he had never heard of the barbarous custom – would have been like serving a haggis with ice cream, candy floss and maraschino cherries.

When, long ago, the sun went down in the summer evenings in Northern Scotland, where it is still twilight at midnight, my Uncle Ezekiel, who was a farmer and knew all about 'hewin' neeps' — hoeing turnips to you damned Sassenachs – he would take up the great hairy cluster of skin and tubes known as the bagpipes.

He would then march up and down in front of his ancient farmhouse near Old Meldrum playing for his own delectation and the lesser delectation of all in the 'cotterhoose' (no translation this time) and every living creature within a range of five miles.

No shadow of doubt ever crossed his rugged mind that to be born south of the Tay was to be effeminate, weak, fickle and wrong.

He drank Scotch whisky on a heroic scale and privileged visitors – whom he regarded as transient friends unless he had known them for twenty years – would be invited to come down and see his cellar.

It was full of empty whisky bottles, thousands of them. When the astonished visitor had seen one of the greatest collections of empties of all time he would turn upon them and cry with pride and joy:

'Wullie!' — or Ian or Donald or whatever the name was – 'I hae drank them aaah!'

In the middle of a dark coniferous wood, he had an old hansom cab – minus the wheels.

Here Uncle Ezekiel read *The Financial Times* and worked out his next investment move. He played the market like the wisest fisherman who ever drew a salmon out of the River Spey and, in the silence of the forest, he grew rich.

He did not actually hate the English, but he certainly despised them.

And he loved porridge with a love that men other than my Uncle Ezekiel reserved for graceful sultry women and for deep brooding wine.

For some strange reason he always referred to porridge as 'them'. He would say: 'Where are they?' – meaning, 'Where is the porridge?'

The plurality I think referred to oats.

'They' would then be served to him in a great blue china bowl with a sprinkling of buttermilk and huge gritty chunks of salt which would lie like saline diamonds on the steaming beige plain of cooked oats.

I will not say that Uncle stood to attention as he ate 'them', but his irreverent, uncompromising heart and his sturdy guts were deeply concerned with the matter.

Uncle Ezekiel has gone these many long years to the thistle-bedecked Valhalla where all the sons of Wallace and Bruce go.

But had he heard that a Laird from the Lowlands, who had reached Number 10 Downing Street, took sugar with 'them', he would have reached for his claymore and come roaring among the Blue Bonnets almost o'er the Border into Ettrick and Teviotdale.

My great uncle Ezekiel once got powerfully drunk, and at an auction sale sold his farm, his farmhouse, his cattle and almost everything he possessed except the great hairy suit in which he stood.

The next morning, when he came to, a brother farmer asked him why he had sold his farm. He said: 'What farm? What sale?'

When the appalling news had battered its way through the hangover, he got into his gig, drove to see the purchaser, and begged him to let him have his farm back and a roof over his head.

The answer was No, No, a thousand times No.

Uncle Ezekiel cleared out, invested the money well and wisely, never did a stroke of work again, never lacked a drink, and died many, many years later a rich and happy man.

The Animal Kingdom

Cassandra loved cats. The fact is well-known. Most dogs he found intolerable: their appalling humility, he used to say, got him down. But he jumped to the defence of all helpless creatures maltreated by man: mice and monkeys in space capsules, and rabbits blinded by the unspellable, unspeakable plague of myxomatosis. There was also the affair of the Stuffed Moose…

In memoriam

November 12, 1957

DEATH

CURLY – In the 2nd week of November, 1957, slowly, painfully
and in the utter loneliness of outer space.

The bitch is dead.

This handful of fur and blood and guts born to the sound of a Pavlov bell has gone.

The Russians have called their little brute a 'Soviet Hero' and then in a sudden shriek of triumph and hate have screamed:

'The London friends of dogs have observed a one minute's silence. But this silence and mourning will not be swallowed by anyone: it will be lost amid the laughter of millions of people, amidst the jubilant voices which salute this great triumph of Soviet science.'

But the tears and the laughter over the death of Curly are separated only by a knife-edge. The guffaw is linked with the weeping; the chuckle is next to the sob.

The scientists, the research workers and the vivisectionists with their hypodermic needles, their anaesthetics, their scalpels, their syringes and their drugs may permit themselves a wintry grin at the global hullabaloo that has greeted the death of this pup. But should one of their own pet dogs die, some shaggy mongrel with a dark and friendly eye, they, too, feel the kick of grief right under the heart.

But in all the slush and the jeering and the sentiment and derision about a dead cur, there is something both terrible and horrible.

The animal was trained, by Purgatory knows what form of coldblooded devilment, to behave like an automaton and learned to live, not without a whimper I suspect, in crouched quietude locked in a harness of steel.

Every dog has its day and sometime before dawn on the morning of November the 3rd Curly had her hideous day. She was taken to her gigantic coffin – all 500 tons of it pointing in the breathless dawn to the sky – and to her celestial death.

There never was a tomb and a kennel like this – the most prodigious aerial torpedo in history, packed with fabulous precision machinery, with electronics, with explosives, with fuel, with pumps, with tele-meters and with Heaven and Hell knows what scientific sorcery brewed in the best brains of the world.

All that and Curly, too.

Charon was the Greek ferryman who rowed the souls of the dead across the River Styx. Curly crossed the Styx in an inferno of flame, of smoke, of steam and white hot gases. Within seconds her needle-nosed tomb ripped through the atmosphere and was away up into the limitless cold and airless void of outer space. The main rocket fell off as the face of earth receded like the ground floor seen from an ascending lift.

The second motor broke away not long after, and Curly – little Curly pierced with tubes for automatic feeding – was where no living creature had ever been before.

No gaol, no solitary cell plunged in endless darkness was ever like this. One small, beating heart, two luminous eyes, a plump little body and four paws were buried alive in the Heavens. Stars all around. A pale moon and a shroud of empty, silent nothingness.

God knows what went on in that small and simple brain of Curly's. Man's best friend – the only animal that has real affection for humanity – was the trembling explorer of the Cosmos within a spinning metal grave travelling at prodigious speed round the earth.

Not with a biscuit or a pat at the end of her journey, but Death, vertiginous death, as her only reward.

When I was very small I was brought up on a hymn that afterwards I came to regard as banal, but at the time it used to comfort and cheer me when I knew no better. I felt that God's great arm was round me. The words were:

All things bright and beautiful,
All creatures great and small,
All things wise and wonderful
The Lord God made them all.

But even now, when I know better, the sound of little children singing this gives me a nudge in the heart and a strained odd feeling in the throat.

I think I'll put Curly back into the department of all creatures great and small.

The cats of Van

December 21, 1964

My cat is the finest cat in Bucks south of a line drawn from Ludgershall to Wendover. There are rival claims, including what I think is a suspect story about a race of super cats, living around Winslow in North Bucks, who are reported to have sent out a challenge to beat the living daylights out of all the cats in South Bucks. Including mine. We shall see.

My cat can purr in his sleep, leap around the tree tops, pinch the best chair and eat more boiled fish or raw meat than any other living creature. He is unsurpassable.

I am prepared to boast endlessly about him but I admit I was slowed in my tracks by some new intelligence about super cats that has just reached me from East Turkey of all places.

I heard rumours about these cats some time ago but information was scarce for the simple reason that their native territory is at a place called Van which is near the Iraq border, where the Turks are notoriously edgy about investigations into their military frontiers or the cats who live near these frontiers.

Now, Miss Laura Lushington has returned from that faraway place with disturbing news for those who brag interminably about their cats as I do.

The Van cats are super cats and they love to swim lazily in the warm waters of Lake Van. One Van cat, according to Miss Lushington, cured itself of stomach catarrh by sitting in a bath of warm water. They purr almost continuously, have long white silky coats, beautiful auburn markings and ginger rings on their tails. Their eyes are a lovely amber colour and their skin is coloured a shell-pink.

These qualities are a formidable challenge to the gifted cats of South Bucks, but there is more to come. The Van cats are enormously affectionate and intelligent.

Moreover they claim the patronage of Mohammed himself. When a Van cat was found sitting on the corner of his cloak, the Prophet cut the corner off rather than disturb the cat.

NOTE: An emergency meeting of the South Bucks Cats-Are-The-Finest-Cats-In-The-World Association will be held tonight.

January 5, 1966

Having been confined to one bedroom for a month and been pretty stationary at that, and after having read all the papers, many of the magazines and barrow-loads of books, one gets a little weary of the printed word.

So the mind, whirling round like a caged rat on a treadle wheel, starts to spin and try to solve the insoluble.

I now know the secret of perpetual motion which defied Wilars de Honecort, John Wilkinson, Bishop of Chester (1614-1672), Johann Bessler, Sir William Congreve, Henry Dircks, and countless other experimenters.

I shall be marketing the machine very soon. I can also square the circle and other trifles.

But I have solved a much more interesting problem while in the dark watches of the hospital night.

For years – nine in fact – I have been trying to weigh my splendid ginger cat, Bulgy, on the bathroom scales. But could I do it? No sir. No sooner had I got the front legs on the platform then the back leg whipped off. I tried to force Bulgy down but the vertical pressure gave the wrong reading.

I tried holding him up like an undignified puss-in-boots and he fought like mad. I tried placing tempting fishy morsels on the scale hoping that he would climb aboard. No dice.

Then recently lying in my lonely bed in the small hours when good things of day begin to droop and drowse while night's black agents to their preys do rouse (all royalties to W Shakespeare), the solution flashed upon the inward eye which is the bliss of solitude (all royalties to W Wordsworth).

Had I been in a bath and mobile. I would, like Archimedes, have leapt out yelling 'Eureka!'

The moment I arrived home I grabbed Bulgy and leapt on to the bathroom scales.

Reading: 14 stones 2 pounds.

I let him go. I then remained on the scales. Reading 13 stones exactly.

Net weight of the finest cat in the world. 16 pounds.

Eureka!

Little dead duck

March 3, 1961

The flags are flying at half-mast and the English are at their very best over the affair.

Indignant. Hurt. Angry. Preposterous.

What happened was this.

In December, 1957, an odd sort of duck was spotted paddling around at Sutton Courtenay, near Oxford. The bird-watchers (usually the kindest of men, although not always, as you shall hear) were delighted.

Their pleasure increased when a mild argument broke out as to whether the duck was a Lesser Scaup from North America – which, as everybody knows, is a greenish black and white craft with nice beady amber eyes – or a Pochard.

A Pochard, of course, is a handsome duck which favours Holland for its home, has a chestnut-red head, a black hull with greyish white below the Plimsoll mark and a touch of pale blue on the beak.

Some said 'Lesser Scaup!' Others retorted 'Pochard!'

What was a discussion became a dispute. What was a dispute came near to being a quarrel.

Meantime, little ducky Scaup (alias Pochard) paddled on his pond.

For three years he mucked about (ducks, like water rats, love mucking about). He was quite happy, not knowing that the little yellow eye of the bird men was fixed upon him.

Then a sinister thing happened. I shall now quote *British Birds:*

'British ornithologists became divided on the matter, many believing that it was a Lesser Scaup, but some considering that it was probably a hybrid.'

The scene darkens:

'As opinions differed so widely, it was eventually decided to collect it.'

Collect it?

For 'collect' read shoot.

'It was shot,' says *British Birds,* on March 3, 1960, under a licence issued to Dr I C T Nisbet by the Nature Conservancy.

The inquest on dead Ducky, no longer ruffling his feathers in the sunlight and no longer standing on his head in a pond, recorded that he was not a Lesser Scaup and that he was the result of a love affair between a Tufted Duck *(Aythya fuligula,* as you know) and a Pochard.

His death solved the problem. The birdmen were satisfied. And Ducky swam in the gravel pit no more.

I have to report that the English are deeply upset. Massacres occur in the Congo, the fear of nuclear extinction wraps its ugly cloak around us, but we are in a temper about a dead duck.

Rightly so.

And if other nations are amazed, puzzled and deeply suspicious that we are a nation of hypocrites – to hell with them.

The gilded sardine

July 18, 1952

All my life I have been dominated.

I am very dominatable.

Anybody can shove me around. Almost everybody does.

It began with schoolmasters, continued through the sporting bossiness of cricket team captains and went on to the more sombre softening-up processes used by masterful employers.

Right now I am dominated by a goldfish called Lucky.

Lucky is two inches long. He cost a tanner and all the skill and resource needed on a fair-ground to toss a ping-pong ball into a jam jar a yard distant.

Lucky got me on edge right away. First of all, I did not want a goldfish. But have you ever seen anybody refuse a goldfish at a fair?

It would take a braver man than I am to withstand the cold contempt of the onlookers at the spectacle of a public goldfish refuser.

So I took him.

I lost no time on Lucky and I started worrying about him immediately.

First of all the jar was so obviously too small. How would I like to be locked up in a pint of water? I wouldn't. How would I like to be left naked in an appalling little glass globe with not even a bit of carpet to creep under? How would I like to be left alone in a wet translucent world where you can never draw the curtains?

I was getting sick with anxiety when I noticed Lucky looking at me with a calm submarine gaze that fairly fizzled with sheer force of character.

I was being dominated again.

Lucky slowly came right up to the edge of the glass and gave a golden sneer. Did I know what goldfish fed on? I didn't.

Did I know whether goldfish preferred tap water or rain water?

Did Lucky like to be covered up with a cloth over his bowl at night on the canary cage principle?

Lucky waved a tiny fin in sheer derision.

I can't get him out of my mind. He swims around my brain in circles of endless reproach. Perhaps the water in the bowl is too cold? Or too warm? But how do I know? Does a cold goldfish shiver? Does a hot goldfish sweat?

Lucky just keeps mum.

There's not room for us both in the same house.

Either this gilded sardine goes – or I go. But where CAN he go? The Thames is near but I cannot face up to the thought of little Lucky (what heartless demon christened him thus in a moment of callous wit?) wandering alone through the watery wastes of uncharted weeds, little Lucky unsuspectingly drifting towards the boiling hell of Marlow Lock. Then there's a pond I know of where lies a giant carp – a tough old brute, who sat out one of those terrible winters we had some years ago when the water froze entirely and forced the carp right down into the mud on the bottom. He survived.

But would this rough old tough like little Lucky? – I mean in a kindly way.

Lucky's latest trick is to grin through the glass. Ever been grinned at by a reproachful goldfish, dear reader? Or aren't you dominated that easily?

July 24, 1952

I could have given Lucky a score of homes and I got enough free goldfish advice to last me until fishes fly and forests walk.

Yesterday morning I decanted Lucky into a jam jar, gave him some breakfast, screwed down a metal cap with holes pierced in it and brought him up to London. He sat on my desk awhile waving a derisive fin and filing me with that tiny submarine sneer of his.

But events bigger than Lucky's impudence were afoot.

The Isle of Wight was reaching out its compassionate arm (in the person of a Miss Tahourdin) and a message was received that if Lucky cared to take the 4.45 train from Waterloo to Portsmouth Harbour he would be met personally.

Further signals were exchanged. (Had Lucky been fed? – Yes. Was he properly jam-jarred? – Yes.) And so we rushed him in a taxi down to Waterloo. The Railway Executive took charge for 1s. 8d. and Lucky, in his pint-sized world, roared out over the lines towards Pompey.

Four hours later from Ryde came the anxiously-awaited telegram: LUCKY SAFELY HERE, VERY SPRIGHTLY AND HAPPY – TAHOURDIN.

Nobody should try to understand the British.

In a world that is half-starving. In a world that is smouldering with war. In a world of napalm bombs and nuclear fission and guided missiles, and every exquisite and fabulously costly device for the infliction of unbearable pain and endless destruction, some of us are

daft enough to worry ourselves sick about a couple of inches of golden sardine.

Excuse me, friends, while I now perform a couple of cartwheels round the picture rail – just to prove that any resemblance to logic and reason that we may show is surely co-incidental.

Brer Rabbit (deceased)

July 20, 1954

I suppose rabbits never did anything worse than knock the green stuff for six. Which they did and do – and in a big way.

But these cuddly, twitchy-nosed, lettuce eaters have raised the ire of peace-loving mankind (what ho! the Japanese fishermen in the Pacific with their harmless hair falling out because of radio-active dust dropping from the H-bomb skies above).

We have attacked these furry salad killers with everything we've got.

Including that unpronounceable, unspellable, unspeakable disease myxomatosis.

This revolting plague which we have spread all over the land has now been reported in half of the fifty-two counties of England and Wales. Thousands of dead and dying rabbits can now be seen in the infected areas. Brer Rabbit himself has been seen beating his lightweight brains out on the side of a barn as he longs to die and escape from this horrible torment.

I wonder what the rabbits think (hell, they don't think but they do know how to feel) in the thudding darkness of the burrows as the descendants of St Francis of Assisi seek them out with this deliberate, disgusting plague.

Silently, softly, stealthily and in a storm of mute pain these creatures are dying by their tens of thousands. Not one of them has had the sense to have a voluble, talkative, publicity-seeking MP.

Brer Rabbit can't write, can't spell and hasn't even written to *The Times*! And no protest meeting has taken place in Trafalgar Square because rabbits are not allowed in Trafalgar Square – by Order of the Westminster City Council.

Poachers who wouldn't think twice about setting wire snares and steel traps are repelled and revolted by this deliberately introduced piece of wicked beastliness.

Brer Rabbit in the spring of 1955 is not the flashing cotton-tail scooting up the mossy bank.

He is something pitiful and obscene to be shovelled up and burnt in heaps.

February 6,1960

I have a disturbing theory that I have held ever since the callous humans inflicted the horrors of myxomatosis on rabbits.

AND THAT IS THAT THE RABBITS WOULD ULTIMATELY TAKE THEIR REVENGE.

The deadly strain of myxomatosis would evolve and develop into that strange and terrible swelling and magnifying disease known as giganticism.

And then what would happen?

I shall tell you.

The time is just before dawn – the hour when executioners test their ropes for the last time; when dawn-attacks are put in on bullet-sprayed hillsides; when the secret police go about their grisly business.

The scene is a lonely farmer's house on the edge of a wind-swept moor.

The farmer has had a bad night from drinking too much sour beer at the local and having had his ears made to ring by a memorable verbal chastisement from his vinegary-tongued wife.

Four years ago he myxomatosed every rabbit within five square miles.

Three thunderous knocks on his door awaken him in near terror as a thin and pallid light puts the faint whiteness of a cadaver on the eastern skies.

He stumbles out of bed, stubs his toe, lights the oil lantern and sleepily unbolts the kitchen door.

There, outside, larger than carthorses, are three enormous rabbits.

Their ears are roof-high.

Their legs are as thick as the boles of your oaks.

Their eyes are the size of soup plates, and their whiskers are the length and the thickness of oars.

First Rabbit: 'Shut up you! Grab a bag. Kick your missus in the face and come with us.'

Farmer: 'But... my false teeth!'

Second Rabbit: 'You'll not need them where WE are going.'

Farmer: 'I never done you no wrong.'

Third Rabbit: 'Gassing was merciful – Belsen by comparison with kindness itself. Snares and gins with their searing pain were almost merciful. But myxomatosis, the almost endless undying death, was worst of all. To the burrows. On your way, Farmer. On your way!'

Exeunt all.

Sound of gigantic rabbits' feet. Ker-lump. Ker-lump. Ker-lump.

Down with Spaniels

July 26,1957

At precisely eleven minutes past eight yesterday morning I reluctantly saved the life of a pudgy, luminous-eyed spaniel that ran out into the road in front of my motor car. The brute, quivering with lust and cordiality, dashed before me and regardless of shrieking brakes, blasting horns and some sturdy oaths from your correspondent, waddled on towards another lascivious looking hound on the other side of the road.

Normally I am very hostile to most dogs because of their cream-puff characters. But I have murderous intentions to all spaniels for reasons I shall now disclose.

If the dog, whose worthless life I saved yesterday happens to read the following, it may teach him to have a care next time.

About sixteen years ago I was at a military training establishment known as an Officer Cadet Training Unit where serious-minded men were trying to teach me the Black Art of Ballistics – a very complicated task in view of the fact that I cannot understand arithmetic, wouldn't be seen dead with a geometrician and believe that algebra and trigonometry should be stamped out – like drug-taking.

My instructors were frankly puzzled by my density. They were used to ordinary stupidity but I had a brand of impenetrable obtuseness that almost frightened them. They would talk about barometric pressures, quadrant elevations and cosines until my eyes were glazed, my breathing stertorous and my pulse very feeble.

'My God,' said one of them in anguish to me. 'Won't the penny *ever* drop?'

All this was bad enough, but horror piled on horror when, like the other inmates, I was called upon to give short public lectures on some abstruse calculations of which I knew exactly nothing. My comrades, kindly men, were fascinated to see how a man who couldn't understand even the rudiments of ballistics could possibly give a dissertation on the complex internal workings of a predictor.

I myself was so appalled at the prospects of these hideous occasions that I even developed a morbid curiosity to see what kind of flap-doodle I would hatch out. I wondered when the Fount of Bosh would run dry. We had been told to make sure that the class understood what we were saying and that we must *never* lose touch with them. The repeated instruction to lecturers was: 'Carry your listeners with you at all costs, and stop frequently to ask them whether they have Any Questions.'

I soon had a few accomplices in the audience who were quite prepared to work with me and planted idiotically simple questions and kept complaining that they could not see the blackboard. I then thoroughly berated them for their stupidity and did valuable time-wasting movements with the easel that drained the agonizing minutes away. We rejoiced over a beer afterwards.

But then I noticed that I was being selected more and more for these mental holocausts and that the Chief Instructor of the OCTU himself appeared whenever I was going to beat the air with my prodigious fatuities.

Now this man, a quiet, rather melancholy-looking major, possessed a dog. A spaniel. A sloppy, lop-eared, maudlin brute of a dog. Whenever I was due to be crucified this wretch would precede his master by at least a minute and would come waddling into the lecture hall and sit down leering at me.

He used to wag his ridiculous tail and say quite plainly: 'Now for some fun! Master won't be long. Boy, do you crease me!'

Then as I struggled into my preposterous Golgotha the revolting canine would smile and grin and jeer.

He would look up at his owner and say: 'This is the stuff! He's better than ever today.'

The major at the end of the performance never said anything, never smiled but just walked sadly away. The spaniel did all the laughing and I grew to hate that dog with a fire of fury that is still white hot within me and I trust will never grow cold.

Years afterwards I met the Chief Instructor in Rome in circumstances where rank meant nothing. He was still looking a little sad and thoughtful and I asked him if he ever remembered me on The Subject of Ballistics?

He said: 'Indeed I do. It was an unforgettable performance. I still relish and cherish the memory.'

I asked him if he had made a point of coming specially to hear me. He replied that he certainly did and that he wouldn't have missed it for worlds.

'What particularly,' I said, 'appealed to you, Major, about my efforts?'

'They were without doubt,' he replied, 'the most concentrated pieces of piffle and meaningless gibberish I ever heard in my life. An absolutely outstanding performance never achieved before or equalled since.'

'Thank you. And the dog is quite well?'

'Splendid.'

'Oh, I am so glad. Please remember me to him, will you?'

Can a duck swim?

May 24, 1949

Just before dawn on the morning of April 26, a two and a half ounce Khaki Campbell duck, later christened Hector, broke his shell and struggled bedraggled and astonished into a glowering world.

The egg that was Hector was one of twelve. But disaster and tragedy were at hand.

No fond beak ever tucked Hector in his shell beneath a feathered breast – only the unmotherly smell of a paraffin lamp in a home-made incubator.

The whole dozen eggs were fertile, but five ducklings never escaped their shells.

They perished miserably, starved to death trying to peck their way out from the little cradles that were so soon to become their graves.

Six finally struggled out – plus Hector.

A day later three died suddenly, without so much as a quack.

Twenty-four hours afterwards two more names were added to the Khaki Campbell Roll of Honour. And on the third day, the toughest, the boldest and the hungriest curled up his webbed feet and died.

There remained but one. Hector.

Hector was exactly one month old at 5 a.m. this morning.

I have, over these anxious four weeks, studied his personality.

It is very ducky. He is cheerful without being boisterous. Confident without being aggressive.

But he is horribly pigeon-toed and, with webbed feet, that spells trouble. Hector falls over himself so often that he has taken to sitting down and looking over his shoulder to find out who tripped him up.

Dry land presented such a problem to him that his worried owners decided to launch him on the liquid stuff.

We filled up the tin bath. Three pailfuls of cold and one kettleful of hot. A nice, tepid, *thoughtful* mixture highly suited to any bird that has recently been heavily bereaved. Hector – three inches high if he is an inch – was placed on the face of the waters. Instantly he grounded.

Alarm signals on the shore clanged out. The dinky duck was standing on tip toes with his neck and head just clear. Rescue parties whipped him out.

The gnawing fear grew that Hector was non-floatable – that he might sink like a stone. Bring in more water. Bucketfuls of it this time.

Hold that duck! He was dripping miserably and fluttering his tiny wings.

Put him in again. Take depth soundings! Ware shoals! Watch that Plimsoll Mark! *He floats!*

More than that he *swims* \

The tiny feet are beating a feverish paddle. A bow wave sets up round the little breast and Hector is off. Buoyant and riding pretty!

Quacking with amazement and utter delight!

Ahoy there, Hector!

No moose is good moose

August 21, 1964

On Sunday, May 17, 1964 (the date is seared on my soul), I was staying with Colonel Howard McClachy of the United States Air Force at his home at Plattsburg, upper New York State.

He said to me: ‘You and I for many years have had a beautiful friendship. Tomorrow you depart for London. A few days later I shall have to leave Plattsburg for Clark Air Force Base, in Manila. Who knows when we shall meet again?’

‘Who, indeed, Mac?’

‘I have therefore decided to mark the mutual respect that we hold for each other and the sad moment of our separation by giving you a small present.

'Just a little thing. A trifle.

'You might call it a tiny bauble but, whenever you gaze upon it, it is my hope that you may say: "Good old Mac!" – in your typically British way. Kindly follow me.'

Deeply moved by this manifestation of Anglo-American friendship, I said, in my typically British way: 'Mac, I think you are a jolly good sport. Absolutely ripping.'

I walked after the Colonel. He took me to his garage. He swung open the doors, and there, with an expressive sweep of his arms he pointed to what appeared at first sight to be an elephant's head growing fur – or a mammoth.

'For you,' he said. 'For you, my boy. Imagine it at Cassandra Towers. The Great American Moose in your English Baronial Hall. A United States tribute from our great dark American forests to the England of Lord Winston Churchill.

'And, d'ya know sumpin' bud? The height of that Moose at the shoulders was over six feet. Moreover, in the breeding season the male Moose, in his fury and passion for the female Moosies, fights with such ferocity with those great antlers of his that he inflicts fatal wounds on any rival Moose that might try to snitch a Moosie from the Big Feller.'

A silence fell.

Chilling. Oppressive. Sinister.

Deep.

I turned to the Colonel and said: 'Mac, I think I shall kill you.

'I may strangle you slowly with my bare hands right here and now in your garage in Plattsburg. The alternative is to grow antlers and then inflict such wounds upon you as will not kill you immediately, but will lead you to a lingering gangrenous death – say in about three months' time!'

'You're kidding!'

'If you burden me with that appalling brute I will land Redcoats on the Potomac. I will be right there back in Chesapeake Bay. I will burn the White House again. And I will personally have you shot in Baltimore.'

The Colonel stared at me with grief, with wonderment, with pain and with profound emotion.

He said: 'Guess the deal's off buster. You win.'

On Monday, August 17, 1964 (the second date is seared on my soul), an American voice on the telephone to me at my home said: 'We have a little item for you, Sir. May we have the pleasure of facilitating this delivery?' (Americans talk like this.)

'And what is the item pray?'

'A Moose. Or what we in Strategic Air Command call the nose section of the fuselage of a vurry large Elk. We'll be vurry, vurry glad to provide transportation.'

'You mean that this Moose is going to be delivered to me at my home?'

'We figure it out that way, Sir. This little item was flown to our base at Brize Norton and directed to be forwarded to you with the compliments of Colonel McClachy of Clark AFB., Manila.'

I think he heard me sob, but he went on: 'Thank you, Sir. We'll be glad to have you have this little item tomorrow morning.'

A blue American Air Force van arrived in our village and I was waiting for him because we don't often get dead Moose where I live. A very pleasant chap got out of the truck and said calmly: 'Got something for you, Sir.'

He was British (a ripping fellow) and when he told me the fell news he announced it with the serenity of a head waiter saying: 'I can recommend the chocolate mousse, Sir.'

That was fine but as we lifted the great hairy head with the lustrous beady eye out of the truck, I thought that this particular decapitation wasn't made of chocolate.

The driver, as we were staggering with Colonel McClachy's affectionate bauble, said: 'Hey! I've seen you before. Seen your picture before. Aren't you...?

Moose-laden as I was, I said nothing. There are times for silence. But I thought that in great disasters as this there might have been even a worse fate. For instance, more than one Moose. Maybe two Mooses – or is it Mice that you call these brutes when they come in marching two by two?

But what can you do with Moose, Mooses or Mice? Where do you put them? What *do* you feed them on?

Sneering villagers, having seen this revolting trophy now crowding out my garage, have already offered to bring in bales of hay – or whatever it is that Moose, Mooses, or Mice eat.

The United States Air Force driver, as he was going, returned to his theme. He said: 'Look, I think I know who you are. Picture in the paper, eh? Aren't you Caas... Cassa...?'

I said, sick at heart and Moose-laden:

'Yes, you've got me. I am Cass... Cassa... Cassanova of the *Daily Sketch.'*

He triumphed: 'Course you are! Got you now, Sir!'

A full day.

No Moose is good Moose.

The Joke Factory

Cass collected puns – excruciating puns.
To be really good, they had to be really bad.
In the end he was forced to invent a sweatshop
for bad jokes sited somewhere in
Penge, SE20. From this Joke Factory
poured a chain of unspeakable *bon mots* - or
rather *mauvais mots* - that found a place in
the column.

Ah, sweet mystery of life

February 6, 1957

Forward into the abyss of unspeakable puns! Look at the ghastly clockwork of this one. It cannot be true, but how I love to linger over the toiling, creaking care of the man who made it up. He went through with it to the bitter end.

Here goes: A nephew of Mr Syngman Rhee – the old gentleman of Korea – emigrated to the United States and got himself a job on *Life* Magazine. He went on a mighty spree one day in New York and vanished.

Life, worried about the welfare of their interesting employee, sent out a search party and sure enough the stray lamb was found dazed but happy in one of the innumerable taverns that used to make Third Avenue the finest street in Manhattan.

The chief rescuer gave a great cry of triumph and shouted: 'Ah, sweet Mr Rhee of *Life*! At last I've found you!'

Thermal barrier

December 7, 1960

The scene is a theatrical casting agency. The boss is a penny-pinching tyrant by nature. He cannot bear even the smallest extravagance and is enraged to see that his assistant has booked by trunk telephone an act by a pair of Persian acrobats that could easily have been arranged at the cost of a threepenny stamp on an envelope.

He bawls out his employee, demanding to know why he has wasted so much money on a long-distance call.

Comes the unforgivable reply:

'I was only trying to bill two Kurds with one phone.'

The black art

January 5, 1961

The Black Art of fishing for the ultimate excruciating pun is still dredging deeper into the abyss to catch new horrors that live in eternal darkness. This is what we fished up yesterday. Get below decks. Close all hatches. Shut the watertight doors. Submerge.

The proprietor of a small soup canteen employed two counter hands to dish out soup and bread.

One wielded the ladle. The other cut up the bread with a small knife.

It was soon apparent that the chap dishing out the bread was only a quarter as quick as the soup server. The proprietor then had an idea to speed things up. He said: 'Why not cut four loaves at a time? – and better get hold of a much bigger knife while you are about it.'

The assistant then went into the kitchen and returned with a large butcher's cleaver. Said the boss: 'What the devil have you got there?'

'Just the thing for the job,' replied the breadman. 'Haven't you heard of a four-loaf cleaver ?'

A Penge Special

February 26, 1962

Red-eyed am I this morning. And if you think that is a disgraceful style of sentence, you are dead right.

But then you haven't been up all night working at The Joke Factory, Penge, SE20. There is something about Penge that seems to suit a Joke Factory specializing in hideous puns.

Last night we managed to build a real stinker.

It is a particularly offensive specimen, but it has the essential characteristic of being laboriously contrived. You can see the rotten laths in the plaster.

Stand by. We're off.

There is a drink called a Daiquiri – pronounced 'Dackery'.

It is made with rum, lemon squash and angostura bitters and is very popular in the United States.

A certain doctor in Savannah (note the geographical touch that has absolutely nothing to do with the story) always used to frequent the same bar where he always had the same drink; a Daiquiri served with a peanut in it.

One day the barman had run out of peanuts and put a hickory nut instead into the drink.

'Hey, barkeep,' said the doctor, 'there's something different about this Daiquiri.'

Said the barkeeper: 'Sure is. That's a Hickory Daiquiri, Doc.'

Eggs and baskets

January 11, 1962

There was a bullfight in Bilbao in the Basque Province of Spain, and all the stands were packed with spectators. One of the stands, over-burdened with the weight, began to collapse and the spectators ran for it. There was only one flight of steps that led from the seats to the back of the stadium.

Comment: 'Don't put all your Basques in one exit.'

I have just heard what you might call the Mark Two version of this story. Like all good puns - and by good, I mean absolutely terrible – it has been conceived with gigantic toil and unlimited sweat.

The scene shifts from Northern Spain to Canada. In a town not far from Toronto (experts will note the careful ploy of fake verisimilitude), a local councillor, who served on a community for charity known as 'The Community Chest', was urging his colleagues not to make several separate appeals to the public for their generosity.

He said that it was a mistake to appeal independently for old folks, the sick, the blind and the sore distressed. There should be one universal call.

Comment: 'We are putting all our begs in one ask-it.'

Drum, flag and stick

December 14, 1962

The Polish Embassy were having a party on their National Day of rejoicing and hurriedly had to hire a pianist to play some suitable music – stuff by Chopin, with maybe a nostalgic piece by Paderewski just for the old folk in memory of days gone by.

When the pianist, in tails and white tie, sat down at the piano, he gave them everything from *St Louis Blues* to *The Young Ones*. But no *Warsaw Concerto.*

When they asked him why, he said: 'That's the way my musical cookies crumble.'

In deep anger, the Poles threw their hired performer out on to the street.

He hit the pavement screaming and cursing. A passer-by picked him up and asked why he was so incensed and so abusive at leaving the Embassy on his backside. He replied:

'Forgive me – but forty square Poles do make one rude.'

Punishment

August 6, 1965

My friend Dick Richards sends me a really punitive example of the triple-decker pun.

This is very advanced technique indeed and needs quite a lot of laborious scene-setting and scaffolding to hold it together. However, here goes.

It is the old situation where a man is trying to tell a funny story to an audience who are resistant to his japes and jests.

However, he plods on until he is brusquely told that they have heard it all before and it is a chestnut with whiskers. He is abashed and furious and one of his listeners tries to console him by saying:

'Never mind old man. A clear case of the tale dogging the wag.'

Pythagoras

May 28,1962

Three Red Indian squaws slept on three different kinds of skins.
The first squaw slept on elk skin.
The second squaw slept on buffalo skin.
The third squaw slept on hippopotamus skin.
Later they all had children.
The first squaw had a daughter.
The second squaw had a son.
The third squaw had twins.
Moral: The squaw on the hippopotamus is equal to the sum of the squaws on the other two hides.

The Good Food and Wine Guide

There are people who swear Cassandra's best columns were about eating and drinking: they could be right. As a chef he was a good engineer. He 'constructed' – not cooked, mark you – some formidable meals, including a 14-day soup and a 48-egg omelette (Pistoia, Italy, 1944) about which he never ceased to boast.

How I like my cabbage

June 30, 1950

O listen to the words:
'BOILED CABBAGE: Remove the coarse outer leaves of the cabbage and cut off the stalk. Either halve or quarter the cabbage and wash thoroughly in cold water. Drain thoroughly and put in a large saucepan with a plentiful amount of salted boiling water. When the water is again on the boil, allow from ten to fifteen minutes' fast boiling, according to size and freshness of the cabbage. Cabbage boiled for longer than this are apt to be flabby and flavourless.'

Flabby and flavourless!

The words are cripples – cripples bleeding to death. Letters hooked and handcuffed together – hamstrung and powerless, flabby and flavourless indeed! The phrase is a crawling compliment.

Boiled cabbage *a l'Anglaise* is something compared with which steamed coarse newsprint bought from bankrupt Finnish salvage dealers and heated over smoky oil stoves is an exquisite delicacy.

Boiled British cabbage is something lower than ex-Army blankets stolen by dispossessed Goanese doss-housekeepers who used them to cover busted-down henhouses in the slum district of Karachi, found them useless, threw them in anger into the Indus, where they were recovered by convicted beachcombers with grappling irons, who cut them in strips with shears and stewed them in sheep-dip before they were sold to dying beggars.

Boiled cabbage!

Yet if you will come into the garden this very night, not earlier than ten minutes past eleven, when the sun is yards deep below the rim of the world and the pale North-West has shut its eye, you will hear something to your advantage if you listen.

It is English cabbage a-growing.

The sound of Harbinger and Jersey Wakefield and Velocity (millionaires' yachts were never named as well as these) and Roundhead and Primo and Cotswold Queen and Daniel's Defiance and Enfield and Beefheart (what a title!) and Myatt's Early Offenham all rustling in the cool and gentle summer night.

Listen!

Hear them!

A rubbery, rustling noise.

The force of delectable greenness on the march.

The muscular sigh of strong leaves growing stronger. The *s-t-r-e-t-c-h* of white hearts bursting out from verdant folds.

Cool night rain may fall long before the June larks set up their intolerable twitter of compulsive happiness and, into the cool crevices of Beefheart (and his consort Cotswold Queen), the diamond splash of cold clear water will run in rivulets and gather in bright globules ready for the morning sun. Here is freshness – springy, moist and crisp.

Here is the young and eager garden life before it is murdered and done to unspeakable death – the corpse of which is called boiled cabbage.

There are thirty-one obvious ways of cooking a cabbage. Not boiling it – but cooking it.

May I play you a little culinary music? Just *one* excerpt?

'Quarter the cabbage, shred very finely and chop.'

Now sit down. Rest awhile and switch off that damned wireless.

Drop that horrible game of cards and come over here.

'Put the pieces into a thick saucepan – thick, thick, thick – and plop in four ounces of butter' (butter from non-psychotic cows, blast you) 'and simmer gently for thirty-four minutes.

'*Stir* constantly. Do not brown!'

What do you think this is – a gas chamber?

'When tender and of light golden colour' (the colour of corn five days after it has been cut from the side of dark earthed slopes facing south-south-east) 'add one ounce of chopped onion and a little chopped parsley' (planted by a lean but lovely virgin with green fingers) 'and simmer for nine minutes.

'Remove from the fire' (smokeless embers glowing a dull red of course and may Allah trample upon all gasometers) 'and when nearly cold add one tablespoonful of white breadcrumbs, two well beaten eggs' (bend down, you Buff Orpington Beauties) 'and season with salt and pepper. Put a clean cloth in a basin. Place the large outer cabbage leaves in it. Fill with cabbage mixture. Tie up. Boil for one hour in boiling water.'

Have a glass of cool dark beer and let the blighters get on with their wretched cards.

'Remove the cloth. Place the cabbage on a hot dish and serve with hot melted butter whilst reciting *The Scholar Gypsy* with compliments to Matthew Arnold.'

And don't forget the thick red rashers of Tewkesbury peach-fed ham and the infant new potatoes ruthlessly murdered in their little cradle-graves long before they were golf ball size.

See what I mean?

The singing soups of Spain

September 17, 1957

As a general principle, hot soup should be eaten on a cold winter's night with the rain beating hard up against the window-pane.

If you are of a malevolent disposition – and some of the greatest soup-eaters have been persons of considerable malice – the soup takes on an additional piquancy if you happen to know that one of your dearest enemies is stranded in the storm five miles from the nearest garage with a flat tyre and no jack.

Yet there are certain hot soups (as apart from the cold soups) that are so delicious that they can be eaten with delight in a heat wave. It is a true test of a soup for it to be able to survive bizarre climatic conditions or strange environments.

I once knew a man who had been to prison and he used to recall with pleasure the soup he had had while being detained at the Monarch's pleasure.

This rather astonished me and I told him that I always associated gaols and workhouses with skilly rather than soup. But he said this was not the case at the particular house of correction (he was a graduate of Peterhead, one of the sterner coolers) where he had served his sentence.

The soup was what he called a 'muscular soup'. Not delicate of flavour, but a strong masculine broth of onions and carrots, of great rough beans; a steaming composition that gained flavour and strength from bone-marrow. He said that he found it particularly appetising after a four-hour session of breaking granite in a snowstorm.

Yesterday in the blazing sunshine at Boulou, near the Pyrenees, I came across a magnificent soup of strong Spanish extraction which was as delightful in the open air under a madly blue sky as it would have been by a log fire at Hallowe'en.

It was properly served as all soups should be served, from a ladle out of a sizeable tureen.

I inquired of the genealogy and soon learned that I was in the presence of what I call a symphonic soup – a gastronomic tone-poem.

Basically it is, I suppose, a chicken consommé, for a young and tender chicken weighing no more than three pounds provides the central taste theme. The supporting contrapuntal motif is two pounds of breast of veal finely chopped.

The giblets, legs and carcass of the chicken, together with the veal, are then simmered in six pints of water for three and a half hours accompanied by two carrots, two turnips, two sticks of celery, two leeks and a teaspoonful of saffron.

Are you with me?

Now, when this exquisite stock is properly cooked, strain it and clarify it with the care that you would give to decanting an old wine. Next, you need the yolks of six fresh eggs and a cupful of the hot stock.

Now pour yourself out a nice glass of dry sherry, or if you prefer it some hock, and either sip it gently or knock it back according to your mood and training. You are doing well and deserve a drink. Good cooks never deprive themselves of something while practising the creative art of the *grande cuisine.*

Now where was I? Oh yes, in the egg section. Beat the eggs up in the hot stock and put them in a decorative mould and cook the mixture. When they are ready take them out of the mould and leave them to cool. Then cut up into small slices.

Now back to the old chicken – I mean the young chicken. You noticed that I said nothing about the wings and breast? The omission was part of the great design. You take the wings and breast and fry them in olive oil. After that remove the skin and the bones. Now add the prepared wings and breast together with the egg to the clear stock. Put in small squares of toast (about four slices) and reheat until almost boiling.

It is a truly princely soup, and is best eaten to the sound of distant castanets. It is substantial but not filling; intriguing but not impertinent; bold but not blatant. And the saffron provides a haunting theme; indescribable but inescapable.

I have dealt with a hot soup of memorable composition and now wish to blow cold (for refrigeration purposes only) upon an iced soup of pure Spanish descent.

It bears the magnificent title of *Sopa De Ajo Blanco Con Uvas.*

Just as excellent hot soup can survive and thrive in hot weather, so, too, I believe that cold soup could be eaten on a frosty night in late October – although as yet I have not tried it.

This particular *Sopa* is not for cowardly persons content with that Anglo-Saxon abomination known as Brown Windsor.

It is a soup with a flair, a cut and a dash.

Stand by for instructions and order yourself a couple of good seats at the bullfight.

Take thirty fresh almonds (you have to admit that this is a stylish start). Skin them, heat them slightly in the oven and grind them up small with a pestle and mortar.

Now muster the following ingredients: five cloves of garlic, a small cupful of toasted breadcrumbs, a pound of grapes from which the skins and the seeds have been removed, some salt, two tablespoonsful of olive oil, a tablespoonful of vinegar and a pint of water.

Mix the almonds and the breadcrumbs into a mortar together with the salt and garlic. Add the vinegar and the olive oil slowly and then put the whole compound into a large soup tureen with the water and the grapes. Throw in three cupsful of crushed ice and leave for ten minutes.

Serve only to intelligent people – preferably under the shade of a large mulberry tree.

The super soup

November 5, 1954

Abandoned temporarily by all my Loved Ones, and in full charge of the catering of an empty house, I have taken a decision that in its breadth of vision, its daring and in its stark courage is in the class of Wolfe storming the Heights of Quebec.

With one glittering, hissing swipe I have solved the problem of my cooking for the next week to come.

There shall be one mighty meal for breakfast, lunch, tea and supper – a super Soup. A gigantic cauldron of spectacular, steaming, bubbling goodness that in its savoury heart-warming integrity will sweep away all the fiddle-faddle about cups of tea, gritty toast, strips of flaccid fish, wet-eyed eggs, gluey jam, hostile soggy buns and all the rest of the innumerable courses of bits and pieces that are lowered down on to the cringing stomach every day.

This decision was taken because of what happened to some sausages the other night, and what Sir Winston Churchill's steward once told me about the maritime diet of that formidable Tinkerbell, when he was travelling on the *Queen Mary* to New York some thirty months ago.

First the sausages.

I was about to cook some chipolatas on Wednesday evening. The pan was heating, the sausages lay there ready to sizzle and in among them I hurled two large spoonfuls of lard from the refrigerator.

Only it wasn't lard.

It was frozen white blancmange.

I decided to give up and follow Churchill's magnificent example. I was told – and if it isn't true it should be – that the descendant of Marlborough liked to start a rough day on the North Atlantic in January with a great bowl of onion soup and a platter of underdone roast beef for breakfast.

So I decided to build my Soup to end all soups.

Rather I should say 'construct' my Soup, for like the Forth Bridge and H.M.S. *Ramillies,* it is an engineering feat rather than some light-hearted confection whipped up by a natty chef in a white hat.

Now the super Soup is the reverse of what that excellent cook, Mr Ambrose Heath, was describing on the radio on Wednesday morning. He was going into gentle delights about a soup made of watercress and practically nothing else. Mr Heath described this as 'a mysterious soup that was quite enchanting'.

My Soup is not mysterious – it is a magnificent, almost brutal, reality.

My Soup is not enchanting. It is overwhelming in the awe-inspiring way that the Niagara Falls are overwhelming. And like the Niagara Falls, it is made to last.

As the fires of coke-ovens burn bright through the years so my Soup never grows cold. It is chuckling and laughing to itself in the grey and thin light of dawn. Its great broad brow steams at high noon. And when the shadows fall it is 'Soup, Soup, beautiful Soup, Soooooooooup, of the evening Soooooooooup'.

What are the plans and specifications (recipe is too modest a word) of the super Soup?

First offer a prayer to Vulcan, Wodin or Thor. Then obtain a cauldron or saucepan large enough to boil a sheep in. Into it throw half a dozen pounds of steak – preferably tough, for this steak has to sit for a long time like a great, rubbery talisman on what we might call the sea-bed of the Soup. Now on top of it hurl (violence is the keynote) a cataract of onions, parsnips, leeks, carrots, turnips (snowball) and tomatoes.

Shower down a storm of split peas, dried peas and haricot beans soaked overnight.

Inform police.

Sling in pearl barley and a scattering of macaroni. Utter the Black Oath Number Six Six Six of the Great God Pan, and with a bloodcurdling (but not soup-curdling) scream toss in a handful of sultanas.

Top up with a few gallons of fresh water, bring to the boil and simmer non-stop for a week.

What is it like?

Stupendous. Superb. Colossal. Excellent. Very Good. Jolly Good. Good. Not Bad. All right.

Have some?

King Hal's Pie

December 2,1955

I am on this occasion the President of a Court-Martial on English Cooking and, as is customary on these military occasions, we show The Flag.

Without further ado, I now announce that the finding of the Court is 'Guilty on all counts'.

Sentence will be promulgated later.

In the opinion of the Court the offence is a compound one amounting to a conspiracy to defeat the true course of gastronomy. It involves consumers, cooks and provender in various degrees of complicity.

Without doubt the consumers – the public – are by far the most to blame.

The British do really WANT bad, coarse food, easily cooked.

They like egg on chips... Millions of young men, battle-trained on hasty NAAFI cooking, have come to worship this elementary dish in which the egg is usually burnt or seized up into a yellowy stodgy mess.

The chips are soused in cottonseed oil with the blackened portions carefully retained to preserve the much-appreciated flavour of rottenness. In seedy restaurants blowsy waitresses serve chemically indoctrinated baked beans force-landed on soggy toast – and the unholy customers love it...

In hotels disillusioned waiters, suffering from gastric-dyspepsia, administer thin watery soups declared free from nourishment of any sort under the washed out title of Clear Soup.

At Masonic meetings adipose manufacturers, consorting reluctantly with their revengeful wives on a Ladies' Night, begin with stale oysters and end with repellent Cabinet Puddings.

Whom do I blame?

NOT the dead food so savagely molested in its grave.

NOT the sad, dispirited waiters who act as pall-bearers to the average English funereal custom known as a meal.

NOT, indeed, the many brave hoteliers and restaurateurs who for years have served excellent meals to undiscerning apes and who in the end have abandoned all their enlightened and gallant hopes.

Reader, dear Reader, I blame YOU who, armed with a palate, a gullet and a belly, neither know, recognise nor appreciate what is good for you.

So I decided to stage a test case... to cook a meal so English, so yeoman, so sauced with the old kitchen flavours of farmhouses in the shires that it could be accounted as a supremely challenging English pot...

One that could be pitted against the mincing delicacies of Paris and the

Auvergne and the sly gastronomic winks and seductions of Boulogne and the Campagna of Rome.

I decided to build King Hal's Pie.

I constructed it from a recipe that was probably being worked out when the bowmen of England were wiping blood from their wounds at Agincourt.

Ho, varlets!

Bring on the minstrels – or, rather, bring on a brassy military band and the Dagenham Girl Pipers – for this is a robust strutting dish which should be assembled to the accompaniment of rough explosive sounds.

Bring me two pounds of self-raising flour, the best part of a pound of suet, mixed herbs and salt and pepper. Mix, mix, mix with two-thirds of a pint of cold water.

Knead and roll until you have a stiffish and slightly sullen paste.

Order the massed bands to play the overture to *Tannhauser* – preferably too loudly and slightly out of key.

Line the bowl with the paste, and mould with loving care a great circular moon of dough to place upon the top of it, like a stodgy cardinal's hat.

Into the gaping bowl *hurl* (not place – for this is an attack not a parade) two pounds of the best rump steak and a pound and a half of beef kidney, both cut small.

Toss in, with a debonair grin, the best part of a pound of field mushrooms, preferably stolen from muggy ground with horses near by.

Insert, while vespers are being said, fourteen (yes FOURTEEN) oysters shoulder to shoulder with seven hard-boiled eggs sliced into moon-shaped crescents.

Add a tablespoonful of parsley, a stick of chopped celery, a saucerful of diced onion, five whole peppers and half a dozen cloves.

Sprinkle with mace (which you, so long after the days of King Hal, may know as nutmeg) and lace with four small slivers of anchovy whose presence in the heart of this majestic Pie will whisper their salty entrancing tale.

Baptise with a dash of Worcester Sauce and then to the fierce clash of cymbals throw in, with a blessing and a curse, a goblet of claret.

If the heart of all this savoury goodness is still a little dry add more claret – and pour yourself a glinting glassful.

Crown with the floury halo of clinging paste.

Seal with a parchment and surmount this Everest of gastronomic joy with a taut cap of pudding-cloth.

Bring the water – preferably in a vast fish kettle – to the boil and then reduce to a slow, contented hiss and simmer.

Lower King Hal's Pie gently and with reverence into the quietly bubbling sea.

Simmer without let-up and with nary a pause for seven hours. Light the beacons on the hills... Set fire to the heather... Order the minstrels to play Handel's *Water Music*.

Then, with the verdure of young sprouts encircling the heated plate and in the company of dark thoughtful burgundy, come back with me to the days when the English could cook and the English knew what was good for them and their robust swelling paunches.

Scrap Cakes

June 24, 1964

I was talking to a few people yesterday when one of our party, a demure young housewife, casually remarked in the course of conversation: 'So I chucked the stewed steak and carrots at my husband and he caught it full in the puss.'

She said this in an offhand manner as if she were telling somebody that his shoe-lace was undone.

One of the party later took me aside and expressed astonishment that such a placid and decorous young lady should serve dinner the fast way to – or at – her loved one.

I told him that most married people threw food at each other and that it was almost as normal a process as washing up dishes.

It gave me an opportunity to expound to him my celebrated lecture, 'The Use of Foodstuffs as Matrimonial Projectiles' which, in its way, is as famous as the Reith Lectures on the BBC or the Chichele Lectures in Oxford.

The first thing to understand is the basic principle that women always do the bowling and the men do the catching – the hard way. The wives apparently find a deep sense of contentment and relaxation watching their husbands wash the gravy out of their ears.

The importance of aim cannot be over-emphasised and the nature of foodstuffs to be hurled must be studied. One young recently-married housewife told me:

'When I first started heaving the groceries at Harry I was an absolute beginner. The very first time I slung a plateful of spaghetti at him I missed. There was a delicious meat sauce with it and, of course, grated parmesan cheese. The stain on the wallpaper is still there.'

Other beginners tend to grab the wrong ammunition.

I heard of a case recently of a charming girl who lobbed a shepherd's pie (½lb. of cold mutton, 1lb. mashed potato, 1oz. of butter, 1 egg, ½pint of gravy or stock, 1 teaspoonful of parboiled and finely chopped onion, salt and pepper), which she had made in a tin pie-dish.

When she got really mad at her man, she gave him the express delivery which doesn't worry about a knife and fork, or the salt and pepper either, and is aimed at the head.

There were minor abrasions and a guarded reconciliation afterwards, but she told me privately she regretted expending the yolk of the egg which she had lovingly brushed over the crust before baking.

'Men as targets,' she said bitterly, 'aren't worth that expertise.'

It is this lack of discrimination when using a cooked meal travelling horizontally at about twenty feet per second to prove a point in the love-nest that disturbs me.

The whole tradition of slinging the grub or the gravy around demands care and sensitive selection. When Buster Keaton and Larry Semon and other exponents of food-pelting in the early days of the silent Hollywood films went to work, they chose the custard pie.

That made sense. The victim stood still – no tell-tale marks on the wallpaper. The target took what was coming to him with dignity.

Then, when he had received his faceful, and his eyes appeared indignantly like dark inkwells through the dripping confection, he, too, seized a custard pie and clapped it squarely, deliberately and unlovingly on the head or face of his also motionless adversary.

Those were the days.

The Marriage Guidance Council should take note of what I have to say.

Young matrons should get advice in the matter of cooked food used as projectiles to correct infuriating husbands. They should hurl handy-shaped meals and they should bung convenient foodstuffs that come easily to the fingers and have a reliable trajectory in flight.

Mrs Beeton foresaw all this in her new edition of *All About Cookery,* when she wisely included her recipe for 'Scrap Cakes' (page 480).

Scrap Cakes: 2lb of fat, 1lb. of flour, ¼lb. of moist sugar, ½lb. of currants, 1oz. of candied lemon peel and ground spices to taste.

From these ingredients you can make from thirty to forty full-sized Scrap Cakes, which should be enough for a two-minute bombardment.

They are convenient in size, fit the hand like a grenade and do not mark the carpet, the wall or the furniture, but, if thrown hard enough, can certainly mark the old man.

In my lecture I always make a plea – an impassioned plea, if I might say so – for more imagination about the choice of artillery food. Not so much of the old steak-pie. Why the eternal fish and chips? Cut out the baked beans. Use your sense of vision.

Take a tip from Mrs Beeton. There was a girl with the eye on the far horizons.

What could be better than to buzz a Jugged Wallaby at the old man?

It's all there (Page 576, same edition).

'Wash and dry the wallaby, and cut into neat joints. Fry in good fat until well browned...'

Welcome, darling hubby – and boy have you got the old high speed wallaby coming in swift and low!

Biggest little omelette in the world

Aix en Provence, September 7, 1957

As is well known and freely conceded all over Western Europe, I am one of the great open-air omeletteers of this century.

This comes, of course, from my internationally recognised feat of designing, organising, cooking and eating (with assistants) a forty-eight egg omelette at Pistoia in Italy in 1944. I have at times been challenged as to whether there were *really* forty-eight eggs used in this golden monster and the answer has been 'Yes' – although I have always been careful to explain that the eggs were on the smallish side as the Italian hens were taking a terrible beating at the time.

I built her (one falls naturally into using shipyard terms with omelettes this size) over a petrol fire in a frying-pan about the size of a dustbin lid and stuffed her with chopped onions – the only vegetable immediately available in those warlike times.

A speech of gratitude and thanks was given to me by the well-filled diners afterwards. I turned down a suggestion to erect a monument to mark the spot.

It was with this impressive recollection well to the fore in my mind that I ran up a tiny little nineteen egg omelette yesterday on a hilltop near St Tropez. She was a dainty thing stuffed with parmesan cheese, chopped black olives, sliced pimento and a few specks of Parma ham.

The accompaniment was, of course, the traditional yard of delicious French bread, the whole repast being washed down with a bottle of Pouilly Fuisse.

This splendid white wine costs only 270 francs here – or about 4s 8d at the present rate of exchange. You can pay five times as much in London.

The occasion was accounted a success.

Shepherd's pie day

April 2, 1959

Had an odd day yesterday.

It was dominated by shepherd's pie. It was permeated by shepherd's pie. It was steeped in shepherd's pie.

All Fools' Day, 1959, was indelibly stamped on my memory with the imprint of minced meat and onions and spuds.

It happened this way.

As a result of some slight domestic dislocation I am staying in my house alone – except for the cat. So I am cooking, serving and waiting upon myself. Good cook. Good waiter. Amusing and excellent guest.

Yesterday I decided to build myself a shepherd's pie. Now don't you make a shepherd's pie or cook a shepherd's pie any more than Sir John Fowler made the Forth Bridge or cooked the Forth Bridge.

He built it.

I rather fancy myself at cooking. I believe I have a natural flair for it. Not exactly pure genius but that essential flash that makes Pablo Casals and Augustus John and other great artists men apart from the rest of the world.

Now shepherd's pie, like many another homely dish, is not quite as simple as it seems. It can be thrown together. It can be played by ear.

But great cooks (I mention no names) prefer to construct it with the precision usually reserved for atomic power stations.

So it was with mine.

Sixteen ounces of high-quality minced beef gently cooked in a large frying-pan on top of which is placed a finely chopped onion. Potatoes boiled and then mashed to silken smoothness with a good hunk of butter and a couple of tablespoonfuls of milk. Pepper, salt, maybe just a hint of grated carrot and a sprig of chopped parsley all bound in good company with rich, dark-brown stock.

The delectable compound is finally sealed in its appetising tomb with the coverlet of bonny spuds. And then away into the piping hot oven (423 degrees at sea-level with normal humidity).

Having got the savoury symphony on its way, I then repaired to the local to do a little quiet boasting.

'Nothing to it old man – you just have to have the KNOW HOW.

'Matter of experience – and a touch of *Je Ne Sais Quoi* (French).

'Some people can do it. Some can't. Just like playing the violin.

'Some can. Some can't.'

Long pause accompanied by low-level gaze at the customers to impress them that you are the Fritz Kreisler of the cooking world.

'Then there's the timing. That's important. Many highly qualified shepherd's pie engineers believe in the stop-watch system. Split-second stuff. I respect them for it.

'But gradually after years of experience you can sense the timing of a shepherd's pie. You feel it in you. It is cooking through the blood. Your heart deep inside you whispers when the pie is done.'

Long pause.

'Thanks. I'll have another pint.'

I then sauntered home.

I opened the door and was instantly confronted with a white haze with visibility down to two yards.

The cat streaked by, hissing: 'Outa the way, you! Let them as can run! It's a gas attack! Either phosgene or mustard.'

I fought my way in. Acrid smoke swirled around. My eyes streamed. I made it to the kitchen and pulled open the oven door. A cloud of dense vapour burst out in a mushroom cloud. I cut the main switch and bolted for the garden convulsed with a coughing fit.

Then I made another foray back into the inferno and opened all the windows. You still couldn't see. The cut daffodils sagged out of their vase with the blanched faces of flowers which have been unexpectedly raped by a shepherd's pie. I retreated into the garden and watched the deadly mists billowing out of the doors and windows.

Two minutes later I struggled back to the oven and there she was.

A bubbling, black crater seething with what appeared to be boiling pitch with red-hot cinders sparkling on the charred crust. This was a culinary Vesuvius with only flying boulders and mud missing. The house stank with the ferocious fury of it. The bedrooms reeked of it. The curtains nursed the noisome smell of shepherd's pie *à la* red hot.

As I was saying before, it is only after years of experience that you can sense the timing of a shepherd's pie. Your heart, deep inside you, whispers when it is done.

Miss Cowie's Porridge

August **15, 1961**

Sir Compton Mackenzie has been recounting how he can remember that when he was very very young he sat on the knee of an old soldier who had fought at the Battle of Waterloo. Sir Compton is 78 and the Battle of Waterloo was fought 148 years ago in 1815.

The remarkable thing about his living link with the past is that Sir

Compton can remember things quite clearly from the age of *eight months* onwards.

There is a heroic note in these stirring memories of Boney and the Duke of Wellington and Blucher and The Scots Greys and the playing fields of Eton.

My first recollection – I was about the age of three – was not of bugles and musketry, the tradition of The Colours and the thin red line.

It was of Porridge.

Miss Cowie's Porridge – and burnt at that.

Mary Tudor said in 1558 that 'when I am dead and opened, you shall find Calais lying in my heart'.

When I am dead and opened you shall find Miss Cowie's Porridge lying in my heart.

'Porridge!' If ever a word describing a food had the sound of its meaning, it is 'Porridge!' – the ship and slur and costive slirrup of the uneatable.

Miss Cowie and her Porridge came into my life when my mother and my father were away. She was in charge of the house, and, submerged below the scum and skein and skin of her Porridge, I can recall the hateful remembrance of her eyes of unwinking blue, her lack-lustring hair like slag, and her mind, so fixed and firm.

The table was up to my neck.

The huge brimming plate with the oatmeal sludge and the swimming Zuider-Zee of milk lay endlessly before me.

Seeing my infantile nausea Miss Cowie said: 'The Porridge will be eaten!' Not mark you 'Please eat up your Porridge'.

Thirty years later, when in the Army, I came across Miss Cowie's same authoritative phraseology. Daily orders did not actually say that 'The Porridge WILL be eaten,' but in the same impersonal Cowie terms they did lay down that 'equipment WILL be blancoed, and that brass WILL be cleaned'.

How I remember that lake of oatmeal slime; far too much for any infantile stomach, no matter how capacious, to contain; a glutinous sea of salt and milk and coarse oats all sludged together under the Calvinistic battle cry of 'It will do you good and make you grow up into a big boy'.

I always wondered about this stuff.

In Scotland, where the crime was first committed, this revolting compound is absorbed after being poured smoking hot into a bowl stirred by 'a spurtle' and quenched with cold milk or sour buttermilk blessed by John Knox and accompanied by a cold lava of coarse salt.

Hair shirts are compulsory.

Great hirsute men, fresh from killing the Monarch of the Glen, have been known to be quite choosy about this criminal mess.

They say that the test of good oatmeal Porridge is that each grain shall be distinct and soft enough to lie level in the bowl, and that eaten in the heather and with the pipes a'skirlin', it should cut cleanly and never cling to the dish or spoon.

Miss Cowie, I was told in later life, was 'A Good Woman'.

But to me, blubbering in a bowl of cooling Porridge with the hot salt tears running down my nose, she was the first implacable frontier of life.

Sir Compton Mackenzie has the ancient chanting of Waterloo about his rompers.

I have Miss Cowie and the smell of stodgy Porridge to be rammed into a parcel of small wincing guts. And burnt Porridge at that.

The prose of sauce

August 4, 1961

I have been a reader of sauce-bottle labels ever since I first got to eye-level with a kitchen table.

Some people are brought up on the works of Keats and Dryden and Macaulay and Ruskin and Coleridge and Herrick. I was brought up on the literature of Heinz and Brand's and Lea and Perrins and Escoffier and Burgess.

There is a splendid archaic quality about the Prose of Bottled Sauce. It is respectful yet lofty; faintly obsequious with the dignity of soft-footed butlers, yet discreetly arrogant withal.

There is the romance of far-off places in sauce labels; of pleasure domes in Xanadu and the magic of Coleridge writing of the Golden Road to Samarkand: 'Aromatic herbs from old-world gardens; rare spices from the Far East; sun-ripened fruits from the orchards of the world.' Author: Messrs. Brand and Co Ltd.

Now and again – bowing slightly from the hips – the sauce boys slip gracefully into French with the shimmering shade of Auguste Escoffier smiling approvingly on:

'Cette sauce de haute qualité est un melange de fruits orientaux, d'épices et de vinaigre de malt.'

Too true – *C'est Le Aiche Pi.*

Then with spinets and harpischords a-chanting in the Minstrels' Gallery, and with powdered wigs well secured, the Saucerers strike the true seventeenth-century note:

'The excellence of their much efteemed Effence of Anchovies ftands unrivalled as a fifh fauce, viz, for falmon, turbot, foals, eels, cod, haddock, and in all ftewed fifh. N.B. Be careful that you are not impofed upon by being fupplied with the counterfeit fort, as many perfons are daily waiting upon country fhop-keepers, offering them an extra large profit to vend it.' – John Burgess and Son, Ltd.

By a splendid Monarchist tradition that would have had Bonnie Prince Charlie cheering in the heather, the British Throne has always been mixed up in Sauce.

According to the labels, our present Majesty Queen Elizabeth II is a proper devil for *'La finesse et la delicatesse de sauce'*.

Buckingham Palace, by Royal Appointment, is never without such popular brands as Crosse and Blackwell; H.P.; Sharwood's 'Green Label' Chutney Sauce; John Burgess's Anchovy Essence (sorry Effenee) and many other fine and rare preparations from old world gardens boosted (out damned word!) with rare spices from the Far East.

Brand's A.1 sauce fascinates me most.

It is a thoughtful and sophisticated garnishment much to my taste and liking. (Advt.)

But it does NOT bear the Royal Coat of Arms like so many of its rivals – and it may well be that it has not gained Prince Philip's approval on dry land – or Uffa Fox's at sea.

But Brand's A.1 does bear a coronet and a fine piece of saucy prose on the side of the bottle:

'H.W. Brand, past-master in the art of cookery, Chef to King George IV, was always seeking new recipes to tickle the Royal palate. He served the King one day a new and subtle masterpiece, a thick fruit sauce. "Brand!" exclaimed his Majesty, "this sauce is A.1."'

This royal occasion has always interested me.

George IV (1762-1830) was one of the most dissolute asses that ever disgraced the British Throne.

When he was not mad he was forgiven for being drunk, but I have always treasured that unforgettable line 'Brand!' exclaimed His Majesty, 'this sauce is A.1.'

Whether the Fourth George, who was a bemused guttural German, ever pronounced that a sauce was 'A.I' might be open to question, but my counter-intelligence squad (whose name is feared in all the Chancelleries of Europe) has a very different version about this deeply tantalising, intriguingly spiced sauce (Advt.).

They report that on Tuesday, July 26, 1881 (watch it boys!) Brand's advertised in the *London Evening News* their A.1 sauce as 'The Queen of

Sauces'. Not the king of sauces, mark you. Brand's then gave this version of how their A.1 came to be named:

'This celebrated SAUCE was invented by Mr H W Brand (formerly of the Royal Household) in 1862 when he was cook and co-manager of the cuisine at the International Exhibition in Hyde Park. It was submitted by him to the Royal Commission for approval for use at restaurants to the Exhibition and pronounced by the Chief Commissioner to be "A.I".'

What! No King? Only a Royal Commissioner of Parks?

That's Okay – I mean A.1 by me.

All stories improve with the sauce of age and the retelling thereof.

And maybe a re-sauced sauce does so too.

Home on the range

August 8, 1962

I first started washing dishes at the age of five. No, that's not quite right. I was drying dishes and putting them away at that age. The higher privilege of actually washing them came later and has lasted nearly half a century.

As I am in reasonably good health, the future is dark with great mounds of greasy plates that will, I hope, be bright when I have finished washing, drying and putting 'em away.

I now see that no less a person than the Chief Inspector of Schools has given his blessing to the washing up of dishes by the young.

'Boys should wash dishes,' he says. 'It is not unmanly.'

Not only should boys wash dishes, but they should also learn to cook the food to place upon the clean platters at the earliest possible age.

My curriculum for young male persons in the Cassandra kitchen begins with a lecture entitled 'The Boiling of Eggs Without the Use of an Eggtimer'.

Medium-boiled eggs are done in the time it takes to sing the first three verses of Hymn 391 (Onward Christian Soldiers). Hard-boiled eggs take the whole five verses.

The course ends with a triumphant exposition. Haddock Soup made with fresh haddock, onions, carrots, celery, butter, olive oil, curry powder, herbs, flour, milk, cream, salt, pepper and white wine.

The graduate from the Cassandra kitchen, after full tuition, can look any Chef in the eye with complete composure – not to say with a secret exultant lilt in his heart.

Fortunately, most young lads these days seem to be able to be at home on the kitchen range.

The other day a young German chap spent a few days in my house. He was a most admirable fellow.

Towards the end of his visit, he said: 'May I do the breakfast? I should like to prepare *Bauern Fruhstuck* – or Peasant's Breakfast – for you.'

I was delighted.

He cooked some new potatoes and then with chopped onions, mushrooms, herbs, sliced ham, a few slivers of pimento and plenty of salt and pepper, gently fried them in a very large pan.

Into each of five cups – there were five of us – he broke an egg.

Then, with that professional unhurried ease that distinguishes an experienced and tried cook from the jittery amateur, he made five separate omelettes which were placed on the savoury plateau in the frying-pan. Yummy Yum. ...

I guess those German peasants do themselves very well.

All young people should be able to cook. Out of the washing-up sink into the frying-pan. And out of the frying-pan into the divine fire that emblazons life with good food prepared with loving and knowledgeable hands.

Marmalade for breakfast

August 27, 1965

The poet Rupert Brooke, when far from home, wondered most nostalgically whether the church clock at Grantchester stood at ten to three and whether there was still honey for tea.

I am glad he did not worry about whether there was still marmalade for breakfast.

To me marmalade, preferably bitter and made by Cooper's of Oxford, is still the foundation of the British early morning way of life.

When all else fails, when the last of the red marks on the maps of the world have been wiped out, and the Bandas and the Kenyattas have come into their surly own, we must hang on to our toast and our tea and especially our marmalade.

In the old days marmalade was marmalade and the sliced imprisoned oranges looked out and winked with glee from the shining pot.

But not now.

The Directorate General for Agriculture of the EEC Commission – what absurd and pompous titles these people assume – have found time to describe and define what marmalade really is:

'Mixture, brought to the appropriate consistency, of sugar and of fruit puree or of fruit pulp and fruit puree, with or without the addition of fruit juice, whether or not pasteurised, deep-frozen, lyophilised or preserved by means of sulphur dioxide, obtained from two of the fruits listed in Annex III, paragraphs 3 and 4, at least one of these fruits being among those listed in paragraph 3, with a refractometric value of not less than 60 and a fruit content of not less than 30 per cent in the finished product, the content of the fruits listed in Annex III, paragraph 4 being, in the case of a mixture of fruits listed in Annex III, paragraphs 3 and 4, not less than 18 per cent; the latter percentage shall, however, be reduced to 10 per cent in the case of citrus fruits and to 7 per cent in the case of ginger.'

Oranges from Seville. The name enchants. The flavour bewitches. Provided, of course, that the refractometric values, the deep frozen pasteurisation, the lyophilised preservatives and the sulphur dioxide values are correct.

Scotch Broth

Strathyre, September 13, 1961

This column, although not quite knee-deep in the heather, is well inside the ramparts of Bonnie Scotland.

We've carried these old bones of ours through the Lothians, and are now heading up into Perthshire to far-off places where the White Sassenach is rarely seen.

Yet nary a drop of Scotch Broth have I had. I've had Mushroom soup from freshly-picked tins. I've had Tomato soup from freshly-picked cans. And I've had a Brown Windsor soup made with freshly-boiled hot water stained to the colour of what the trade calls 'dark oak'.

But not Scotch Broth.

This does not worry me, but hitherto, when I have been in these parts, Scotch Broth – like porridge – is almost a compulsory dish. I do not care for it, and I class it as an admonitory soup. It is an imprecatory soup, and it carries with it that ominous warning so often applied to many unappetising dishes that 'It is good for you'.

If I could be assured that it was bad for me, maybe we'd get along better.

The recipe is a lazy one.

Take a 2lb. scrag of mutton – *there's* a delicate, piquant start for you – and hack it into great chunks, as your guests are liable to be tossing the caber in their idle moments. Chuck it into cold water – say, three pints.

Boil, and try not to get the dry heaves or the vertiginous nausea as the bubbling scum seethes and spumes. De-scum.

Now simmer – and ye should be fair scunnered by the noo. Add diced carrot, leek and turnip – the latter, incidentally, is called 'Neeps' by the kilted cognoscenti.

The *potage* of the bagpipes is now beyond redemption; quantities of pearl barley, soaked from last Hogmanay, plus too much coarse salt and black pepper, will make the brew sufficiently inedible to qualify for the taunt that 'it will do you good'.

Mind you, there IS a good Scotch broth.

I invented it. Or, to be meticulously exact, I invented it with the aid of senior military accomplices in 1944.

The scene was an Italian hillside below the snow-line, and my guests were a rough, outspoken crew much given to depravity. With the aid of a petrol-fire, a great iron bowl and a large number of tins thoughtfully supplied by the RASC I set out to build them a nourishing soup that would at least be hot, if nothing else.

The main ingredients were M and V (short for meat and vegetables), diced carrots, dried powdered potato, some horrible string beans, and a can of lurid, sliced beetroot.

These I boiled until it was so hot that I thought that any sense of taste on the part of the consumers would be scalded out of them. My biggest mistake was, of course, the beetroot, which stained this high temperature *potage* into a hideous mauve mess.

I had a near mutiny on my hands.

So I tossed the lot away, and rebuilt the whole thing minus the beetroot. They objected to the beans – so I skimmed out the beans.

They said the carrots were bad. I removed the carrots. I re-heated, and then, with a touch of desperation and near-genius in equal quantities, I gave the whole concoction a sharp shot of whisky from a considerable reserve that we had obtained by stealth from some rather simple Canadians.

One soldier, renowned for his grudging ill-will, said that he didn't mind it so much now, but could I take out the meat?

I did.

I injected more whisky.

Men began to Oliver Twist on me 'What about chucking the veg out?' asked a thin, weaselly sapper.

Somehow I sieved the pale seaweed out.

I reinforced with more whisky.

Men's eyes began to shine. The hard lines of life were being rubbed out.

Geniality replaced rancour. Magnanimity replaced pusillanimity. Private Jack was a damned sight better than his master, Major John.

Coarse songs filled the freezing air, and we opened another bottle. And that's how REAL Scotch Broth was born.

The Black Ribbon

May 21, 1963

Unhesitatingly I award the Cordon Noir to Dr Sidney Schwartz, the American physiologist, who is engaged on research work in the United States to land a man on the moon.

The Cordon Noir is the reverse of the Cordon Bleu.

The Cordon Bleu is France's highest award for chefs – originally restricted to female cooks by Louis XV, who was one of France's greatest gourmets.

My Cordon Noir is awarded to Dr Schwartz for having debased the culinary art to its lowest possible abyss.

This assassin of good food has invented – perpetrated is probably a better word – 'edible structural material'.

He has committed the ultimate gastronomic crime and has produced a recipe for structural material to be used in the building of space ships that can also be eaten.

Dr Schwartz – how happily he is named for the Black Ribbon of astronomic-gastronomic murder – says that he received his inspiration for eating the framework of space ships 'from reading of how an Arctic explorer left mounds of dried fish behind him, which served the double purpose of marking his trail and feeding his sled dogs on his return'.

The determined Dr Schwartz then went to his local grocery store and bought small quantities of white flour, corn starch, powdered milk, powdered banana and hominy grits. For those who are lucky enough not to have had hominy grits, they are a debased form of boiled maize served up, usually for breakfast, in the Southern States of America in what appears to be a cold white slush of pasty glue.

The hominy grits, explained this grim scientific chef, served the same function as gravel in concrete. He then baked these sombre ingredients for nine minutes in a hydraulic press. The result was a dark brown crystalline substance nearly as hard as ivory with a 'compressive' strength of 7,230 pounds per square inch.

This almost granite-hard dish can be machined, sawed, drilled and tapped. It can also be moulded into instrument knobs.

To serve the meal (no dim candlelight, elegant silverware of Chateau Yquem required), you reconstitute the dreadful fossilised rocks by soaking them in water at 180 degrees Fahrenheit for two and a half hours.

'The flavour,' says Dr Schwartz, 'is not unlike that of breakfast cereal' and in a pre-cooked state on a lunar expedition can be a valuable material for landing gear to be discarded on the face of the moon – which may, in my opinion, be a good place to leave it.

Delicious, Dr Schwartz, delicious. Kindly accept the Cordon Noir.

'A' for Asparagus

June 14, 1961

This column today is dedicated solely and exclusively to Asparagus, and if you want to take to the hills and beat it to the wild blue yonder you go with my fond farewell.

Charles Lamb knew about capital A for Asparagus when he said that although he appreciated the force of the maxim that 'a man cannot have a pure heart who refuses apple dumpling' he personally preferred Asparagus.

'It seems,' said Mr Lamb, 'to inspire gentle thoughts.'

Charles Dickens too was of like mind.

He makes his *Flora Finching* refer to her late husband as 'an estimable man and a most indulgent husband' to whom it was 'only necessary to mention Asparagus and it appeared'.

I took up Asparagus seriously eleven years ago. I was wondering at the time whether for the sake of posterity to lay down a good cellar or to lay down a chain of Asparagus beds.

I built the beds and, such is the lasting nature of this splendidly succulent plant, I can safely rely on my goodly plantation to last for another ten, twenty, thirty or even forty years right up to AD 2000.

At this very moment the tips are pointing triumphantly to the moist and laughing sky and they will be there long after I am gone.

Over the interior of the North Door in St Paul's there is an inscription to Wren which, being translated, reads: 'If you would see his monument look around.'

When I am departed and you ask for a monument to me there will in the Asparagus beds be a triumphant raising of spears and a loud hosanna 'Look around!'

There are some twenty-three doubtfully established ways of cooking and serving Asparagus.

You can crucify it in a tart with a coffin of pastry and bechamel sauce with grated cheese laid on like a shroud.

You can put it in fancy dress with long thin slices of dark Italian ham and a drizzle of chopped olives.

You can hack the noble stalks into tiny pieces the size of a pea, cook for five minutes in boiling water, drain, melt butter, add sugar and stir in cornflour.

You can, also in the same ugly mood, murder your grandmother.

You can go on to rob a bank or desecrate a grave and while the antisocial madness is still upon you, you can make an Asparagus Soup.

With the gelignite in your pockets and your boots still muddied with graveyard soil, you can besmirch the Asparagus into the shameful cauldron.

Cut the stalks into short pieces and simmer for half an hour.

Rub recklessly through a sieve, for devil's work is afoot.

Stir in a gill of cream and, for all I care if the madness will not leave you, add slips of yew silver'd in the moon's eclipse and eye of newt and toe of frog and wool of bat and tongue of dog.

There is but one way to serve Asparagus.

Old Mother Beeton knew it all. In the index to her Holy Scrolls of Cooking she pauses between Artificial Respiration ('Quickly make sure that the casualty's nose and mouth are free from obstruction') and Asphyxia ('Drowning is not a common accident in the home, but falling asleep or fainting in the bath does occur') to deal with Asparagus.

Her recipe is simple, unequivocal and classically clear.

It rings out like those silver trumpets which the Rev Sydney Smith said should be the accompaniment to eating *foie gras* in Heaven.

'Take a bundle of Asparagus,' commands Isabella Beeton, 'with some salt, two ounces of butter and lemon juice.'

No bits of interloping Italian ham, no impertinent olives, no cloying sugar, no clogging cornflour or sluppy cream.

'Wash them in cold water,' runs the writ. 'Tie them in small bundles with the heads in one direction. Keep them in cold water until ready to cook. Cook very gently with the heads off the source of heat, in just enough salted boiling water to cover.

'When tender (in about 15-20 min.) drain and serve on a folded table napkin. Serve with melted butter, seasoned and lightly flavoured with lemon.'

In no other way can A-for-Asparagus delight the soul, cherish the heart, enthuse the stomach and give that tranquillity which Charles Lamb knew was the inspirational cradle of gentle thought.

The Scotch Goose Egg

May 2, 1963

A man who knows me too well for me to conceal my guilty load of secrets from him easily said to me yesterday:

'There's been an indefinable air of smugness about you – the smear of a quiet self-satisfied grin on your face that I find intolerable. Come on, out with it! What are you so pleased about?'

I said: 'When Michelangelo completed the ceiling of the Sistine Chapel, when the final stone was lodged on top of the Pyramid of Cheops, when Galileo first peered through his telescope and saw the wonders of the firmament, and when Beethoven wrote the last crashing chord of the *Eroica* Symphony, there was no false humility around the place.

'I, too, have looked upon my work and found it not wanting.'

'And pray what have YOU done?'

Answer: 'I have designed, composed and constructed the world's first Scotch Goose Egg. It is the result of, if I may say so, characteristically big thinking, simple thinking, visionary thinking.

'I do not believe that anybody has ever made a Scotch Egg with a Goose Egg before.

'In spite of the fact that the ingredients are easily come by, no one has trod the culinary path before me. The touch of classic boldness which places me far above the ordinary run of cooks is in achieving the obvious and that is the rarest virtue of all.

'My completed Scotch Goose Egg is about the size of a Rugby football, and the final ovoid form, with its irresistible meaty cloak, follows the elliptical shape of the mighty egg within.

'The pork sausage meat came from well-adjusted and scientifically integrated pigs.

'The parsley grew under the shade of an old monastery garden wall.

'The sage was wise in its soft flavour, and the lemon thyme came from a noble strain of aromatic plants.

'The Goose Egg itself, the heart, the inner citadel of this symphonic poem of succulence, was laid by a high-born feathered lady near Sherborne in Dorset whose name is Arabella Bianchardine Phyllada – known to her intimates as Lydia.

'It weighed 13 oz. – at least a quarter of a pound above the Dorsetshire average – and I boiled it for seventeen minutes as laid down in the laws of Goosey Goosey Gander.

'The sausage meat was bound together with a lathered-up clutch of seagulls' eggs and the whole nest of pure delight left for a few minutes to set, and then coated with a loving confetti of breadcrumbs, all being consummated in a fiery bath of deep boning fat.

'Back to your telescope, Galileo. 'Back to your Sistine Chapel, Michelangelo.

'There's hot scientific and artistic and culinary competition afoot.'

Talking turkey

December 24, 1983

Now look, what you do is this.

Get half a pound of dripping; four rashers of bacon – preferably fat; chestnut and veal stuffing; one pound of chipolata sausages; some watercress; bread sauce; green salad; chipped potatoes (slice 'em thickly) and a pint and a half of thickened gravy.

Oh, and a turkey – I nearly forgot.

Make it about a fourteen or fifteen pounder. Now are you with me?

Wash the giblets and put them on to simmer. Stuff the breast and the body of the bird. Place the bacon over the breast and cover the turkey lovingly with greased paper and put on a grid in a baking tin with the fat. Cook in a hot oven for an hour and then cook more slowly for another three hours.

Baste frequently. Grill the sausages. Prepare the thickened gravy.

Then grab the darn turkey and sling the lot away.

Yes, you heard – dump the brute.

What a shocking fraud the turkey is.

In life, preposterous, insulting – that foolish noise they make to scare you away! In death – unpalatable. The turkey has practically no taste except a dry fibrous flavour reminiscent of a mixture of warmed-up plaster of paris and horsehair.

The texture is like wet sawdust and the whole vast feathered swindle has the piquancy of a boiled mattress.

Turkey is nowhere as good as chicken – even muscular chickens that do Swedish exercises in the dark are better than turkeys. And chickens are nowhere as good as the dark-fleshed and kingly goose.

The goose however gives way to the guinea fowl, the guinea fowl gives way to the partridge, and the whole darn lot of 'em give way to roast pheasant – emperor, czar and monarch of the poultry world.

The green green grass of home

December 24, 1964

One of the things that has defied the scientists for so long is the production of food in quantity from some basic substance that is available in abundance.

Grass has been the subject of many experiments and as long ago as thirty years, scientists were trying to cut out the cow and go straight from the green stuff to butter and milk.

So far no dice.

I remember there was a wonderful chap who, I believe, used to live near Mitcham, and who was a great grass-eater. We corresponded for a long time.

He seemed to live on the stuff and would discourse learnedly about the flavour and edibility of various types of lawn mowings, and he was particularly well worth listening to when he was expounding on the tastiness of a slice of good rich compost right from the gooey depths of the hot heap.

Now I see that large-scale experiments are taking place at the University of California to manufacture food from seaweeds and extract nourishment from the brilliant bright green scum that you see on ponds.

I don't know whether the boys over there in California know it, but one of the shortest cuts to getting sustenance from seaweed is to eat it as it is.

In my time I have gathered it from the rocks on the shores of County Derry, where it is known as dulse. You collect it at low tide.

You can eat it raw or boil it and serve with whelks or haddocks.

You can even roast it on tongs.

I have no hesitation in saying that this slimy meal is the most revolting mess I have ever tasted.

Back to plum pudding.

Overturned eggs

February 9, 1962

My life is caught up with eggs – a yolky-yallery golden web from which I cannot escape. I am proud to know a man who overturned a van near Basingstoke and broke the best part of his cargo of 18,000 eggs.

He was by way of being a bit of a cook himself and said:

'Mrs Beeton has a recipe which I sometimes make. You get half a dozen eggs, some breadcrumbs and butter, salt and pepper. Then you butter six patty pans and coat them thickly with breadcrumbs. Break an egg into each and season lightly. Bake gently until set then turn them over on to a hot dish.'

He asked me whether I knew what Mrs Beeton called this dish.

'No,' says I.

'Overturned Eggs,' says he. 'Had I had forty loaves, a hundredweight of butter, a stone of salt and pepper and a portable furnace, I could have made you a rare dish of Overturned Eggs on the road that day.'

I have boiled, scrambled, fried, poached, baked and sat on eggs.

I have eaten hens' eggs, ducks' eggs, geese eggs (sound a fanfare of trumpets), guinea-fowl eggs, turkey eggs, plovers' eggs and gulls' eggs.

I have had fresh eggs, Lion eggs, pickled eggs, dried eggs, curried eggs and scotch eggs.

I have seen venerable eggs used as the artillery of criticism at political meetings and I once knew a Buff Orpington called Jessie kept by a pawnbroker. It laid spherical eggs.

He said he regarded it as a graceful compliment to the traditional sign of his trade.

Thus anything to do with eggs commands my attention, and it was with interest that I read the tale about how a woman in a Chinese restaurant in Leicester protested over the slow service.

She broke two sugar bowls, two ash trays, two lanterns, one chair, eighty plates – and smashed sixty eggs.

I don't query the shattered bowls, the ash trays, the lanterns, the chair or the plates. But I do query the eggs. Those who, like myself, get mad with slow service in restaurants should take an egg-timer to measure the inefficiency of those who fail to serve.

When the sands have run out they should record their disgust with, say, enough eggs to make a medium-sized omelette for four people.

None of this sixty or this eighteen thousand stuff.

Hen-fruit is worthy of better use.

Master and man

May 15, 1958

I have been studying the subject in a masterwork called *The Management of Servants* by 'A Member of the Aristocracy'. It was published in 1890.

Breakfast was a shade more than thin dry toast, weak tea and spots before the eyes. Writes 'A Member of the Aristocracy':

'The only eatables placed upon the breakfast table are dishes of rolls and fancy bread, and plates of thin bread and butter, glass dishes of preserves, and honey in the comb, fruit, clotted cream, dry toast, a stand of eggs and muffin dishes containing muffins or buttered toast.

'The sideboard is covered with a cloth and rows of knives, forks, and tablespoons, one or two dozen plates are placed upon it, also the cold viands, tongue, ham, game-pies, potted meat and the like; the hot viands are placed upon a side table such as eggs and bacon; dressed fish, kidneys, cutlets, broiled chicken, savoury omelette and roast partridges.'

The staff required to run establishments that were content with such crusts as these were laid down by the 'Member of the Aristocracy' on the following scale:

'A house steward; a groom of the chambers; a butler; a valet; a man cook; three footmen; a head coachman; a second coachman; three grooms; stud-groom; pad-groom; and one or two under-grooms; a steward's room boy; and a servant's hall boy.'

The serving distaff side in this Help Yourself Establishment looks like a badly attended meeting in a disused light-house:

'The women-servants consist of a housekeeper; a head lady's maid; an under lady's maid; young ladies' maids; a head nurse; a cook; two under laundry maids; a head kitchen maid; a scullery maid; a nursery maid and a schoolroom maid. Dairy maids are not included in this description, the dairy being comprised in the home farm.'

The 'Member of the Aristocracy' (who was also the author of *Manners and Tone in Good Society)* gives an interesting tariff of the wages paid to domestic servants in the eighteen-eighties.

The butler received anything from a pound to thirty-five shillings a week.

The cook got as much as two, or even three quid a week.

The first coachman collected up to twenty-two shillings a week and two free suits of livery.

A plain cook took home not more than twelve shillings a week and much more likely seven shillings every Friday.

And a schoolroom maid was lucky if she got four bob a week and compulsory Divine Service not more than twice on Sunday.

On the grave matter of 'Opening The Door' the 'Member of the Aristocracy' devotes a full chapter. It is a tremendous piece of protocol, the importance of which is indicated by the ominous words: 'There is no surer indication of the manner in which a household is conducted than is conveyed in the act of opening the door.'

Stand by for the old Welcome Mat:

'If a servant were in doubt as to whether the call is a friendly or business one, it would be correct for him to say: "I beg your pardon, ma'am, but do you wish to see my mistress on business?" And if the answer were in the affirmative, he would then say: "I will take up your card, if you please."'

On delivery of the card, the Door Opener would then say to his mistress: 'A Person has called to see you, ma'am, and is waiting in the hall.'

Butlers were always suspect by 'A Member of the Aristocracy'.

'Again, the wine under a butler's charge is a temptation to a married man whose wife is ailing and very much in need of strengthening things. Half-bottles of wine and even whole bottles of wine are under such circumstances not unlikely to find their way to the butler's home.'

Nursemaids had to be particularly careful of their pronunciation:

'Although it may amuse members of the family when she talks of "Master 'Enery's beautiful blue heyes," it is not perhaps quite so amusing when Master Henry himself informs his mamma's visitor that he 'as 'urt 'is 'ead" and pinched 'is 'and".'

One final word from these savoury, steamy Turtle-Soup Days.

'In the country the housekeeper helps in her mistress's charities to the poor, carries out her orders, and attends to their wants.'

What ho!

A pauper's outing

November 16, 1962

I once knew a young man many years ago who, when he was wining or dining and felt that he was not getting enough to eat or drink, or that the quality of the solids and liquids was inferior, used to let out a great roar of:

'What's all this – a pauper's outing?'

I was reminded of him when I recently got mixed up in a social war against a friend of mine, that may be of interest to students of one-downmanship.

It began when he rather expansively invited me to lunch at the Savoy Hotel.

We had a drink there and, with the prospect of the caviar coming into sharp focus, I was enjoying myself.

Then, with a swift, ugly blow to the stomach, he suggested that we should eat at a far less sumptuous place than the Savoy. We had inferior cottage pie that I suspect included a heavy ingredient of boiled sawdust faintly flavoured with creosote.

After this carefully contrived gastronomic humiliation and with strict regard to the courtesies (and an eye on a reprisal), I invited him out a week or so later, suggesting that we should meet in the downstairs bar at Simpsons-in-the-Strand.

My guest was within smelling distance of the saddle of mutton, when I briskly told him that I knew of a much more interesting little restaurant near by.

His face clouded with pain as I took him to a filthy little soup kitchen where I ordered some coarse fish that had long forgotten about the sea and a sultana pudding that tasted strongly of warm putty, flavoured with cheap perfume. The texture of this hairy slush was that of a ball of sodden wool.

He got the point.

At our next encounter at which I was the guest, he dispensed with all pretence about fixing some lush meeting point before The Great Diversion and escorted me straight to a public house that specializes in discomfort and squalor. It is an establishment where they are very loath to serve you a drink, and when they do condescend to do so, they have a positive flair for short-changing you or blatantly overcharging you.

My host said that he strongly recommended the tinned salmon sandwiches.

It was no idle threat.

They were dried up pieces of grey bread protecting a layer of pink, sullen ptomaine poison.

The pace of this Lucullan war is quickening, and although my opponent is no mean tactician in The Unhospitality Stakes, my menu for the next two engagements may teach <u>him</u> a severe lesson.

I have planned a new Belshazzar's Feast. You, being well brought up like myself (Daniel, Chapter 5, verses 1 to 9), will remember that King Belshazzar 'made a great feast to a thousand of his lords and drank wine before the thousand'.

The King and his princes, his wives and his concubines 'drank from golden vessels that were taken out of the temple of the house of God'.

This time I am going to give my sly friend Belshazzar's Feast – in reverse.

Making sure that it is pouring with rain, I shall invite him to meet me in a bus shelter.

There we will share a bag of inferior crisps – without the salt.

The next, and probably final, Pauper's Outing will be held in Oxford Circus Underground Station at the peak of the rush hour in the evening.

The menu will consist of a sticky piece of stale chocolate that I have been carrying about in my coat pocket for a fortnight.

That'll learn him to live it up.

Fried Za-Zas

June 15, 1960

The Admiralty and Harrods have many things in common. They range from impassivity to adequate supplies of Naval pink gin plus the fact that they both have the same impressive address which doesn't bother with trivia like streets or squares, it just says 'London, SW1'.

This week they have come up trumps again. Harrods publish a bulletin called *Food News* and on one page, which deals with convalescent foods and meat and vegetable extracts, they have a final section which is headed: FOR THE GOURMET.

It is magnificent – all mixed up as it is on the same page with pappy stuff for pale pink stomachs hemmed in by ulcers.

FOR THE GOURMET should be read to the accompaniment of a fanfare of silver trumpets – Ta-ra!

'Roasted caterpillars 1½ oz. tin 2/6
Chocolate-covered bees 2 oz. tin 6/-
Fried grasshoppers 1½ oz. tin 2/-
Seasoned bumble bees 3½ oz. tin 5/-
Fried silkworms 2-3 oz. tin 4/-'

And finally 'Seasoned za-za insects' which sell at 4s. 6d. for a two ounce tin and which must not be confused with 'Fried za-za insects'. They are a bit special and cost 4s. 3d. for a one-ounce tin.

I am normally of a leaden disposition that has had all the curiosity eaten out of it long ago. But a za-za insect!

I got on to Messrs H of London, SW1, and spoke to their Mr Miller, who is the buyer of the Grocery Department. He was quite magnificent. Calm, Informative. Polite.

He said: 'Za-za insects are like small wasps and they come from Japan. However, they are no longer obtainable as, for some reason, all the za-zas have emigrated to China.'

Mr Miller went on: 'The Chinese do not export them. The supply at Harrods is a very limited one and the future is dark, for no more can be obtained after the present supply has been sold.'

We thanked Mr Miller and, as we parted, he said in a grave, courteous voice – 'That's my story and I'm sticking to it!'

That's why I like Harrods.

Private and Personal

Cassandra on Cassandra could be hilarious, the stuff of some of his best columns. But now and again he wrote of private and personal things that revealed an astonishing depth of tenderness in the man: the Celtic seam, no doubt. It would be wrong to omit from this section two little classics by Cass – MANHUNT and THEY MADE ME WELCOME.

On hangovers

About 1937

He found that he was suffering from what he (counsel) said was vulgarly and commonly known as a 'hangover'.'
'A what?' asked Mr Justice Hawke.
'I am just as ignorant as your Lordship,' replied counsel.
Mr Justice Hawke then severely rebuked people who laughed at this.

– Court Report

May I hasten to help his Lordship? A hangover is when your tongue tastes like a tram-driver's glove.

When your boots seem to be steaming and your eyes burn in their sockets like hot gooseberries.

Your stomach spins slowly on its axis and your head gently swells and contracts like a jelly in the tideway.

Voices sound far off and your hands tremble like those of a centenarian condemned to death.

Slight movements make you sweat, even as you shiver from the deadly cold that is within you.

Bright lights hurt the eyes, and jeering, gibbering people from the night before seem to whisper in your ears, and then fade with mocking horrible laughter into silence.

The finger-nails are brittle and your skin hangs on you like an old second-hand suit.

Your feet appear to be swollen, and walking is like wading through a swamp of lumpy, thick custard.

Your throat is cracked and parched like the bottom of an old saucepan that has boiled dry. The next moment the symptoms change, and your mouth is stuffed with warm cotton wool.

When you brush your hair you are certain that there is no top to your skull, and your brain stands naked and throbbing in the stabbing air.

Your back aches and feels as though someone is nailing a placard to your shoulder blades.

Knee joints have turned to dish water and eyelids are made of sheets of lead lined with sandpaper.

When you lean on a table it sways gently and you know for certain that you are at sea.

Should you step off a kerb you stumble, for it is a yard deep and the gutter yawns like a wide, quaking trench.

You have no sense of touch and your fingertips feel with all the acuteness of decayed firewood smeared with putty.

The nostrils pulsate and smell the evil air.

You believe that you are in a horrible dream but when you wake up you know that it will all be true.

Your teeth have been filed to stumps and are about to be unscrewed one by one from your aching jaw.

You want to sleep, but when you close your eyes you are dizzy, and you heel over like a waterlogged barrel crammed with old, sodden cabbage stalks in the Grand Junction Canal.

When you read your eyes follow each letter to try to spell the words, but in vain – no message reaches your empty, sullen brain.

Should you look at a simple thing like a tree, it will appear that the bark is gradually crawling upwards.

Lights flash and crackle before you and innumerable little brown dwarfs start tapping just below the base of your skull with tiny, dainty hammers made of compressed rubber...

O Death, where is thy sting?

Manhunt

January 27, 1948

Exactly twelve days ago at 6.10 p.m., an elderly gentleman put on his fawn-coloured raincoat, his grey cap and set out to go to the local choir practice two and a half miles away.

He had done the journey many times before, was cheerful and in good health. At five minutes to seven he was noticed within a hundred yards of the church.

From that moment when he was seen standing at a crossroads, he has not been sighted again.

Here in this year 1948, with its enormous mechanism of identity cards, passports, flying squad patrols and all the rest of the careful documentation of human activities, a kindly old chap just disappears. He has six pounds on him, and a gold watch engraved with his initials, WHC. He was happy, liked walking and had no worries.

There are near-by woods into which he might well have strayed, but they have been repeatedly searched by the police, by RAF squads, and by as knowledgeable a crowd of farmers, gamekeepers, beaters and poachers as ever set an appreciative eye on a cock-pheasant.

There is a river a mile-and-a-half farther on but it has yielded nothing. Bus drivers, postmen, tradesmen, roadmen and lock-keepers have all been questioned. They have also seen nothing.

Outbuildings, sheds and hayricks for miles around have been examined.

No result. No trace. No clue.

THAT MAN WAS MY FATHER.

Here in a newspaper office we deal in this sort of thing. It makes news. To me it is a part of my trade – provided it comes normally and impersonally over the ticker tape, the telephone or by mail. You can look at it critically, weigh up its value and assess its interest – always provided it is someone else.

But when it comes crashing in on the quietude of your own home, it makes you feel more than strange – even plaintive. And you think 'Out of all the teeming millions of this overcrowded isle, why pick on me?'

And when the National and Evening papers get you on the telephone (not knowing you are in the trade) and ask you with tact, good sense and even sympathy (Royal Press Commission, please note) you feel slightly disembodied as you go over the familiar, mournful description again: 'Name, William Henry Connor. Age 75. Last seen at Hambleden, Bucks, 6.55pm. January 14. Fawn raincoat. Grey cloth cap. Walking-stick. Brown shoes. Clean shaven. Height 5ft 10in. May be suffering from loss of memory.'

You might think that contented old gentlemen just don't disappear these days.

You might think that the network of modern registration has too fine a mesh to lose ordinary, law-abiding citizens going quietly about their business.

You might think that efficient, friendly police and good neighbours prepared to give days of their time in combing the undergrowth and ranging the fields would have some luck attendant on their efforts.

But you would be wrong.

For they haven't. Not yet...

Dear God

January 29, 1959

'Dear God, I wish to be a Christian. Which brand do you recommend?

'Yours very truly,

'A Would-be Believer.'

I could write that letter in all reverence and sincerity and I would be interested to know the answer.

Both the Pope and I am concerned about it, and His Holiness John the

Twenty-third has shown his anxiety over the vast array of the different forms of Christianity by calling an Ecumenical Council, which is a grand way of saying one united brand of worship is better than fifty-seven varieties.

If you go into the Christian shop and ask which brand do they recommend, you get a very startling answer.

'Well, sir, there is C of E, which is very reliable and is under Royal patronage, or, if you come from farther North, we can recommend the Church of Scotland which has a valuable Presbyterian Additive.

'Or perhaps you might incline towards what we call "the Free Churches" which give you a useful choice of being Methodist, Baptist, Congregational or Presbyterian.

'Some of our best customers do not, however, care for the big name brands and many of the Top People insist on Quakerism or Salvation Armyism, both of which, in rather different fields, have an excellent reputation.

'If you want a particularly strong brand of Christianity – and most of the patrons having sampled it rarely give it up – I can sell you Roman Catholicism which has a very distinguished clientele amounting to over 423 million customers. This vast company is under the guidance of Pope John, who is one of the most promising managing directors that the concern has had for several centuries.

'He is said to be engagingly human, which is no bad thing if humanity is your business.

'But if the mixture is rather concentrated – and many customers find it's a little strong – we can offer you quite a wide range of other Christian makes. There are the Plymouth Brethren, the Christian Scientists, the Unitarians, the Buchmanites, the Peculiar People, the Pentecostalists, Seventh Day Adventists, the Jehovah's Witnesses, the Foursquare Gospelites, the Missionary Allies, the Christ-adelphians, the Hutterites, the Old Believers, the Mormons and the Nameless Ones.

'Christianity is sold in many packets and some of the cheaper varieties, which we do not recommend, have lost the old Galilean flavour.

'But make your own choice, sir. Some of the ten chapel brands often come up to cathedral quality.'

Nellie Dean

January 8, 1957

I am without doubt the worst piano player in Fleet Street.

I don't say this with reckless triumph or with thoughtless boasting. I say it with the calm, cool tranquillity of a man who understands what he is talking about and is completely sure of his facts. I know it is an enormous claim to make, for Fleet Street has the worst piano players in the world, but nevertheless there is no more execrable and intolerable piano player than your humble servant.

Why I am such an appalling affront to the ear is that I can play the piano really badly in such a large number of different styles.

You want to hear me (by gum you wouldn't!) butchering my way through a fragment of Bach. Once the awful contrapuntal hash-up has got on its way you will understand what I mean – unless you get trampled to death in the rush for the door.

Then there's the way I tackle Paderewski's *Minuet.* I can get the full mincing horror of this with a blundering bass that has to be heard to be believed. It's like a berserk bull let loose in the minstrel's gallery.

Also there's Rock 'n' Roll.

I had a go with this as a duet with Paddy Roberts the other night. Paddy (tunesmith of *Softly Softly, Evermore, Bluebell Polka, Lay Down Your Arms,* etc. etc.) Roberts was mad enough to share a keyboard with me until he could stand it no longer.

The blood ran from his face as I got to work and he cried aloud: 'For Pete's sake change gear or we'll all be killed!'

But I suppose it is with *Nellie Dean* that I work the most terrible havoc. Men and women who have undergone the experience of listening to me playing *Nellie Dean* have never been quite the same again. Some, of course, go grey-haired within a few minutes, but most of them never mention the fact that they have been present at a performance. I am told by survivors that it is like being terribly burned in an air crash. You just don't talk about it.

It is my favourite number.

The death of dear old Gertie Gitana who sang it into the heart of the world has left me very sad.

Nellie Dean is an absolutely outstanding number in that it is almost a grave offence to sing it completely sober; for the public houses long ago adopted it as their signature tune. It has an exquisite woozy character that flourishes amid lashings of black pints of mild. *Nellie Dean* has a magnificent lurching quality that is at its best about a quarter of an hour before closing time. It is the moment when complete strangers speak to each other; when charladies take on a new motherly charm and when barmaids become radiant.

It is at this zenith of alcoholic joy that I apparently reluctantly take the piano stool before an instrument which I insist be out of tune and preferably in some state of disrepair. Usually there is a sudden hush such as used to occur just before a major air raid. The customers are hypnotized and horrified and, if they are not very considerably fortified by malt liquors, they either abandon ship, take to the boats or dial 999.

The atmosphere is unbearably tense and there is a wave of primeval fear and fascination as I make the first tremendous assault. It is a musical Battle of the Bulge. I am Marshal Ludwig Beethoven Montgomery. I am Marshal Johann Sebastian Rundstedt.

The force and the incredible violence with which I hit the wrong notes, get the tempo all snarled up and massacre the melody with my bare hands is like Myra Hess, Rubinstein and Artur Schnabel in reverse. Medical specialists say it is one of the most punishing experiences known to the human ear.

The final excruciating climax is when I burst into song. This is a harsh metallic cry that is a cross between the sound of a drunk bittern booming in an Essex marsh and a factory hooter connected to a boiler that is about to blow up.

With blundering hand and brutal throat I split the quivering, wilting air.

I shall always remember one of the finest tributes ever given to me after I had finished with *Nellie Dean.* It came from a foundry worker who used to be a riveter and knew something about the harsher sounds of life.

He was trembling slightly as he gripped my hand and he murmured: 'Unforgettable.. and absolutely unforgivable.'

Speechless in NW3

April 16, 1957

Did I ever tell you about the night that I slayed them in NW3.

The time that I had them rolling in the aisles?

The time the old spellbinder within me burst into flames?

The time I played the audience tenderly like Pablo Casals caressing his 'cello? The time I chiselled the heart out of them like Epstein in a moment of monumental glory? The time I transfixed them, harpooned them, hypnotised them and had them eating out of my hand?

No?

Sit down, old friend, and mark my mournful words.

Some long time ago I received an invitation that was pressing, flattering and precise. Would I do a certain party the great honour and favour of addressing a select audience on the subject of The Press?

I consented. I said 'Yes'.

The rendezvous was a lecture hall in London, NW3. Now as a lecturer I consider myself superb in W1 brilliantly constructive in SW2, engagingly roisterous in SEI, sagacious beyond compare in N22 – but an unknown quantity in NW3.

I was prepared to take the risk.

The time was 7.30 on a Sunday night in NW3. I had the letter of invitation (signed: 'most cordially yours'). I knew the address and I arrived there at 7.25. The first thing that disturbed the renowned lecturer was that there were no milling crowds outside. No endless rows of parked cars. No policemen keeping the mob back. Only the local kids played in a raucous whirligig round the lamp-post.

Two Indians with dark, flashing grins were polishing a white Jaguar near by.

I retired to a pub, checked the invitation by place, time and purpose, felt my bundled notes in my right hand raincoat pocket and returned to the hall. All correct.

But still no lights. No crowd. No crush. No welcome. Nowt.

I banged on the door. A hollow echo came from the darkened within. No reply. A small pane of glass on the door, heavily barred inside, showed in the fading daylight a vestibule leading to a larger hall. A fierce little notice under the doorbell outside which I had not noticed, said primly: PLEASE DON'T RING UNLESS YOU HAVE AN APPOINTMENT.

'By God,' said I, in a fury of doubt and anger, 'I HAVE got an appointment.'

Ring, ring, ring – and again no response. I re-checked the letter. I looked up at the address. I walked to the nearest street lamp to verify and re-verify that I was the bloke, that here was the place and that this was the time. It was.

Surely nobody, no committee, no student-group could be so recklessly mad as to forget this important, this intriguing, this potentially historical date on which I was due to address the North West Three-sians on the subject of The Press?

Could be? Banish the perishing thought.

At this moment two middle-aged women came up the steps where the jubilant rally of NW3 was due to take place and I said to them anxiously: 'Is this where the meeting is due to take place?'

'What meeting?'

'The meeting to discuss The Press.'

'There is no meeting here tonight,' said the elder of the two. 'I am the housekeeper here. There is nothing in the engagement book.'

'There MUST be a meeting. I am the principal speaker.'

She looked at me sadly, and said: 'There may be a mistake. Please do come in.'

We went into the hall and the Notice Board laden with joyful information about DANCES, DISCUSSION GROUPS, DEBATES and HOCKEY MATCHES contained not a word about the lively, intelligent, scintillating occasion on which I was to be coruscating star.

'Is there nobody here?'

'Ah, they have gone away. All the young people have disappeared until next term.'

'But they INVITED me.'

'Strange, but I suppose they forgot. Let me see the letter.'

I showed it to her with mortification, humiliation, anger, sorrow and pique boiling up within me.

'It is too bad. Much too bad. Will you join us in a pot of tea?'

'No, thank you.'

'Please do not wound so easily. Will you take a dish of *Gefullte* fish?'

'What is *Gefullte* fish?'

'Stuffed fish seasoned with my own delicate onion sauce such as I would not serve to young people who forget their invitations and their guests.'

'Madam, you are too kind and I am grateful. But there are occasions NOT for *Gefullte* fish. This, I assure you from my bleeding heart, is NOT a time for the delicate *Gefullte.*'

And that's how I wowed them on that memorable night in NW3.

Extinct my foot!

May 25, 1948

We'll have foot-drill today. Fall in the following: Dr Samuel Johnston, John Wesley, Charles Darwin, Martin Luther, Alexander the Great, Pitt the Elder, Lord Tennyson, Isaac Newton, Kubla Khan – and Cassandra.

Now then, Squad – squad 'shun!

Nothing happens. Nobody moves.

We just stand there glumly looking at our feet.

Can this be mutiny?

No, sir, it is gout.

I am in famous company – bound by the red hot Great Toe to soldiers, sages and scientists of all ages.

It is curious the things that make human beings happy, for whenever I mention to people that I have had gout, their faces light up and they guffaw with glee.

I ask them if they have ever had toothache in the foot. They hold their sides shrieking with joy.

I explain that gout is like walking on your eyeballs. The tears roll down their cheeks.

I describe the crushing, terrifying weight of but a single sheet upon the tortured foot. They cry with ecstasy.

I recount to them the example of the fly upon the ceiling.

The victim lies in bed in splendid agony watching the accursed thing. As it stamps its way across the plaster, the Great Toe, ruddy and glazed, winces at each reverberating clomp. Now the buzzing brute has taken off. It dives, circles and zooms. Fascinated and afraid, you watch it until freezing anxiety that it may land upon your foot almost wrenches the mind from its sockets.

At this description of clotted pain, my friends, half-crazed with sheer happiness and pure delight, beg me to continue so that they may die in a last convulsion of glorious laughter.

Gout is commonly believed to be directly connected with port bottles and great juicy steaks.

'Many have lost their gout with their fortunes,' moodily observed a Dr Hosack, but alas he was talking through his stethoscope. I know savage teetotallers whose eyes light up at the mention of the Metropolitan Water Board, and embittered vegetarians who run amok among the lettuce beds; they, too, have fallen for the disease.

This malignant, mordacious, venomous, virulent disorder strikes the libertine and the ascetic alike.

'Cut out meat, fish, game, gravy, cheese, butter, most vegetables, all soups, beer, whisky, wine, gin and brandy,' says one school of thought, 'and your foot may yet touch the ground again.'

'Stick to eggs, white bread, potatoes and dandelion leaves,' cries another miserable crew.

A third party, writing recently in *The Lancet,* boldly recommends that we wretches should try three glasses of Cockburn's '28 after dinner. While yet a fourth authority, this time the *British Medical Journal* in 1932, announced blandly (and blindly) that 'gout is almost an extinct disease!'

Extinct my foot!

One consolation alone attends the victims of the Blazing Toe. 'The association of ability and gout,' writes Havelock Ellis, 'cannot be a fortuitous coincidence. The genius of the gouty group is emphatically masculine, profoundly original and pre-eminent in intellectual ability.'
If only we could stand up, we'd bow.

The good old M.O.

January 1, 1959

The official history of the Royal Air Force Medical Services tells, among other things, how during the early part of the war men were called up and sent to France while suffering from such diseases as cancer of the stomach and inoperable hernia.

Presumably they did the same thing in the Army for I personally knew men suffering from blood pressure (the luckless chap died), semi-blindness, permanent lameness and mental sickness.

The final discharge medical examination could also be a very cursory affair. I was interviewed by a very young medical officer who didn't trouble to look up when I came into the room. The following conversation took place:

Medical Officer: 'How do you do?'

Me: 'Very well, thank you. And how do YOU do?'

M.O.: 'Okey-dokey.'

Still without looking up he wrote under the heading 'General Condition of Health.' 'Excellent'.

Then he glanced up and saw that I was a man of substantial, if not portly build. Said he: 'Strewth! A fat basket.'

He then crossed out the word 'Excellent' and substituted 'Indifferent'.

'A very good day to YOU,' says I.

'And a very good day to YOU,' says he.

The B.M. and the I.C.

June 17, 1960

Like war between the sexes, the struggle between bank managers and their clients ceases only with the grave or the bankruptcy court.

A chap whose style of living might be called robust was summoned by his bank manager to discuss all that red debit stuff that was disfiguring his account.

The bank manager, hereinafter to be referred to as the B.M., was pleading with his roistering client to introduce a strong note of asceticism into his life which, he said, would result in welcome economies in his bank account.

The indigent client, hereinafter to be referred to as the I.C. protested that he was scrupulously careful in his way of life; that wine, women, song and caviar had no part in the thin, bitter and emaciated existence that he led.

The B.M. was not convinced.

He said: 'Take the question of lunches. It is only a small thing, but how much do you spend on a meal?'

Without waiting for an answer he plunged on: 'Why not cut down? One lager instead of half a bottle of burgundy. Why not a sandwich occasionally, instead of the escalop Holstein? Or perhaps a simple plate of cold meat and salad in one of the excellent cheap cafes that abound – instead of the minestrone, the mixed grill, the strawberries, the gruyere and the slow, soft, sleepy port?'

This infuriated the I.C. who retorted: 'You don't know what you are talking about! Come and lunch with me. I promise you that you will not starve. I eat well but I can tell you that I get the best value for money and don't spend a penny more than is necessary. You lecture me! Now come and eat the proof of the economical pudding!'

He named a first-class West End restaurant and said: 'Monday at ten past one.'

'Done,' said the B.M.

'It's a date,' said the I.C.

He then left his tormentor and rang up the manager of the restaurant, booked a table for two and said: Mario, I've got a guest on Monday. Odd sort of chap who is agin good living. Don't let him get a glimpse of the prices – either now or for evermore.

'Whatever happens make the bill out for, say, nineteen and fourpence for the pair of us and I'll send you the balance by post.'

Came the day and the B.M. and the I.C. sat down to a spartan meal of asparagus, smoked trout, *sole Bon Femme, a* sly but memorable cheese and a glass of smiling brandy. The bill for the pair of them, as planned, was only nineteen and fourpence.

The waiter struggled with his grin.

The manager let down a slow cunning wink aimed solely at the I.C.

Four days later Mario rang up the I.C.

Said Mario: 'You know that friend of yours you lunched with the other day – the nineteen and fourpenny job? Well, he's here right now with a pal and so far, in spite of the fact that they are not yet on the last lap, the bill is about five pounds eighteen.

'You'll settle later – I take it?'

The April 26th Club

April 27,1959

I was fifty yesterday. I don't feel a day older than sixty, and when I'm really on form with every ounce of strength mustered and respiration clearly detectable by the mirror-to-the-lips method I feel fifty-nine.

Being fifty is the age at which you can really settle in and enjoy predicting disaster. When you put your fingers together, stretch your legs and say with an air of finality: 'No good will come of it,' the young folks really begin to listen. 'Rum old devil,' they say, 'but he's seen a thing or two in his time.'

From now on, so far as I am concerned, not much good is going to come of anything and I shall survey the hopeless scene with expanding pleasure.

I have been doing an intensive piece of research on my birthday trying to find out what other great events have occurred in the past on the twenty-sixth day of April. Surely the day of my nativity must, down the years and the centuries, have been accompanied by equally outstanding events.

Let us call upon History to read the Scroll.

'Great Chronicler of Events please read the record of April 26th. What happened?'

Great Chronicler: 'Practically nothing.'

Me: 'I beg your pardon.'

G.C.: 'Of all the days in the calendar, April the twenty-sixth is among the most barren.'

Me: 'You mean to tell me that it is not a day of great events and of great men?'

G.C.: 'Do you want to hear the record?'

Me: 'Pray proceed."

G.C.: 'Well, there's virtually nobody on the horizon so we'll start with Alfred Krupp. He was born on April 26th, 1812.'

Me: 'You mean that ferocious old buzzard from Essen who made a fortune out of cannon, armour-plate and the resultant death?'

G.C.: 'Precisely. One of Krupp's most murderous toys was the first 100-ton breech-loading gun. And fittingly enough April the twenty-sixth is notable for people who died on that day rather than those who were born on it.'

Me: 'Cheerful, aren't you?'

G.C.: 'Well, you asked for it. Defoe died on April 26, 1731. Jeremy Collier died on April 26, 1726. Sir Eyre Cooke, the soldier, died on April 26, 1783 and the Great Plague of London started on April 26th, 1665.'

Me: 'Is there no ray of hope?'

G.C.: Not much except for the fact that on April 26th, 1564, William Shakespeare was baptized in the Parish Church of Stratford-on-Avon.'

Me: 'Anything else?'

G.C.: 'Not much. How about the fact that conscription in Great Britain began on April 26th, 1939.'

Me : 'Getting pretty thin now. What else can we members of the April 26th Club celebrate? '

G.C. : 'Well, there's always High Tide.'

Me: 'What do you mean?'

G.G. : 'You can always fall back on High Tide at London Bridge to celebrate. There was High Tide at London Bridge on April 26th, 1909, the day you were born. There was also High Tide at London Bridge yesterday at 5.07 p.m. on your birthday.'

Me: 'Any other totally unexpected events happen on April 26th?'

G.G. : 'Well there's always lighting-up time. 8.43 in London yesterday.'

So there you have it.

April 26th is the day of utter nothingness.

I don't suppose there is a bleaker festival. Just the ghost of old Krupp toasting me many happy returns in a glass of hemlock.

As sweet as I am

August 5, 1959

This is William Connor, licensed to write a column five days a week under the name of Cassandra (and also licensed to run, operate and maintain an overhead tramway and to whammel trout for profit in open sea estuaries) reporting back to you after a month's absence.

Or rather this is the original Cassandra minus 12lb 4oz returning for duty, and if you think you aren't getting full weight for your money you are dead right.

There are but a bare 14 stones of me left.

But I have been far from idle. When not reclining on the operating table, with deceptive grace and calm, I have been rebutting a grievous charge laid against me in the law courts. This incorrect assessment of my character (honeyed words come easily to me these days) was made by the formidable and venerable advocate, Mr Gilbert Beyfus, QC, in the course of a recent legal crossness I had with a piano-player.

He said that what I wrote was 'violent, venomous, and vindictive'.

Now although I know that it is the bounden duty of all counsel to use the tarbrush with all their accomplished might and main against their adversaries, and conversely to use the bucket of whitewash to cover up any defects their clients may possess, I felt that Mr Beyfus was being a bit hard on me.

How was he to know that he was treading on my dreams? Stamping on them? Pounding them with his ironclad hoof?

For the truth is that I have always regarded myself as distinctly sweet.

Just a ball of glucose.

Professor Saccharine himself.

And so I am.

And, moreover, I'll prove it to you.

There are certain routine procedures to go through before surgical operations these days, and when in my case these had been achieved and the results examined, my nurse looked at me and said with that sidelong curiosity that goes unnoticed in leper colonies: 'You been feeling all right lately?' 'Yes, Ma'am.'

'Well, we'll have to take a blood test, all the same, you know.'

'Yes, Ma'am.'

This they did with some speed.

Very shortly a doctor appeared and said briskly: 'You are in the soup all right.'

'In the soup?'

'Well, not exactly. In the sugar bowl would be more accurate. Bags of it. Diabetes.'

It seemed that apart from the fact that I was wearing pyjamas it was medically difficult to tell me apart from a toffee apple ; a one-man Tate and Lyle factory; a human Mr Cube; just a couple of yards of barley-sugar. Sir Syrup in person.

This complaint of surplus sugar was no skin-deep icing. It was in the blood. Scratch me now and it is a question of 'one lump or two?'

So when next some sharp (I nearly said acid-tongued) lawyer calls your old friend a vinegary, sour, corrosive, virulent, tart-tongued crab-apple, just remember that he can't get his facts right for toffee.

Anyway, the text for today is Judges, chapter 14, verse 14.

'Out of the strong came forth sweetness.'

Famous last words

November 24, 1961

I don't know what I shall be saying with my dying breath, but I hope it will be something utterly banal, like William Pitt's farewell.

His friends reported that the great man expired saying: 'My country! Oh, my country!'

But a more reliable source said that Pitt took off for The Great Blue Yonder remarking cheerfully: 'I think I could eat one of Bellamy's veal pies.'

A certain amount of research on Last Dispatches from the edge of the tomb has been made, but I feel that there has always been a strong tendency on the part of the imminent mourners to tart the script up a bit.

Now comes a useful addition for all anthologists of the final communiqué.

It is a book called *Famous Last Words* by Barnaby Conrad, and is published by Doubleday in the United States.

It is a splendid mixture of the heroic and the mundane.

On the silver-trumpets-sounding-for-Paradise theme, there is the famous theologian Isaac Barrow crying: 'I have seen the glories of the world!'

It is offset by the dying English playwright Sir Henry Arthur Jones who, when he was asked whether he would like his niece or his nurse to spend the last night by his bedside, remarked briskly: 'The prettier! Now fight for it!'

There is the tremendous self-satisfaction of the preacher Lyman Beecher quoting St Paul and-expiring to this swelling crescendo:

'I have fought a good fight. I have finished my course, I have kept the faith; henceforth there is laid up for me a crown of righteousness, which God, the righteous judge, will give at that day.

'That is my testimony – write it down – that is my testimony.'

Mrs David Garrick, practical to the end, snapped as she accepted her last cup of tea from a servant: 'Put it down, hussy! Do you think I cannot help myself?'

Rupert Brooke, the poet who believed in the relaxed attitude to life – and death – looked up when he was dying of food poisoning and said weakly to his friend Denis Browne: 'Hallo.'

Which may be the perfect farewell.

In the same laconic tradition and as a last, last word, there is the final brevity from a certain Dr Joseph Green.

His surgeon, who had been urgently called to the bedside, examined his patient, gave his diagnosis and said simply: 'Congestion'.

Dr Green then took his own pulse, waited for a second and said equally crisply: 'Stopped.' He was dead right – and dead.

Dearly beloved bomb...

March 29, 1964

On March 1st, 1954 – the date may yet be the most dreadful or the most joyous of the 20th century – the United States Government exploded their latest hydrogen bomb at Bikini. What exactly happened there is not yet known. But what is certain is that the explosion startled and appalled those who set it off. It was greater and more terrible than they had calculated – 600 times more powerful than the first man-made hell dropped on Hiroshima.

Welcome, Dear Bomb. Welcome and bless you.

Bless those who made you. Bless those who set you roaring and flaming and vaporizing the face of the earth.

Bless the hellish heat of you. Bless the bursting heart of you. Bless the lethal cloud that arose from you and rained atomic dust on Japanese fishermen seventy miles away; that covered them with sores; that rotted their hair away; that even poisoned their cargo of fish.

The crew of the Fukuryu Maru looked to the west early on the morning of the first day of March and thought they saw the sun rising; 'We saw flashes of fire as bright as the sun rising to the sky. They rose about 10 degrees from the horizon and the sky around glowed fiery red and yellow. Someone yelled to the men below: "The sun is rising in a strange fashion. Hurry up and see it!"

'But what we were watching was not the sun, for the light was coming from the west. The glare lasted several minutes and then faded like a dull red piece of iron slowly cooling in the sky. A pyramid-shaped cloud billowed up and changed colour many times.'

Mankind was serving notice upon itself that time was getting short.

Little man made in the image of God, you have been warned.

Welcome, beloved bomb, Greetings, Great Bomb, made to a recipe that not more than 100 men and the Devil himself alone know.

Flesh and blood never held a secret like this before. Hydrogen, lithium, uranium, tritium, plutonium and Satan-knows-what, all compounded into the death sentence – or the salvation of the world. Cities collapse and fall into rubble at your embrace. A hundred thousand square miles are rendered unfit for human life. Dreadful and beautiful bomb!

Little man made in the image of God, you have been warned.

Welcome, hellish, but also heavenly, bomb. Children unborn smile upon you and the maimed of two world wars shout for joy and raise their crutches to salute you. For man at last has accomplished with his own hands not only the means of his doom, but also the shining hope that he will never dare to accomplish it.

War as we knew it in 1945 has gone for evermore. One bomb, one missile 25ft. long and weighing less than 10 tons, now has more destructive power than the sum total of all the bombs cast in the last world war.

Whose is the unimaginable madness that would seek to use such, a weapon?

Little man made in the image of God, surely not yours?

Where then are the profits of a hydrogen war?

In land and territory gained?

The face of the earth would be a contaminated desert.

In the power and glory of conquest?

There would be no victors – only the vanquished.

Can universal suicide tempt the human race? Can inevitable and overwhelming ruin encourage an aggressor to launch an attack?

Who would sound the trumpet for the grave?

Who will raise the flag for the tomb?

Little man made in the image of God, surely not you?

The Angel of Death is also the Angel of Peace, out of dark destruction comes the light of salvation, the threat can also be the promise.

The choice is not war or peace. It is extinction or peace.

Russia knows it. America knows it. We know it. We all share the same fate.

It can be atomic power to transform the peaceful world, to give us limitless heat, light and power, to slave for us as no horse has ever toiled for us before.

Or it can blot us out in a trice. Who in the name of Mercy could take the second choice?

Little man made in the image of God, surely not you?

In hospital, Cassandra wrote this most moving article for the New Statesman. *It was reprinted by the* Sunday Mirror *with acknowledgments.*

They made me welcome

June 6, 1965

It was absurdly like arriving at a party very late and knowing that it was all over and that everyone who had any sense would be in bed.

They were, and the place was almost in total darkness.

Mind you, they made me very welcome.

The public ward (Surgical) of a hospital just before midnight is not the gayest of places but I had valid admission tickets: a fractured skull; blood from the left ear (a very good credential); a high temperature; accelerated respiration; post-shock shivers; and, almost certainly, concussion.

Peter Sellers was, of course, the late-duty-house-doctor-receptionist and was brimming over with the dusky charm and real concern of his kind that sometimes contrasts sharply with the brusque impartiality of the paler brethren who, occasionally, I have found, are inclined to regard illness or accident as a matter of guilt on the part of the patient.

How did it happen? asked Mr Sellers. What a shame. Where did it happen? What a pity.

No, don't worry about the blood on the pillow. Just relax. We'll take care of you. All will be well.

My heart did not go pit-a-pat but my head went honkety-tonk all right. Then on to the rubber-tyred trolley and head foremost towards the ward.

Nurses waiting and the Night Sister in the background. Again the polished charm, the practised efficiency, the enfolding silence and the comforting dark.

I roll on to one of those absurdly high beds that later I am told by a nurse is not so damned silly as you might think. Making beds is back-breaking work, especially with people lying in them.

The lower the beds are the more spine-twisting they are for those who have to make them. Can I have another pillow? No. Head injuries should lie flat in bed. May I have a sleeping tablet? No. Not allowed in cases like yours.

I have never felt more alert, more detached, more clinically observant. Maybe that cloud on the head is doing things for me. I feel I can step outside myself and just watch; watch, with interest, watch with amusement, watch with pleasing self-disdain.

There are twenty-five beds in the ward. On the left three prostates (you soon learn to separate the maladies from their owners in hospital), are breathing heavily and a fourth, a motor-cycle mix-up suspended in the inevitable rigging, is gently snoring.

I learned later that prostates were 'done' early that morning and were making swift recoveries from this once fearsome operation.

On my right was an old man in his eighties called Harry, who was sleeping peacefully.

He later introduced himself to me in a gruff, friendly voice with a splendid touch of old-fashioned formality: 'Neighbour on my left!' he shouted. 'My name is Harry. What's yours?'

'Bill,' says I.

I tried to get to sleep but the mental light inside me glowed maddeningly brighter.

You know you can't sleep. You know exactly why. Within seven paces of the foot of your bed there is a man dying.

An old, old man – nearly eighty-five years of age as it turned out – is coming to the end of the road. This is the last big sleep. He was hit by a car five days ago and has not recovered consciousness.

The mind, already buried, is dead in the tomb of the failing body. With him, night after night, has been his son. A burly impassive figure keeping the last pointless but brave vigil. He stands almost motionless and rarely sits down.

The curtains are drawn round the dying man but there is a wide gap left open. Above his head is a light covered with a red duster. He rests high on the pillows and his face, flushed and sharp, has an angry look.

I am told by people who know about these things that the last expression on people's faces, especially those killed in accidents, is often one of surprised indignation.

They wear the why-should-this-happen-to-me look. The dying man breathes fiercely, harshly and at double the normal speed. So regular and so noisy is his respiration that you get the impression that he must be in some mechanical iron lung. One… two… one-two-one-two like stamping feet on a parade ground. In-out-in-out-in-out, chest heaving. The minutes crawl by to the accompaniment of this terrible rhythm. The lone relative – the shadow against the curtain – looks on.

The old life that began in the 1880s is gasping its way to the last rendezvous.

Disraeli had just died when he was born and his mother first looked on her little male child. Gladstone had nearly twenty years to live. Stage coaches were running regularly in the Lake District and between London and Brighton and London and Oxford. Tallow candles were a penny a dozen and Robert Louis Stevenson was describing electric light as fit only for the corridors of lunatic asylums.

Hiram Maxim was hard at work on his machine-gun and John Henry Newman had written *Lead Kindly Light.*

This was the surrounding dawn of the beginning of the life of the aged man so near to me. He was in his late teens the night Mafeking was relieved.

He was a fully grown man when the guns in France could be heard in London in the summer of 1914. He was just sixty when the Second World War sent 30,000,000 people to their graves before their time.

When he was born there was no motor-car, no flying machine, no radio, no television, and during his eight decades man increased his travelling speed from eighty miles an hour in an express train to 18,000 miles an hour encircling the globe in eighty minutes.

Now the tumultuous years were ending.

As the pale water-colour wash of dawn lightened the east windows of the ward the stertorous breathing suddenly stopped.

Silence.

You felt the whole ward was awake, roused by the ticking of the clock that had abruptly ceased.

The Sister was at his side within seconds. The nurses, with ballet precision, tallest on the left, shortest on the right, stood outside the curtain looking in. The soundless scene was frozen.

The breathing cut in again as suddenly as it had cut out. They held his pulse, moved silently away from the bed and resumed their seats at the table.

Three minutes later the tearing, wheezing sound stopped again. Had the old heart really failed this time? In a trice the oxygen cylinder on its rubber-tyred cradle was wheeled in. A faint hiss.

Some thirty people were listening. Not a sound. The mind cried out for a whimper, for a prayer, even for the tolling of a bell. Anything but this aching nothing.

A nurse switched on her torch and the thin searching beam flickered up the wall to the ward clock. A professional touch to read the time of death – 4.33am.

Still the freezing quiet.

Then from the bed next to me, Harry spoke – a gruff, whiskery voice that said hoarsely but loudly: 'Gorn!'

There was no emotion. Just a dispassionate observation.

Harry, with terrifying matter-of-factness, was simply recording the fact that the old man had gone.

It so happens that recently I attended the exultant and splendid service of Sir Winston Churchill at St Paul's, perhaps the most triumphant farewell in the history of mankind, with flags flaunting, trumpets sounding and a great congregation singing defiance of death – not lamentation.

Here in this hospital ward was the obverse side of the coin of death inscribed with surely the tersest of all epitaphs – 'Gorn!'

Depending on how you think about these things, a life was snuffed out for ever, a soul was winging its way to Paradise, a spirit was adrift on the River Lethe.

The faithful son, the silent Absolom, gathered up a few of his father's pieces and disappeared.

With a strange little secular ceremony they pulled all the curtains around our cubicles when they wheeled the old fellow away. Soon they washed us. They fed us.

The paper boy came in and Harry greeted the new-born day with a rousing description of the Soccer virtues of West Ham and the motor-cycle smash-up case chattered with endless cheerful idiocy about Sandown Park. I think they know how to do these sombre things in the public wards. Arm in arm, dispassion and compassion go rather well.

Handy about the house

February 2, 1966

Am I handy about the house? Leaky taps? Laying the lino? De-bunging the bunged-up sink?

I'll say I am.

I'm your man.

Did I ever tell you how I changed the needle on the old radiogram that ended in the ever-intensifying struggle that civilisation brings –The Battle Between Things and Us.

I had in mind buying a new needle for about five bob, but the salesman winced when I said this and insisted that a super sapphire job for about twenty-five shillings was the only thing that a perceptive, sensitive music-lover like myself would tolerate. 'First class service for a decade,' he said. 'No mush, no hiss – only the deep purple of absolute silence.'

I bought it.

I also purchased on the way home a watchmaker's screwdriver to slacken the small grub-screw that holds the needle.

It worked perfectly but the screw fell out and landed, I thought, on the floor.

I couldn't find it. I then searched for it on the carpet with a small table lamp.

The shade fell off.

I dropped the lamp, there was a blue flash and all the lights went out. I found the remains of an old candle and blundered across the darkened hall, tripping up over a chair. The candle snuffed it.

I relit it and plunged into the cupboard under the stairs where a colony of fuse boxes nest together like the bats in a barn. Finding *The Lost Chord* is child's play compared with looking for a burned-out fuse wire under the guttering twilight of one candle power – especially when you stand on brooms that bounce back and bust you over the beano like emaciated Indian students being clubbed by riot police wielding lathis.

Finally I found the burned-out metallic gossamer of what had once been a fuse and reconnected with 5 amp wire where 10 should have been. The lights came on. Back to the carpet. No screw. Heavy breathing followed by a strong ale.

Finally located screw that had gone to earth under the turntable. Tally ho! Tried to dig out with the aid of a ruler.

No joy. No screw. Nothing.

Then tilted the whole radiogram to get the screw to roll out.

One leg snapped off like a rotten carrot. Lights go off again. Back into the broom cupboard, fighting mad. No spare fuse wire. More blows in the darkness and Indian riot still raging. Reconnect with wedge of silver paper.

Lights on again. The Fleet's all lit up. On a radiogram four legs are fine, but three, two or one leg do not help unless the whole ship is listing 45 degrees to starboard.

I snap off remaining three legs. The madness is upon me. Music box now on even keel.

No screw but if it's a fight you want I'm your man. Bell sounds for round five.

Why not lift the turntable up? It must pull off.

You heave ho.

Turntable won't budge. One final heave and turntable DOES budge.

So do yards of wire entrails and a whole digestive system of condensers and grid-leaks and a shower of volts, amps and ohms. So you won't play, huh?

Grab hulk of wrecked radiogram and stagger to dustbin. Crash wreckage down on rim.

Too large for dustbin so force it down and batter it until it does fit – in instalments.

Heavy breathing again followed by what that snivelling limb of Satan

described at the shop as nothing but 'the deep purple of absolute silence.'
Victory to Things. Defeat for Us.

L-shaped room

March 9, 1966

Last week a man from the telly looked into my room here in the *Daily Mirror* building with, I think, the object of taking some pictures of me at work.

He was very polite but left almost immediately and if ever there was an expression on a man's face that said: 'Gripes! Does he work in that there dump?' that expression was on that man's face.

Now this incident interested me very much for I have always held that the offices in which people work are one of the most revealing things about them.

It was therefore with dismay tinged with regret that I recently read the views on these matters by Mr William Davis, who is the enlightened financial editor of *The Guardian* – and not as you might think the sales director of Maple's or Heal's.

'I hope I don't sound too frivolous,' writes Mr Davis, 'if I say that this matter of office accommodation is very important – in business as well as in politics. Most tycoons spend vastly more time at their desks than at home. Why shouldn't they enjoy their surroundings?'

The main reason that rich businessmen spend huge sums on their offices is to impress their visitors, and a chairman looking at a Monet, by himself, for the pure delight of it, is as rare as a salmon fisherman on the Mersey at Widnes.

The number of apparently successful businessmen sacked from their jobs, not because of their inefficiency but because of the misguided opulence of their surroundings, would fill the Necropolis at Woking.

One of the best chaps I ever knew in the newspaper business parted company with his employers because he was forced to work in a room with no air (a trivial complaint in this business) and had to bring his own oxygen cylinders with him.

He pined away for black velvet curtains and a rubber tree plant.

I, in my physical surrounding, have always modelled myself on a brilliant advertising man who really understood the intrinsically frippery-phony-value of Chippendale, Tompton and Toulouse-Lautrec in offices mixed up with the effluent and the profits of a prosperous chemical works.

He worked in a large bare room at a rough deal table with not a telephone in sight although, when I last heard of him, he was toying with the idea of having a chipped enamelled megaphone to look after telecommunications.

There were no filing cabinets, no carpet and only some coarse worn linoleum purchased at enormous expense from Brown's Hotel where they really know what goes on and supplied from the lang toon of Kirkcaldy, where they make the best lino.

There was no hidden buzzer under the lino to summon his staff, but an old brass school bell stolen from Howard Gardens School, Cardiff, in 1927.

He wore dark glasses on the gloomiest winter's day because he said that he couldn't stand the sight of his most important clients, and in front of him he had a single sheet of paper with one freshly sharpened pencil. Nothing else. Not even a paperweight.

Later he had the design of the room changed to become an L-shaped room because of forbidden but delectable thoughts that he had about that lovely actress Leslie Caron.

He was without doubt the most successful advertising man of his decade.

That, Mr Davis, is my idea of a really efficient tycoon's room.

Time clock in the turn

April 12, 1966

A funny thing happened to me on the way home from the hospital – funny that is, if you have a much greater sense of humour than I have.

My time clock slipped six hours.

The cogs seem to have stripped their teeth after serious internal repairs and adjustments had been made.

Instead of going to sleep at night at about ten or eleven as is my custom, I could not sleep until four or five o'clock in the morning. It was not a question of wakefulness being interrupted by quick cat-naps which often delude the slumber-hunter into thinking he has been fully conscious all the time – I was ceaselessly on the reluctant alert.

The medicos stepped up the sleeping pills gradually until I was on the verge of mild hallucinations. But to no purpose. The unsleeping eye and the all-hearing ear continued their nocturnal watch until the grey water-colour wash of dawn tinged the skies in the east and the birds began blasting off from the boughs.

I was just living on another segment of the clock, dozing at breakfast, being roused by the guard when arriving in the morning train to Town, stumbling through a soporific haze until midday and then – bingo! – salute the happy morning that begins in the late afternoon.

'All you have to do,' said a friend, 'is to put the clock back six hours.'

A fortnight ago I clambered aboard the only time-adjusting machine I know – a big jet aircraft that travels at 600 miles an hour – and headed west for New York.

There the time is six hours behind London Summer Time. When it is my old bedtime in London, it is four o'clock in the afternoon in New York. When it is bedtime in New York, 10pm, it is four o'clock in the early morning in London – my new bedtime.

In New York and also Toronto which I visited, and which is also on the London-minus-six time-schedule, I slept the innocent sleep that knits up the ravell'd sleeve of care.

Deep dreamless sleep and normal again. Back in London I am now on the night shift once more. I hear the old house where I live creaking in the chill small hours and the mind, bright and luminous, burns uneasily in the dark.

If this goes on I shall be like the Hungarian playwright Ference Molnar who slept by day and worked only in the hours of darkness. The old Owl of the Danube they called him.

Once when he was forced to break his routine because he had to appear in court, he gazed around him at the people thronging the streets of Budapest and remarked in wonderment: 'Are all these people witnesses?'

The built-in time clock is a mysterious thing.

The senses of sight and sound and touch and smell may tell you that you are walking along Forty Second Street over three thousand miles from The Strand but Old Man Time, controlling the appetite and all the vast weird chemistry of the body, says: 'It may be time for a hamburger in the bright Yankee sunlight up there but it is three in the morning and real dark down here. Belt up.'

When I was younger the brain said to the body: 'Get in line there, chum. No, we are not having steak and kidney pudding for late dinner at dawn. Nor porridge for tea.'

It now takes me two or three days to get all of me marching in step.

What goes on in the internal arrangements of Space astronauts who may experience up to sixteen dawns and dusks within twenty-four hours, the Heavens they fly through with the greatest of ease only know. People can adapt themselves to nocturnal life but as a rule they don't like it. I was astonished in what was then called Tanganyika to find the rare roads and tracks in the bush often crowded with people including small children at two or three in the morning. The reason was simple. It was far too hot to get about when the sun was overhead but it was pleasant and cool especially on a moonlit night long after midnight.

In northern polar lands where in summer the sun shines all round the clock and it is unending daylight, the Eskimos and the people who live within the Arctic circle tend to keep the sleeping habits of the rest of the globe where daylight and darkness alternate.

Plants and flowers, too, tend to cling to their old a.m. and p.m. habits.

They keep up their original daily rhythm when they are transplanted into caves, where there is unending darkness and a constant temperature, opening and closing their flowers and leaves at the same time as the roses and the daffodils do far above them in the sunlight.

Butterflies and birds and insects are also clockwatchers unwilling to change the habits that their species learned a few hundred million years ago. A consignment of bees, normally very orderly and precise in their habits, was flown in a sealed box from London to New York. There was consternation among the colony when they were transported across the Atlantic, but once they were taken back to Paris, although the time but not the scenery had changed, order prevailed as before.

How the air-crews fare in their daily longitudinal lives I do not understand. When they go west they are flying away from food. Breakfast is at 2am destination time and lunch is at 8am. Coming east you fly into food. Lunch at breakfast departure time and dinner at lunchtime.

It is all very bewildering. In my new world the lark should be singing at siesta time and tea served just before midnight.

Good night sweetheart – I mean, good afternoon.

The most personal and poignant of Cassandra's comments on his insomnia came in six lines at the end of his last column. It was dated February 1st, 1967, and it was headed:

Plenty of Time

He wrote:

'Normal service in this column is temporarily interrupted while I learn to do what any babe can do with ease and what comes naturally to most men of good conscience – sleep easily o' nights…'

He died on April 6th.

Lightning Source UK Ltd.
Milton Keynes UK
UKOW031939170413

209396UK00015B/568/P